MEMC … ISLAND GIRL

W…

Published … ig

DEDICATION

I dedicate this book to my children, grandchildren and their children through generations; to my siblings and their children; to my cousins especially to those who paid a big part in my upbringing, and to my dear friends who have always stood by me.

Thank you all!

ISBN 978-1-7396620-0-4

MEMOIRS OF A SMALL ISLAND GIRL

MEMOIRS OF A SMALL ISLAND GIRL

CHAPTER 1

MY FAMILY WERE MY JOY

One day, in the year of 1946, at the age of four, there I was sitting comfortably on the floor in a corner of our veranda with my sisters Selda, Christa and brother Victor. Mammatee, our mother, sat on a chair holding our baby brother, Harren. Sitting beside her was our uncle's wife, Isha, who everyone called sister Isha. Sister Isha often stopped at our house on her way from Kingstown- the capitol of our little island, St Vincent, for a short rest and a chat with Mammatee before taking the High Road to her house. At times other people stopped there too. Our house was pleasantly and thoughtfully designed, I do not know who the architect was; It was built on an ideal spot between top and bottom Lowman's Hill in the parish of St. Andrew. The only one of its kind with a shelter for weary travellers. Many people rested there on the way to their homes at the top, where almost all of my relatives lived. It also provided shelter from the rain for people going up to the mountain and to Kingstown, just one and a half miles down.

On this day of 1946 while we were on that veranda, two ladies passed by. They had to be strangers. I could not remember seeing them before; one was tall and elderly, the other was short, young and friendly-looking and they were both smartly dressed. Surprisingly, they greeted Mammatee and sister Isha, not at all like strangers, which puzzled me, my eyes and ears were opened to their every word and motion, and my ever-enquiring mind was on the go. "Tee! Another baby? What are you going to do with all those babies? Which one are you going to give to me?" asked the older lady.

"Don't know." answered Mammatee. "How about the dark one in the corner?"

I suddenly became afraid, and I cringed in fear. My head found my knees, my eyes shut tightly, my ears no longer heard, and my mind went blank. When I opened my eyes, the ladies were leaving. I thought that the old lady's request to have me was just her dream of the moment.

On school opening day sister Christa was the last of my siblings to set off for Lowmans Hill Government School. I guess she was late, perhaps she had too many chores.

"Take Sheva with you they might let her in, she is such a *Kitty Question*." Mammatee said to her.

Mammatee often referred to me as *Kitty Question* because I questioned everything. Well, my face stretched with a big grin of happiness. Christa took my hand and on hearing the last bell of call we ran all the way. School was not far from home. When we got to the door a lady, who I suppose was a teacher, stood at the entrance.

"Mammatee has sent my little sister," said Christa to her.

"How old are you?"

"I am four."

"Well, you are not yet of school age, you cannot come in."

My grin instantly changed to a frown followed by tears.

Christa comforted me with a big hug. "You have to go home. Can you remember the way?"

I nodded, and she pointed me to the direction we came and told me where to turn. Getting back was quick and easy; I ran and cried all the way. When I got back to Mammatee she smiled and said, "Never mind!". *I wondered how did she know what happened, and why did she smile? How could she smile when I was crying?* I soon settled down with my brother Victor who was two years younger than me. I was tenth of fourteen children; the expectant one would total fifteen born to both our parents. Dad was blessed with two others from another mother. Having Mammatee, Pappahen, siblings and especially my baby brother was great and better still were my grandmas, grandpa and lots and lots of relatives. It seemed as though everyone in Lowmans were family or friends. There were times I was scolded by some for talking too much; they would say, "Sheva Da, you ask too many questions, you are a chatter box." When I was not called by my name it was usually *Chatter Box* or *Kitty Question*.

Some others were delighted to hear my questions and when chatting with me they often remarked, "Sheva you are so bright!" Some rewarded me with gifts, which made me happy. Unknown to me a drastic change was about to take place. They had plans to send me away.

DON'T SEND ME AWAY!

One day just before my fifth birthday Mammatee hugged me and said, "Your Dear Aunt wants you to live with her."

"Dear Aunt? Who is she?" I asked Mammatee.

"The Lady that passed and asked for you to live with her, she is your Papa's aunt; your Papa and I agreed to let you go. They live in a nice house on a big farm."

"No! No! I don't want to go! Please don't send me!"

"You will come back and visit with us, and Selda will visit you but now you have to go up high Lowmans and say goodbye to your grandmas and the others up there, your sister will take you," said Mammatee. Which sister, I can't recall. I do remember that gone were my chats and smiles, they were replaced with tears, sadness and pleas. I was hugged and kissed by everyone, they all said the same thing to come back and visit us soon.

My last goodbye was to my parents and siblings. Words I no longer spoke. I tightly hugged my immediate sister Selda, we were like one. To all others I gently waved and that was the way it stayed with everyone I passed. My eldest sister Dorada, I think, carried the little case packed with my things and held my hand.

I ENJOYED THE JOURNEY

We walked to the town and to the bus stand with the sign saying 'Windward'. My sister looked for the bus to Stubbs Village. I was lifted by a man up into the high wooden bus he must have been the footman or bus conductor. It was my first time on a bus. When the bus was full, the driver started the noisy engine; he then turned the big wheel and the bus started moving, slowly at first until we were out of the very busy streets and town. Then it went faster and faster. I began to lose my sadness as I viewed things and places we were passing. It was as if everything was moving, the trees, the houses, the people along the road, even the valleys with some plantations, and in some parts the clear blue sea was a long way down as the bus climbed elevated roads. This turned out to be an amazing big day for me, a little girl. The bus stopped in different villages along the way. Finally, we got to Stubbs Village, the second stop was ours. We descended the bus to see big double gates attached to a high wooden fence and joined to evergreen hedges; perhaps they were there to keep unwelcomed people out. My sister rang the bell, and someone quickly came with a big key, unlocked the gates and opened them wide. As time went by, I was told that the person who opened the gate was the garden attendant.

CHAPTER 2

THE WELCOME

Four people appeared in the gallery of the big, beautiful house, two of them I remembered. We all exchanged greetings, I became very shy and withdrawn. The occupants went back inside, and my sister and I were left alone sitting in the gallery for a while, perhaps to get acquainted with the surroundings. A young lady about the age of my sister came out with a tray, on it was a glass of milk and a biscuit for me, a glass of coconut water and two biscuits for my sister. The young lady laid it on the little table beside us and said, "I brought this for you two," then she left. We enjoyed the refreshments, and I began to relax. About fifteen minutes after, she returned and cleared the tray, we both thanked her. My sister said that the lady was the house maid and that she might be the one to look after me; well, that was good because she seemed to be a nice lady just by the way she smiled at me. The occupants of the house returned; my sister and I were asked to join them in the lovely large drawing room. The first thing that caught my eye was the enormous grand piano and then the huge wall clock; I thought to myself one day I would learn about them, but now it was time for the introductions.

INTRODUCTION

"Sheva," came the voice from the old lady that Mammatee said was my Dear Aunt who wanted me to live with her and her family. "I am your great aunt, your Pappahen's aunt. You will call me Dear Aunt. Come and kiss me". Nervously I did. She then pointed me to the old man in his rocking chair, "That's father, go and kiss him and here is your cousin, Dorawa. You will do whatever she tells you." I felt drawn to cousin Dorawa. I was next introduced to Franado, but was not told to call him cousin, however my sister soon told me that he was our first cousin, our uncle Tom and sister Isha's son. Instantly I loved him, especially as I figured that I would soon be joining him in school, and we would be the only two in the village with the same surname. It took about three years before I knew how cousin Dorawa and I were cousins and gradually I picked up information about father and Dear Aunt, which I shall come to later.

GETTING AQUAINTED

The house maid was called, Rosalie. I later learned from her that she lived two houses down with her family but sometimes she stayed over. Dear Aunt said that Rosalie would be helping to look after me, but cousin Dorawa would instruct her on what she needed to do. This was good news because I liked them both. My sister stayed a week, and we shared a bedroom. There were four bedrooms surrounding a lovely drawing room, and a trap door discreetly hid the stairs that led down to the double dining room and pantry, and out to the kitchen and garden. By the time my sister was ready to leave, I knew everywhere except one bedroom which was always locked. When the day came for my sister to leave, she cuddled me, and tears flowed. Cousin Dorawa moved me into her room. It was good that they all loved and cared about me, but it did not stop me from wanting to be with my Mammatee, Pappahen and my siblings, especially Selda as we were so close. A few days later cousin Dorawa said that Dear Aunt had asked one of the neighbours, the parents of a nice girl of my age, called Carmody to be my friend and that they agreed. Cousin Dorawa further said she would be good company for me. When I was introduced to Carmody we liked each other at first sight.

CHAPTER 3

SETTLING IN

The first duty of the day as a family was our daily devotions- reading scripture, praying and singing songs to music played by cousin Dorada on the big piano was like sunshine to my soul, especially when I sat beside her and watched her fingers move in time with her toes. The best was being left alone at the end of devotions to practise the scale. Playing with the keys, listening to the sounds of the notes and forming my own music. I never wanted to stop. Eventually came the call, "Sheva, that was an excellent tune! Now it's time for breakfast." Going through the trap door and down the stairs to the dining room was always fun. First in view was the reception hall, then the kitchen maid entering with the breakfast trolley, covered with a crisp white towel. Rosalie would wheel the trolley into the dining room, and place it next to Dear Aunt, at the long dining table where everyone was seated, waiting for me. The table was always nicely laid with dainty vessels and cutleries.

My eyes had a way of dilating at the sight of the lovely dishes. All meals were tasty but when poor father was ill, he constantly sneezed. I would cry, cringe, hide my face from the sight and refuse to eat the arrowroot porridge, the details of which I leave to your imagination. Thankfully, I was usually excused from the table to eat elsewhere. Some days, after breakfast, I helped Dear Aunt tend to the little lambs.

CARING FOR THE LAMBS

"Come on Sheva," Dear Aunt would say, "you hold the bottle for this lamb, so that I can take care of Rickets." *Yes!* I was on my best behaviour when feeding the lamb but in no time the milk was all gone. I waved my hand and said, "Shew! Shew!" The little lamb then scampered off to the pasture.

Dear Aunt took good care Rickets as we called her, because she had fallen into a ditch and had broken her leg. Dear Aunt, cleverly made splints from wood, picked special leaves known for healing which she soaked in brown vinegar. These leaves she applied to Rickets' broken leg, wrapped with brown paper and bandages, then used the splints as supports. Every day Dear Aunt looked at Rickets' leg and added more vinegar. One day, she removed the bandage, and Rickets ran off with a limp, looking rickety, but sounding happy, we knew by her bleat. So that's why she was given the name rickets.

CHURCH LIFE

After lunch we sometimes went to the village to visit our church brethren. They all lived in lovely homes. But how they all came to be teachers in the same school and preachers in the same church puzzled me. Other times, with the exception of father, we all went to the banks of crossroads and riverbanks with our tambourines and played music as we sang songs about Jesus and his love. Many people joined in, some others hated to hear our message and threw water or stones at us as they laughed and mocked. There were times we had to run, nevertheless, we kept going back.

Sundays were all about church. Communion service in the morning, children's bible school in the afternoon and evening songs at six. Tuesdays and Thursdays were for fellowship and Bible study, Friday nights were prayer meetings, Saturdays were cleaning days. Dear Aunt and father owned the church, so it was like our second home. After Sunday night services I was carried home by Franado, never being able to stay awake and only becoming aware on reaching the gate. It was nice being carried but was Franado happy to carry me? I never knew and he was not allowed to say. Although tall, he was only eight years older than myself and, I guess, he carried me for about a year; that would have been a long time.

MY BIRTHDAY

23rd of October 1947 was to be the beginning of many birthday treats for me. After breakfast, while we were all still sitting at the table, cousin Dorawa stood up and said, "Sheva, come and stand here!" she pointed me to the spot beside her. My mind wondered, *what have I done wrong?* "Happy birthday!" they all chanted. Cousin Dorawa handed me a bag. My eyes lit up. I bowed my head and curtsied the way in which I was taught to do when I was given gifts at Sunday school for answering questions correctly. I kissed everyone before peeping into the bag. Dear Aunt said, "Now Sheva, off you go and play in the near garden!" I could not go far even if I wanted, I was too anxious to see the contents in the bag. I went to one of my favourite spots to the side of the house at the back of the kitchen and there I sat, discovering the contents of my bag. It contained sweets, balloons, a colouring book and a drawing book with pencils. There was also a very colourful kite and a mouth organ. Filled with joy, I ran back to father, with my kite held high in the air having real fun. I met up with Franado and he showed me how best to fly the kite so that I would not lose it in the wind.

When I got to father, I blew my mouth organ for him to hear. I think he was happy because he smiled. I shared my sweets with everyone. While sucking my sweets, I made drawings of teacups, saucers, pots and pans. In fact, I drew everything I saw in the kitchen and dining room. And in the evening, I drew little boys and girls and named them after my siblings, those closest to my age. I also drew Carmody.

THE FIRST VISIT

'Ding dong!' came the sound from the bell at the gate. I left my gifts and ran in the direction to have a quick look. *No, it can't be Selda!* "Selda!" I shouted and jumped in excitement. With her was one of our older sisters, Karen or Manda, I cannot recall. When the gate was opened for them, we kissed and cuddled not wanting to let go. We went into the house, and they were greeted by Dear Aunt and the family. My surprises continued as they presented me with birthday gifts from my Mammatee and Pappahen. First came black and gold shoes exactly like the ones Selda was wearing and two beautiful dresses. Selda also wore a dress like one of them. "Go and try them on!" said my senior sister. The dresses made me look really nice. Mammatee was a lovely seamstress, styling us all alike, girl's dresses and boy's shirts all from the same material. Sadly my lovely shoes did not fit, they were too narrow for my wide feet. I cried, "Please, please can you take me to the doctor so that he can cut a bit off my foot for the shoes to fit?" "Hahaha!" they all laughed. "Don't cry, I'll take them back and bring a bigger pair for you," said my older sister. I calmed down, but kept remembering that promise, and waited for the day to receive my pretty shoes but they never came.

Not being able to wear the shoes did not spoil my joy that day. I had my sister Selda, so all was well. We had a whole week together. Words cannot express the joys we had in flying my kite, drawing, colouring and the fun of just playing. However, the days passed quickly. I tried hard not to think that my sisters would soon leave, yet every so often my mind drifted off to Lowmans. I visualised Mammatee and Pappahen sitting on the moonlit veranda, watching some of my siblings playing in the front garden.

Before my sisters left, I was taken to Stubbs Government School where I was introduced to the headmaster. I was allowed to look around and say hi to some of the pupils in the beginners' class.

I realised that I was no longer a Lowmans girl but a Stubbs girl. I knew then that my place was with Dear Aunt, Father, cousin Dorawa and cousin Franado, with no one of my age apart from the occasional visit from Carmody. It was not what I wanted but there was nothing that I could have done to change things.

On the eve of my sisters' last day, I gradually became withdrawn. I did not want to play or eat. Dear Aunt thought I was ill and sent me to bed. Selda laid beside me. "What's wrong?" she asked.

“I want to come back with you.” I said.

”Ok. When I get back, I will tell Mammatee that you want to come home,” replied Selda.

Finally, the day for parting came. My sisters packed their cases and after breakfast goodbyes were said, then we all stood at the gate waiting for the big bus that would take my sisters to Kingstown on their way back to Lowmans. I kept telling myself *I will not cry! No! No! I will not cry!* Eventually the bus came and stopped at the gate. Final hugs from my sisters and into the bus they went. Selda was helped on by the bus conductor. We stood there until the bus drove out of sight, then I went and occupied myself with the joys of my kite. Suddenly, I remembered my beautiful dresses and decided to take a look at them. I ran to the bedroom opened the wardrobe door and looked between all the clothing, but those dresses were nowhere to be seen. I thought that perhaps cousin Dorawa or Dear Aunt had put them away in that locked room, for special occasions only, but I never saw them again.

CHAPTER 4

MY WATCH DUTY

“Father.” I gently called to him as he sat in his chair beside me.

“Yes, my child.”

“It's so good standing on this veranda, looking through the trees and over the tops of the houses. I can see the buses coming down the road on the hill.”

“Yes, it is a lovely view. I loved to watch when I was able to stand for long, now that my legs are failing, I must sit. It is now your job every morning, except Saturdays and Sundays, to watch carefully for the blue and white bus. That's the school bus to take your cousin Dorawa to school. As soon as you see it, go and tell her it is coming so that she won't be late!”

I felt as if I had been given a very important job, which I carried out with delight, and always got it right. Meanwhile, Dear Aunt kept herself busy with the staff or the animals.

COUSIN DORAWA

Cousin Dorawa attended the girls high school in Kingstown. She boarded the bus at seven in the morning on weekdays and returned on the same bus at five in the evening. I had no problem knowing what time the bus was due. The grandfather clock on the wall always kept me informed- Ding-Dong Ding-Dong Ding! But I did not rely on the dings and dongs. I made sure I learnt every Roman number; I always nagged away at someone to teach me, until I got it right. I could not let my cousin Dorawa enter the gate without me being there to welcome her. It was so nice having her home. Yes, I was always at the gate to greet her, but all chats had to wait until she changed out of her navy and white uniform and did her homework in her favourite quiet spot in the garden. When I noticed she was done and packed her books away back in her bag, I followed her around like a little puppy. Most days she went to the kitchen and helped Dear Aunt and the maid with cooking supper, or she sometimes made the dessert. I was allowed to look and learn. My favourite desserts were stewed guavas with custard and cake with custard.

FRANADO

Franado went to Stubbs Government School, which also became my first school. I never saw enough of Franado, he always disappeared into the nearby field after changing out of his school uniform. I thought that perhaps he was tending the sheep and feeding the dogs and the pigs. I found out later that I was correct in my thinking.

When Franado was not at school he went up to the high country on his bike with one of his mates who also had a bike. They returned in the evening, each carrying a large bag that contained various vegetables and fruits. Some of the produce they brought were different from those grown on our farm. I soon picked up from their conversation that they went to a village far up in the country, and that the soil there was better for those produce that we did not cultivate on Dear Aunt's farm. Up there, crops grew in abundance and were sold cheaply, so Franado and his friend were sent there to buy. Other times he went there to collect Dear Aunt's and Father's medications. He also collected medication from another pharmacy not far from Kingstown. I gathered from his conversations with cousin Dorawa that while he was on errand, he took the liberty of riding to Lowmans to visit families. I was a 'chatterbox' the name I was sometimes called, but not once did I speak about the conversations that I overheard between cousin Dorawa and Franado. I loved them too much and hated seeing them being flogged with that awful whip, which they themselves had to cut from a tree remove the leaves and twist the strands. As I look back, it's rather funny. Those who knew that he went to visit family were happy for him. *Who could blame him?* Everyone knew that we lived a restricted religious life.

At this point I paused from writing and called Franado for a quick chat. He now lives with his beautiful wife and family in New York. Our memories brought us tears of laughter.

MY CHAT WITH FRANADO

On our call I explained to Franado that the shut-down due to the Corona virus pandemic afforded me the time to reflect and to write, which is something I always wanted to do. After our lovely long chat, my mind wondered back to supper times and cousin Dorawa's dessert making.

THE LONG WAIT FOR SUPPER

Waiting for supper seemed like forever, especially as I helped to stir the custard, but it was well worth waiting for. As I waited by the kitchen door for our meal to be taken to the dining room, I sang a couple of choruses that I learned in Sunday school. The words of the first one were - 'Sowing in the morning, sowing seeds of kindness', and the other were – 'Bringing in the sheaves, bringing in the sheaves, we shall come rejoicing bringing in the sheaves'. Mealtimes were special. We had three-course dinners, quite a treat! Although portions were small; we were fortunate. Most people on the island had only one course, their potions were large or small depending on what they were able to afford. I know that some had ice cream at three in the afternoon or a seasonal fruit. No matter how long the meal took to get to the table we were not allowed to eat before prayer was said. Our hungry tummies were trained to wait, and proper table manners were vital. Pick up the wrong knife, fork or spoon and the long whip came gently down on the hand by none other than Dear Aunt.

AFTER SUPPER

After supper I was allowed some playtime, and when the sun went down there were always frogs and toads along the garden porch. It seemed as though they played hide and seek games with me. I loved to watch them. Actually, we became friends. There were usually three together, they looked at me and went, "Cluck, cluck, cluck!" I answered, "Cluck, cluck, cluck!" They fascinated me and kept me so engrossed that I never heard when my maid came and stood beside me. At times she tapped my shoulder and caused me to jump. Other times she gently took my hand and said, "Come on now it's time for your bath."

"Oh no! Not yet! Please! I am talking to my froggies!"

"You will talk to them again tomorrow."

Just as well because they disappeared.

MY BATH

The bathroom was adjacent to the house and was accessed from the garden porch via the dining room, just a step up from where I played with my froggies. My maid Rosalie was so lovely. As she washed me she said such nice things, while she tickled me and caused me to laugh aloud. One evening Dear Aunt heard me laughing and later asked me,

"What was all that laughing in the bathroom about?"

"Rose tickled me." I said,

"I'll have a word with her."! I did not want Dear Aunt to do that, I knew that telling her would get Rose into trouble but what was I to say? After my bath I had to quickly run naked and shivering back to the garden porch and through the dining room. At times there were unexpected moments which made me feel uncomfortable. Yes, those times when I had to run past father's son, by his first wife, sitting in the porch chatting with father. I wished I could have ran back, but I could not, so I bolted past without acknowledging them. Yes, I know that was rude of me, but I was too embarrassed to think. I just hurried to the dining room and up the stairs, through the trap door to the bedroom that I shared with cousin Dorawa. She was always there, waiting to massage and powder me, finally she would hand me my night wear, kiss me and leave the room.

FAMILY NIGHT PRAYER

I slipped into my nightgown and sat quietly in the armchair next to our big four poster bed, waiting for the family to gather in the pretty drawing room. Everything in there was built in the same wood, dark mahogany which shone from regular polishing, a job that within months became my weekly duty. Well now, with my ears pressed to the bedroom door, I listened for footsteps entering the drawing room and for the sound of voices. I made sure that they were all there, then slowly and quietly I joined them as I was told by cousin Dorawa to do. They all welcomed me with smiles and nods of approval. I took my seat next to cousin Dorawa, and Father began the night prayer. We had no written prayers to follow. After opening prayer, someone was called upon to read some verses from the Bible. We used the old King James version. When it was my turn to read, I stumbled on some of the words, especially the names, but no one seemed to mind, they gladly helped me along. I began to look forward to the prayer meetings. Eventually I was asked to pray. My eyes moved in fear, and because of my delay Dear Aunt said, "Just tell Jesus whatever you're thinking." Well now, I needed to be smart, because I had lots of thoughts that I could tell Jesus, but could not, since everyone would hear. I think I said, "Jesus, I want to tell you that I love you, and I thank you for being my friend, bless all my family." I was trying to think of more to say but everyone said, "Amen."

CHAPTER 5

FIRST CHRISTMAS IN STUBBS

I thought, *Wow!* I had never seen that many movements. Everyone was doing something different, and tables were packed with all sorts of boxes and things. I wondered *who was that lady helping our maid? I had never seen her before.* "Sheva, this is a very busy day, you cannot be in here. Go and practise the scales," said Dear Aunt but not once did I get the tune right. *What are they doing downstairs? Go on, sneak a peep!* I obeyed my inquisitive mind and got caught.

"I see you," came the voice of Dear Aunt, "it's okay you can stop playing now, go out to the front and do some runs."

"Thank you, Dear Aunt." I replied, and thought, *Oh yes! Good!* I loved to run, touch the stones and back again several times. On my run I met Franado carrying a tree, "Where did you get that tree and what are you going to do with it?" I asked Franado.

"Girl, you ask too many questions, you'll know in time."

By suppertime, the tree was stood in a large pretty box at a corner of the dining room right next to my seat. "Oh Franado, so that's where you put the tree! Why did you put it there?"

"Stop asking questions!" said Dear Aunt.

STRANGE THINGS

The boxes and things on the table had disappeared, I wondered what they did with them. That evening after supper I was not allowed playtime but was given my bath as usual and put to bed to read my Bible Story book. I wondered again, *what about tonight's prayer meeting?* but I thought no more of it and tapped into my book. I loved to read the stories of Jesus. While reading, there was the most delicious aroma, smelt like baking. I took deep breaths, *umm!* More deep breaths and filled my lungs. Next, I knew it was morning.

Christmas day! I took a big stretch, arms up and touched something unusual. *Oh my! What's this up above my head*? I said to myself. To my surprise it was a stocking. *A stocking! Dear Aunt's stocking filled with things and hanging over my bed head!* Then I thought, *yeah! Father Christmas came and left it for me! But where did he get Dear Aunt's stocking?* I wondered. *Oh well, never mind about that! just look inside!* cupcakes were first in hand, too tempting not to eat one. *Yum, yum, umm! That was nice!* I said.

THE TEST

I then jumped out of bed ran to the trap door and down the stairs with my stocking firmly held and shouted. "Look, look, everyone! Father Christmas came and brought me this stocking, filled with nice things." They looked at each other and smiled. "Well tell us what he left you?" they all seemed to have said those words together. That was when I searched through the contents of the stocking and exclaimed, "I've got sweets, balloons, mouth organ and cupcakes!"

"How nice! How many cupcakes did he leave you?" asked Dear Aunt.

"Three" I said, and they all laughed because they knew there were four and that I had lied. Cousin Dorawa later told me she added the cupcakes to the stocking that Father Christmas left. They were actually testing my honesty, while not wanting to spoil my future fun of the expectancy of Father Christmas. Once more my eyes beheld the tree. This time it was beautifully decorated, and every branch held a gift. It was easy to see that most were mine, as none were wrapped.

THE JOYS

First presentation of gifts was after breakfast, the second after lunch and the final one was after supper, then Franado removed the tree. That was the first Christmas I recall. It was wonderful and many more followed. I must admit I lived an upper-class life, the envy of many. Yet, I longed for my family in Lowmans especially those siblings that were closer my age.

CHAPTER 6

JOURNEY TO SCHOOL

January 1947, day and date I cannot recall, but I do remember the excitement on that morning; my first official day at school has always been engraved in my mind. The anxiety, nerves, and joy all had rolled into one. I also recall this feeling when cousin Dorawa told me that Carmody would also be starting with me, and that we would be able to walk along together. Carmody's house was about six hundred metres from mine in the direction of school which was about quarter of a mile away. The journey I was to make twice daily and back for seven years. The first year I left home hand in hand with Franado. The responsibility for my safety on each journey was placed on him. Dear Aunt watched us from the window to see if we were in the company of other children. One day, Franado caught her looking. Their eyes met and from then Dear Aunt moved from looking out of the window to spying from the hedges. She conveniently cut a discreet hole and perhaps thought that from there, she would not be seen spying on us. But one morning our neighbour's son spotted her at the hole and told Franado, as they were good friends. Franado and I came to an arrangement that worked well. When we got to just passed Carmody's house, out of Dear Aunt's sight, Franado went with his friends and Carmody and I held hands. When we were late, we ran all the way. When we were early, we hugged, sang and danced to the rhythm of our song until we got to school. People who passed by stood and stared, and shopkeepers laughed. I am sure we lifted the spirits of many. We were free spirits.

CARMODY AND I AT SCHOOL

Back to the first day, when we arrived at school. We were put in the beginner's class with other new starters. As we were the smallest, we were given front seats, so side by side we sat. We could not believe the easy work we saw on the blackboard for us to do, we both did it in seconds, others struggled. Immediately we were moved up a class stage one. We still had to sit in the front row because the children there were also taller than us. After one term we skipped stage two and went into stage three. And that was the way it was for us after each exam term, until we got to standard six, at the age of twelve. If we had failed an exam, we would not have been promoted. Most children got to standard six, the last class at the age of fourteen, which was the age for leaving school.

Life at school had its ups and downs, teachers were lovely. Carmody and I were teachers' pets, which aggravated some pupils. Can you guess who they were? Well, I'll tell you. They were the slow learners who always looked for ways to cause trouble, the ones who sat at back of the class. At times they did everything they could to distract me. One boy in particular leaned over the seats in front of him just to pull my hair and untie my ribbons, trying to wind me up. I was good at maintaining outer cool, little did they know that I cried inside. Why did they do such things to me? Possibly because I was not from the village and also because I lived with strict Christians? When Franado was around, I had no problems.

AFTER SCHOOL

We left school at twelve noon and went home for lunch. We had to be back by one. Our day at school ended at three o'clock. Carmody and I always aimed to be the first ones out the door, then we ran until we were out of the sight of other children for fear of being bullied.

Bullying was terrible. Everyone in the class who walked the same road was blackmailed by the ring leader, Lyn G. If you did not do what she demanded, you were in for trouble from those who sucked up to her. No matter how hard Carmody and I tried to stay away from trouble, Lyn would set someone up to get at us. Sometimes it would be to catch up with us along the road and usually they grabbed my books, scribbled on them, or wrote rude words. I did not always see what they wrote in my book and when Dear Aunt checked them, she asked,

"What's the meaning of these words?" I no longer replied to these questions because when I said that someone else wrote it, she flogged me for being in their company. The only way to stop the gang and be on their good side was by giving Lyn a gift. She actually told me that that was what I had to do. It was never easy finding gifts, it meant sneaking fruits and peanuts from home to take to her. And whenever I found pennies around the house, I stole them and bought coconut drops to share, and, as if by magic everyone displayed affection. I was never sure how long that friendship would last. I was always cautious, and finding gifts was difficult.

One day everyone seemed as nice as pie, but the next day it all changed for no apparent reason. The worst times were when Carmody and I were not speaking to each other; she would be in with the group and I would be alone, or vice versa. How that happened we never knew. Thank God our division never lasted long, but they were hell days for me. When we made up neither of us mentioned our separation. We were both sorry and ashamed, but words were not necessary, we saw into each other. Eventually Lyn and the gang would come one by one bearing and sharing gifts which we accepted to be at peace. The other girls in the group were fairly quiet and peace loving and when Lyn was absent from school the atmosphere was brilliant.

Another good thing, Lyn was one of the first to branch off the main road having to take the rough road that led in the direction of her house. When she left, we all relaxed and felt the peace. Three others lived close to Carmody. With the absence of Lyn we sometimes chatted together on the way. My house was the farthest. When I could not see Franado to walk me home and when he was no longer at school, Carmody walked with me a few yards passed her gate to accompany me a little closer to mine, then we would both run in opposite directions. Her legs moved swiftly back and mine forward. The truth about Lyn, she was spoiled by her father, she did all kinds of wrong and was never rebuked and if anyone tried, he defended her.

CHAPTER 7

FRANADO RETALIATES

Franado continued to hold my hand as we left the house on our way to school and on our return as we neared home. But he was growing up and became weary of the strictness under which we had to live with gratitude, so he retaliated by taking another route home after school. Some mornings he went his own way to school, and I left home alone. It turned out that most days he was late home after school and had to face the whip. One day when I got to the gate his books were there on the grass, *why were they there? Where was he?* I wondered, I did not take them in just in case he was around somewhere, so I went in and said nothing about his books being at the gate, not wanting to get him into trouble. One hour passed and Franado was still out somewhere, everyone began to panic, and a search party was sent out to look for him, but he was nowhere to be seen. His books were discovered at the gate by someone else and brought in. *So where was Franado?* He went home to Lowmans, how he got there, no one knew. But the following day his dad returned him. My poor cousin said that my uncle whipped him so badly, his mum wept for him and cried, "Don't kill my child," but she could not stop my uncle. He was too furious with Franado for running away.

From then on Dear Aunt became so cross with Franado that he was even more unhappy and distanced himself from us. It appeared that Dear Aunt was no longer able to keep Franado under strict control. He spoke up for himself regardless of the whip.

SISTER DORADA CAME TO STAY

One day sister Dorada came to stay. She brought a baby with her. I am not too sure if it was a boy or a girl but, thinking of the year, I believe it was her first son, Prince. I would have loved to help her with him, but she did not allow me. One evening while I was about to have my shower, sister Dorada had just finished bathing the baby. I picked up the oil to anoint him but accidently dropped the open bottle. *Gosh!* I clearly remember the heavy spanking she gave me on my bare bottom. Franado was preparing to go to Lowmans the following day, in tears I asked him to report my sister Dorada to Mammatee for spanking me. A few years ago, he reminded me that my message, while crying, went as follows, 'Franado, when you go home tell Mammatee that sister Dorada beat me y'hearrrrr.' Sister Dorada did not live with us for long. Why she left, I did not know.

END OF TERM VISITS MAMMATEE KEPT HER PROMISE

I thanked God that Mammatee kept the promise she made that Selda and I would exchange visits during school holidays, although it did not always happen. I was grateful when Selda was brought to me for one week by an older sister, I think Manda or Karen, I was never quite sure. They usually stayed overnight. Selda and I always had real fun together, we were like twins. She always brought me new dresses and we dressed alike. She was well liked by lots of people in Stubbs, even those who deliberately caused me grief. Some said, "Why don't your Dear Aunt keep her and send you back? She is so pretty!" But Selda just hugged me closer. Each time Selda left Stubbs my pretty dresses disappeared, I did not get to wear them, and I never figured out where they went. Dear Aunt believed that Christians were to be simply dressed in plain clothing and especially no jewels. She made my dresses with the help of cousin Dorawa, but they were not dressmakers, and I did not like the clothes they made for me to wear. I had no say in the matter.

THE INCIDENT AT END OF TERM

During one of Selda's end of term visits, we were happily playing hide and seek when I accidentally ran into the staircase and bumped my forehead. Instantly, a lump appeared and covered my left eye. Strangely, although Selda did not bump her head, a lump also appeared and covered her left eye. Consequently, I was not sent to

Lowmans with Selda that year. I tried explaining to Dear Aunt that I was not in any pain and still wanted to go but without success. Our time together was short lived. You could imagine how tenderly I was treated, just like a baby, and that's how it was whenever I was ill. I was often put to bed with an ice pack on my head.

ILL BUT MANAGED TO ACT AT END OF TERM

Another end of term I had the leading role in a play at the school concert. That day I really was not well but the teacher asked Dear Aunt, "Please can you allow Sheva to perform her act and then go home?" I was so happy that Dear Aunt said yes. She then called a friend who had a car and he drove me to school. I acted my part well. Everyone clapped, stamped, and shouted, "Hurrah! Hurrah! Encore! Encore!" Some said, "That was brilliant!" I wanted to stay as I felt much better, but I was not allowed to, so it was home again on Franado's shoulder and straight to bed. I lay there visualising the continuation of the concert because I knew every song and act. Eventually I went off to sleep.

END OF TERM WITHOUT SELDA

Some days during the holiday period, when I was without Selda and not well enough to run around and play, I sat at Father's knee, held his hand and asked him to pray for me to have some babies to care for like my sisters did. I said, "Whenever I go to Lowmans there is a baby in the house, so why can't I have one too?"

He looked at me and said, "Don't worry my child you will have many babies."

"Father, how do you know that?"

"I can see it in your eyes, you are just like your mother."

"In my eyes!" I blurted excitedly "You can see babies in my eyes?"

"Yes," he said.

"Oh, let me have a look in the mirror!" I said, and off I went to look. I looked and looked but I did not see any babies. I ran back to Father. "Father! Father! I can't see any babies in my eyes!" I reported.

"When the time comes, they will be there," he said. "Now off you go and leave me be."

So off I ran in search of butterflies.

I think my parents realised how lonely I was, because Selda visited more frequently. Some of my other sisters came as well, also uncles, cousins and occasionally Mammatee and Pappahen came at different times. Those visits seemed to have started from the time Franado ran away to Lowmans and was brought back by his dad.

MY END OF TERM VISITS TO LOWMANS

My visits to Lowmans did not start until I was about six. I guess they wanted me to be well settled in at Stubbs first. Cousin Dorawa always took me. She left me with my family and continued to high Lowmans to her mother who was my great aunt, one of Dear Aunt's sisters. Cousin Dorawa spent a day or two with her before returning to Stubbs, and when my time was up, she came back for me or one of my sisters took me back. Each time I was in Lowmans I gathered more information about my family and how we became connected. I got to know that my sister Dorada went to live with Mamma El, Mammatee's mother, after she left Stubbs. She then got married and had four more children. I adored them and had much fun playing with them especially the baby Denny. Sister Dorada handed him to me after she had given him his bath, I guess because I was older now, so she felt comfortable giving him to me. This was unlike when she lived in Stubbs, and I wanted to help with her first baby. I held Denny high and sat him on my head, where most times he did a wee. It ran down my face but that was all part of the fun, soap and water was on the spot.

I never knew my Mammatee's dad, he died before I was born. I was fortunate to have had a brief glance at Pappahen's dad, Grandpa Toni, short for Constantino. To me, he looked huge with white skin, whiter than Pappahen's. I later learned that they were of Portuguese origin, hence our surname Da Silva. Pappahen explained to me that the correct spelling for our surname was two dashes under the first 'a' followed by a space and a capital 'S'. I believe Grandma Georgi, Pappahen's mum, was a black Carib. The family had an Afro/Indian look about them, and I presume that Mammatee's mum was from African descent judging by the English surname, Morgan, perhaps given during the slave trade.

One day, on one of my visits, we were sitting on the veranda when a handsome man came to the house. "Who is he?" I asked Selda.

"He is Brother," she replied.

But I soon gathered that his name was Franklyn. We called him Brother to show respect because he was our eldest brother, the same reason that 'Sister' preceded Dorada our eldest sister. I could not recall seeing Brother when I lived at home. He came crying to Mammatee, "Mammatee, forgive me please! Please forgive me!" what for? I did not know. I just knew that I felt sorry for him as Mammatee took no notice. I watched him go still crying, and my heart went out to him.

On another visit, while in High Lowmans, from a distance I spotted a tall white man. I asked my sisters who were with me, "Who is that tall white man?"

"He is our grandpa" I was told.

I don't know why but I remembered feeling scared. I did not get close to him as he disappeared towards the river. I never saw him again. As I grew older, I gathered that down by the river was his private workshop, where he made illegal rum, he called stale dew or moonshine, but when the police found out he had to stop.

This had to be this same year I witnessed an awful incident. One of my little brothers had an accident. Selda, Victor, Chelly the baby and myself were playing in the playroom. Selda ran to the toilet and asked me to keep an eye on Chelly, but he quickly ran to be with her. Instantly he toppled over the garden wall and fell on his head. Within seconds Selda was beside him. On hearing the commotion Karen and Mammatee rushed through the back door from the room where they were sewing to take care of Chelly. God knows they did everything to help him. The hospital also tried but all efforts failed. At one point, Chelly tried to crawl up the partition above the bed were he lay. Mammatee said that Chelly's movement was caused by the sudden flow of blood to his head. We were all in tears as he slid back onto the settee and sadly died. He looked so peaceful in his tiny coffin that was placed in the front garden for viewing. At his funeral we all sang the hymn, *'There is a friend for little children above the bright blue sky, a friend who never changes, a friend whose love will never die...'*. Poor Mammatee could not go to the cemetery, she sat in her chair and rocked in deep sadness. Those who were present may tell this story differently, but this is my memory.

On my next visit the following year, another of Mammatee's babies died soon after birth. It was so sad and worse, I imagine, for Mammatee. However, being in the family home with so many others was comforting and re-uniting with the wider family and friends around the village was exciting. I was always warmly welcomed, and many presented me with little gifts that they kept safe for me when they heard that I was home and would be visiting. Their kindness and generosity made me feel well loved.

This was the year I got acquainted with my second eldest brother, Sonday, and his fiancée, Claire, my half-brother, Tony, and my sister, Thelma. I was told that Sonday lived with our grandmother, Mammatee's mum, whom we called Mamma El. Sonday was never there when I went to see her. Perhaps he went to the mountain, where Mamma El had her farmland, to take care of plants and animals or to his fiancée in the village where she lived. I got to know Tony when he stopped at our house with Pappahen most evenings on his way home from the mountain. Being the 'kitty question' as they called me, I found out that he was my half-brother and he had another brother, who was also my half-brother, who died. I then enquired about their mother and went with Tony to meet her.

How did I get to know Thelma? One morning, Mammatee and a couple of my siblings were on the veranda. I stood on the step that led to the veranda viewing the sea in the far distance when my eyes beheld two of the most beautiful girls I had ever seen. They were coming up the road carrying small bowls of fresh fish. I asked Mammatee, "Who are those two beautiful girls?"

"Don't be so stupid, you know one is your sister."

"No Mammatee, I did not know," I replied. Mammatee did not seem to realise that Thelma never visited me in Stubbs, and it might have been that each time I went home she was out working hard. I later discovered that she was extremely hard working. However when Thelma got close to me, I asked her, "Sister Thelma, do your lips bleed?"

She laughed, and said, "No why?"

"They are so pretty," I said. To me they were a lovely pinkish red. Even then Thelma did not stop to chat as she went to clean the fish and was soon off again. Unfortunately, during those early years I never got to know her well.

After Christmas one year, during another visit, I got to know a lot about my brother PJ's character. I had always seen him but briefly. Like the other older siblings, he worked hard and was in and out, but the day that I got close to him was a Boxing Day, a day for fun or just to take things easy. On that holiday I took my best Christmas present with me, a board game called micky mouse. It had twelve stations and took up to twelve players but could have been played by just one person, which was what I did. The rule was to choose a station, spin the wheel and hope that it will stop on your station. When PJ saw me playing it with some of the others, he was fascinated and came close to watch then joined in. When he got knack of it, he asked me, "Can I borrow it for an hour, I will take it to Shop Rock (a local hangout joint) and make you some money from the guys at the rum shop." I was not bothered about the money; I was just happy to share my lovely toy with my big fun-loving brother. I got to learn that he was into all kinds of sports, especially cock fighting, and that a cock that was given to me by my god father when I was christened got killed in one of PJ's fighting games. Well, as for my mickey mouse game, it too got broken and never came back to me. When I returned home to Dear Aunt, she asked, "Where is your mickey mouse?"

"I gave it to my brother PJ because he loved it." She knew how happy I was when playing with mickey mouse, but she simply smiled. I knew that she was happy to see my selflessness in giving away my favourite toy.

BACK TO STUBBS AFTER MY VISITS TO LOWMANS

Each time I got back to Stubbs after my holidays in Lowmans, Dear Aunt sat waiting for our usual hug and kiss. Then she would ask, "Well Sheva what news do you have for us?" The first time she asked, I spoke naturally about the things Selda and I did together, and my trips to see the family. Every year I had more news to report to Dear Aunt because I kept gathering more information, and she loved it. She and Father taught me to always ask questions, the complete opposite of my immediate family, to them I was 'kitty question.' After I revealed to Dear Aunt all the news from Lowmans, I always hurried to greet Father. His regular spot at that time of the day was on the porch. He seemed to appreciate when I hugged and kissed him, stroked his head and play with his long fingers, but that was just for a bit. Then I would go to my usual pastime, which was to find my frogs, pick wildflowers or catch butterflies.

MEMOIRS OF A SMALL ISLAND GIRL

CHAPTER 8

FROGS, FLOWERS AND BUTTERFLIES

Four years had passed, and my frogs still looked at me with shinning eyes. When I was alone on the porch, they came out of hiding and cluck, cluck, cluck! came their usual sound. I responded as before, cluck, cluck, cluck! We kept this going for a few minutes. I had always wanted to touch them, but Dear Aunt was so protective of me she forbade it. Sometimes tiny toads followed them, they were adorable. To me they were my creature comforts, they seemed to love playing appearing and disappearing games, but where did they go? This was a mystery to me, for when I removed the stones under which they went they were never there, and I did not see any holes. Funny though when I turned to leave, they often came back. But if adults were about, they steered well clear.

I was allowed to pick wildflowers, an adventure I enjoyed, but it took some time before I knew the wild ones from the planted ones. Once, I picked a little bunch of crawlers that ran along the path, pleased with myself I took them to Dear Aunt and said, "Dear Aunt, I brought these beautiful flowers for you!"

"Oh yes! They are very lovely, but you are not to pick these again." I was a bit sad, so she then told me where to go to find the wild ones next time. While I walked through the garden in search of wildflowers, I touched, smelt and talked to the roses and the other flowers. I often danced and sang all kinds of songs that I was taught in Sunday school. My favourite one was, *'The birds upon the treetop sing their song. The angels chant their chorus all day long. The flowers in the garden bend their hue. So why shouldn't I? Why shouldn't you? Praise God too.'* I was also good at composing my own songs and my body moved to the natural rhythm of the song. Our garden was delightful, there were many colourful butterflies. Why did they allow me to catch them and tie sewing cotton around them? They could not have known that I wanted to make them my own, to watch them fly and bring them back to me. And to think of the many caterpillars I put into jars, watched them change to butterflies and fly away. My fun had to be their torture, I never thought about that back then, even though I had a heart of love for them.

The death of frogs made me sad. They did not die in their hiding places but always somewhere to be seen. Dear Aunt said I had to bury them. It was not fun, but I had no choice. So, in obedience, whenever one died, I buried it. They had their own special burial ground, and after the burial I planted wildflowers and sang one of my songs. Afterwards, Dear Aunt would ask, "How was the funeral? Did you plant some flowers and sing a song?"

"Yes, Dear Aunt, I did," was my usual reply.

At one funeral my best friend Carmody was with me, she was still the only friend allowed in my house, and by invitation, which was very seldom. Carmody loved to laugh when she saw how I buried a frog, put flowers on its grave and sing. She just laughed and laughed; she was in hysterics. I did not think it was funny, but Carmody's laugh was so infectious I could not help but join in. Well, that was a real happy day and together we sang, *'O happy day! O happy day when Jesus washed my sins away...'* We sang and danced all the way back to Dear Aunt. She was pleased when she heard and saw us. "Well done!" she exclaimed. After washing our hands, we were rewarded with cake and a drink.

OVER THE HILLS

My ever-enquiring mind always kept me busy. *I must go over to the hills today to watch that ship go by*. I had always seen it from the porch, but I wanted to have a closer look. I was never taken over the hills when the ship was passing.

And this was how it began, "Dear Aunt, please can I go over the hills? I am a big girl now; I will be careful."

"Alright my dear but keep far from the cattle!"

"Oh thank you, Dear Aunt!" I was so excited, I set off singing. I did not get far when I saw snakes, lots of them. I had no intention of going back. *How will I get past these awful garden snakes all on my own? And why must they spread themselves along the path as if it belongs to them? Well, I need to get a move on before it's too late to see the ship*. In desperation I ran, jumped and watched my step as I tried not to disturb the horrible creatures, but to my surprise it seemed that they were more afraid of me. *Gosh look how quickly they disappear into the bushes. Hahaha!* I laughed. And congratulated myself saying, *I'm the winner!* I never thought I would have been so brave to face those snakes and scare them all away. *Dear Aunt would be so proud of me when I tell her*. I didn't even think that she would have allowed me to go, with her being so strict.

Well now no time to waste, I've got to get to the top of the hill, but oh dear, the cows are coming after me! And so is the big bull with his long horns. What shall I do now? There's a guava tree. Go on, climb quickly! Up, up, I went. Well, I could not believe they no longer came after me but seemed to be fascinated by my climb. They fixed their gaze on me and I on them. To my surprise, relief and joy, they were all chained and fastened to stakes. *Why did I not see those chains before or hear their rattling sound? Too scared! Ah well, now I know the length of their chains, I can keep my distance and they can only watch*. I hoped and prayed that none would become angry, pull hard, break the stake and come after me but they stood still all in one accord. Again came the thought, *I must hurry!* I quickly jumped over each row of sweet potato plantation and ascended my climb. "Yes, I've done it!" I shouted! I never got to the top with Dear Aunt, she could not make the climb and whenever Franado was going he always said I was too young and that I would keep him back. I was so happy to be at the top of that green grassed hill alone with Jesus, my invisible friend.

It was an awesome sight. I watched the sunrise above the blue Caribbean Sea down below where the water looked like jewels of many colours. Sea gulls were there having fun, and birds sang sweetly in the treetops on the other side of the hill towards east. As I looked down to where I started, I beheld the wonderful view of the distance I travelled. I saw my house and many others with their brightly coloured paint and their galvanised roofs, they shone like diamonds under the sun. Close to the houses were flower gardens each displaying a beauty of their own. Behind the flower gardens were different kinds of vegetable: potatoes, cabbages, lettuce, tomatoes, spinach, cucumbers, each bordered by a variety of short growing fruit trees: coconuts, mangoes, breadfruit, soursop, guavas, and some others, and among them animals grazed. The branches of the trees swayed to the soft gentle breeze. Birds landed on the backs of the cattle. Fowls scratched the ground in search of worms. I wish I had a camera back then but thank God the scene is photographed in my mind, which reminds me of the reggae song with the words, '*Written down in my mind...*'

Hold on! came my inner voice, *Listen!* I heard the sound, *Tootoo!* Ah, it was the ship. It sailed fast. I wondered whether it would it be possible for a sailor to spot a little girl eight years old dressed in blue dungarees. I'll wave my stick and see, *Oh yes!* He spotted me and quickly he waved back but all too soon the ship sailed passed. I watched as it went around the next rock to the north and out of sight, on its way to dock in Barbados, one of the nearby islands. Well, I did not know that until I shared my story with Father. Father, as he was called by everyone including me, was really Dear Aunt's husband, my great uncle-in-law, Ephraim Halaby. He was always delighted listening to the tales of my little adventures. He also took pleasure in educating me. I guess he observed my love for nature, history, biology, geography, and art; they were my favourite subjects in school.

You'd better make tracks back, said the silent inner voice, *before Dear Aunt send out a search party*. Going back was easy and so much fun jumping over each potato bank. The big bull and the cows stood and watched, they even seemed to have enjoyed my fun. *No snakes!*

Whoa! Were they really afraid of me? Safely back on the porch I shouted, "Dear Aunt, I'm back! I went all the way over and up to the top of the hill. The awful snakes had lined the track, but they slid into the bushes when they heard my footsteps. And on the way up I was afraid of the cattle, I thought they were coming after me but then they stopped. I watched the ship go by, waved my stick to the sailor and to my surprise he waved back and in no time the ship was out of sight!"

"Sounds like you really enjoyed yourself," said Dear Aunt.

"Yes, I did, and the scene from the top was beautiful."

"My dear little bizzy body, I am so glad you had fun. Now what next?" That was when I ran off to be with Father.

Around that period, I needed Father more than ever because cousin Dorawa was no longer a pupil at high school but a teacher in Georgetown, High Windward. She left earlier in the mornings than when she went to school and got home later. I was not able to watch for her bus in the mornings from our veranda because coming from Kingstown, the view was blocked by trees and houses. When she was late getting out of the house, I stood at the gate and stopped it for her, and I no longer watched for it in the evenings as I had little jobs to do. I was shown how to wash my smalls and was sometimes sent to the shop on errands. Whenever I went to the shop Dear Aunt had a way of timing me. She made bubbles between her teeth with her spit, spat it on a stone and said to me, "Be back before my spit quails." By this, she meant before the bubbles in her spit disappeared. I was stiff scared and ran my fastest. One or two people that I passed along the way said, "Girl slow down!" But I never took any notice. When I got to the shop, I tried hard to draw the attention of Father's son because he owned the shop and he knew that I could not wait around, so he always left off serving others and tended to me. I was off again like lightening and always got back to the spot I left Dear Aunt. When my eyes beheld her spit unquailed, I smiled and she praised me. God knows I dreaded the whip.

CHAPTER 9

HOME AFTER SCHOOL

I had no idea that getting home from school with untidy hair and ribbons undone would put me in trouble with Dear Aunt and cause me pain. *Surely it was my hair! Why did she speak as if it belonged to her? And why did she not believe that I did not touch 'her' hair, as she called it?* It was unwise to try and explain that the children sitting in the row behind me were the culprits. I never knew which one, whenever I turned to look, they all laughed under their breath. I came to realise that it was best not to reveal truths to Dear Aunt or show annoyance when she formed her own conclusion putting me in the wrong. I knew she expected my character to be higher than those of all the other children, so as to be a good example to them. I certainly did my best in that respect, so why she assumed that I loved being in the company of bullies, I never knew. One thing I did figure out, say less and receive fewer spanks. Talk too much and you end up with lashes. Worst of all, after the spanking or the lashes was the demand from Dear Aunt to thank her for the discipline and not just a 'thank you', but to reward her with a kiss using the words 'Thank you Dear Aunt for beating me.' This I had to do with a cheerful face. Luckily, she could not see the hurt in my heart. Strange how Dear Aunt loved for me to talk but only when it suited her.

Everyone knew that Dear Aunt was very stern. Some people called her wicked or stupid, which was always to my distaste, for they did not really know much about her. I got to know that she was a very educated person. She worked for the best part of her life in the USA in the nursing profession, retired as superintendent and returned to the beautiful island of St Vincent in the Caribbean, our homeland, where she married Father. They settled on a fairly large farm of their own and employed workers to cultivate it and to care for the animals they bought and reared. When it was harvest time, the last pick from every crop was not to be reaped and sold but, in keeping with the law that God gave to Moses in the book of Leviticus, it was left to be gleaned by the poor to do whatever they wanted to do with it.

People nearby heard about the harvest and came early to glean. Dear Aunt kept a watchful eye and always took some produce away from those who gathered too much. They did not seem too pleased about that but there were others from afar who came late when the field was almost bare. Dear Aunt tenderly asked, "How did you do my dear?" I watched as they showed her their little gleanings. She always topped up their baskets from that which she took from those who had taken too much, and when that was gone, she gave from our own storeroom. So, going back to those who thought that Dear Aunt was wicked and stupid was far from truth. To me, she was kind and generous, but over possessive of the children in her care. Having no children of her own and wanting the best for us, her rules were even more strict than most parents in those days. She was guided by words from the Bible, as in Proverbs chapter 13, verse 24, meaning, don't spare the rod and spoil the child.

Cousin Dorawa was my guardian angel. Quite often when she knew that I was in for the whip, she made me aware of the wrong I did, gave me a little spank and said, "If Dear Aunt calls you for lashes, tell her that I have already whipped you." I was usually in for the whip when I ate something between meals that was not given to me, like fruits I gathered from under the tree or groundnuts left on the vines after harvesting, or late home from school. At times Franado also stepped in and shielded me from Dear Aunt's whip. Sadly, there was never anyone to help them when it was their turn for lashes. They were not aware that I peeped through the keyhole of the locked door and spied as they dodged and danced around the big four poster bed to escape the whip. I think I had it the easiest being the baby of the family.

I also found comfort in kneeling at Father's knee, crying on his lap asking him to pray for me. I also went to him during my happy times provided he was not ill, because he easily snapped when he was not well. After all, he really was old. I knew that he wanted to entertain me but when he found it difficult, he shook his stick and said, "Go away." Then cousin Dorawa or Dear Aunt would appear saying, "Sheva, leave Father alone, he is not well." Father had his own special chairs and walked with stick. His coffin was already built, waiting for him, and stood upright to the wall, in an area curtained off between the ice pantry and the dining room. I was afraid of it at first, but I later became accustomed to it being there and at times when my sisters came, we played hide and seek in it. I found it hard to stay away from Father, or to be still, so off I would go in search of my frogs or butterflies. Other times I did my school homework or secretly chatted with our maid.

One evening, I decided to play on the cosy trap door. It was surrounded by rails and looked like a baby's cot when the door was shut down. As a matter of fact, it was made up as a bed for me for a short while. From there, I heard and saw most things. Yes, I heard my name. Cousin Dorawa and Dear Aunt were talking about me. I quickly slipped from my spot in the cot and pressed my ear to the gap under the door. I managed to grasp the last of the conversation from the report cousin Dorawa brought back from her day trip to Lowmans. "Sheva's eldest brother is dead. He died on the Island of Dominica where he worked as a surveyor." My body went cold. I did not know much about Brother, I just remembered the day when I was in Lowmans, and he passed to ask Mammatee's forgiveness.

Although I had only seen him once, he was my brother. I cried to myself. Later that evening Dear Aunt was very gentle as she informed me that my brother was dead. I don't think she wanted to, but I guess she felt she had to. She knew I would have heard on my next visit or when my sister visited. Nonetheless, that was when I got the full story of how Brother died. He went for a bath in the river after a hot day's work, caught a chill and died within days. By the time Mammatee got to Dominica he was already buried, all she received were his belongings. Another hard time for Mammatee, to lose her first son and miss his funeral.

Mammatee was such a strong woman, everyone admired her. I worshipped the ground she walked on. One day while at home in Stubbs, Dear Aunt called a church sister, Mrs Jack, from the village of Cedars to take me to see a private doctor in Kingstown. Dear Aunt said I was ill, but I felt great. However, I smiled at the chance to go into town, especially with Mrs Jack, she was a lovely lady. While in Kingstown I spotted my Mammatee. I pulled my hand away from Mrs Jack's and sped off to meet Mammatee.

"What's wrong? Where are you going? Don't cross that road!" Mrs Jack shouted in panic, but I took no notice. I just ran to Mammatee and buckled my arms around her legs - well, she was a tall lady, and I was about eight.

Mammatee shouted back to Mrs Jack, "It's Ok! I am her mother! Where are you taking her?"

"To the doctor, her Dear Aunt thinks she is not well."

Mammatee said, "She is fine. Although her aunt was a nurse for many years, she knows little about children. Her problem is she worries too much but you better take her to put her aunt's mind at ease."

When we got to the doctor, he also said I was fine, yet he gave me an injection for the sake of my Dear Aunt's peace of mind. I cried at the pain and when we left the surgery Mrs Jack cheered me up with an ice cream from the ice cream cart along the side of the street. When we got back to Stubbs, Dear Aunt was pleased that whatever she thought was wrong with me would be cured.

CHAPTER 10

ACCEPTING

"Please Dear Aunt," I asked, "can I be baptised with those who are going to be baptised?"

"No Sheva, you are here to watch," she said, but the more the crowd sang and prayed, the stronger were my feelings. Cousin Dorawa was one of the candidates for baptism, along with other members from our Gospel Hall. We all stood by the river side where the water from the river flowed into the sea. It was a wonderful experience witnessing the candidates being dipped three times under the water by the church elders. On the first dip, the leading elder said, "I baptise you in the name of the Father." The second time he said, "and of the son," third time he said, "and of the Holy Spirit." I truly wanted to be one of those candidates, but Dear Aunt kept saying I was too young. Yes, I was only nine, but Jesus was my friend, He lived in my heart. He was actually my secret friend. The candidates declared their love for Him and that they wanted to follow Him. Well, so did I. But then I thought *perhaps Dear Aunt feared that I might have drowned, her being so protective.* Then what would she have said to my parents? Eventually I kept quiet and accepted that my baptism was not to be, not then anyway. When the candidates had changed from their wet garments into their nice white outfits, we all went to the Hall to continue the service. Church was always good. There was one lovely girl my age, when she was not seated with her mother we sat together.

There were many special occasions in our church fellowship. The one I loved best was our yearly conference at the large main hall in Kingstown. Busloads of members gathered from around the island, and some elders came from other islands, I think as far as Plymouth, where the ministry first began called the Bethel Plymouth Brethren. The conference went on for about three days, but I was only taken for one day. That day we were given lunch in a brown paper bag. The bags were packed in large wooden trays and were distributed by a team of about twelve members to every attendee. They contained a large homemade roll filled with beef, lettuce and tomato and a drink. These rolls were made by my aunt and her team at our house. The first time I saw so many women in our kitchen cooking I wondered what they were doing and why were they making so many food bags.

It began with a cow being slaughtered by men in the field. I was not allowed in the field on that day nor for a few days after. No one told me what was taking place, but I overheard from the servants that a cow was to be slaughtered. I also heard the wail from the cow. That was the day the women came and prepared food in our kitchen and had me wondering where they came from and why they were all so busy. I knew by the aroma from the kitchen and pantry that whatever they were making my tummy was awaiting, however, it had to wait until the day of the conference when my food bag was given to me. The roll made by Dear Aunt and her team had a filling that was about two full tablespoons of the meat from the cow that was killed, dressed in lettuce and tomato. The meat was seasoned well and cooked to tender so that it was minced. The roll was delicious.

I also went on some good outings that did not involve the church. A couple of times Dear Aunt and cousin Dorawa took me to Kingstown to visit another great aunt that no one in Lowmans seemed to know about, yet she was one of Dear Aunt's sisters, also Pappahen's aunt. She was very old and bedridden and had a daughter who had many children. We took them gifts although I did not see what those gifts were, I guess my pretty outfits from Mammatee. If that was the case, they needed them more than I did. They lived in such poverty, and I believed they would have been most grateful.

Another lovely day out was on a school trip to South Rivers to the hydroelectric plant. I did not think that I would have been allowed to go but to my surprise Dear Aunt was pleased to send me, perhaps because it was educational. We were shown the stages and the elements through which water passes to produce electricity. Dear

Aunt sent me off with a lovely packed lunch, enough to share with some other children. I shared and we all enjoyed. Such a great day that was but you can imagine Dear Aunt stood at the gate, anxiously waiting for my return.

There were times when cousin Dorawa and Dear Aunt went to Lowmans for an overnight stay. One day they forgot to ask our neighbours daughter to comb and plait my hair for school. Franado decided that he was quite capable doing it for me, but I did not want him to. Boys did not plait little girls' hair. He thought it was fun, he held the comb saying, come on Sheva! I stood there in tears. Father took his side, I could not believe when Father said, "Now Sheba sit still and let Franado fix your hair, or you won't be going to school." Franado had fun, he laughed as I sat still while he plaited my hair, but unknown to them when I got to the neighbour's house, I told one of the girls and she quickly redid it for me. You will have noticed that father called me 'Sheba'. He said my name was not Sheva, and he did not know why I was called, Sheva. I suspect he preferred to call me Sheba because there are references to this name in the Old Testament. I later learnt that the name Sheba means the same as Sheva because there is no difference between 'B' and 'V' as with 'I' and 'E' in Hindi it is Shiva. Sheva also means seven in Hebrew, God's whole number. Genesis chapter one tells us that God created the world in six days, He rested on the seventh and hallowed it. Dear old Father knew so much, it was not possible for him to explain it all to me.

I had slowly accepted my life in Stubbs but there were some things I just did not come to terms with. There were three sisters from the lower part of the village, it seemed as if they enjoyed tormenting me whenever I walked past the bank along their garden. I wondered how they knew the exact time I was passing their house, as it was not close to the road. I prayed that they would not see me. When I did not see them, I thought *great, they are not there*! but then they would suddenly appear and one by one they shouted, "Here comes chest to the front Sheva." Then they laughed "Hahaha!" I took no notice, how could I? They were adults and I had to respect them. But at the time I wondered why were they so horrible to me. My aunt taught me to walk with my head held high, chest forward and shoulders back and that I did. When Carmody was with me she held me close and said, "Don't worry with them." After some time, they left the village, and I was relieved. Just a few years ago I was told that they had had a difficult life, and that I was not their only victim. Sad that they did not know of better ways to deal with their troubles, I was also told that they became Christians, glory to God!

Father's legs had become weak. We needed to walk him to the latrine, which was not too close to the house. He fell twice when I was with him, and I had to run for help. When he ascended the stairs through the trap door, one of us walked behind him, his words were always, "Hold me up me stick! hold me up me stick!" Not once did he fall going up or down those stairs, there were many rails. With one hand he held his stick, with the other he held the rail and once he was safely seated in his chair he smiled. After some time, he was no longer able to use the trap door stairs and had to walk along the garden path to the wide steps onto the veranda then through to the drawing room.

THE UNEXPECTED

Father's health did not improve, within a few months he was confined to his room with a special carer. I saw little of him and missed him dearly and worst of all cousin Dorawa had left teaching and joined the nursing profession in Kingstown. It was vital for her to live in the nursing quarters because it was walking distance from the hospital. Thankfully, she came home on her days off. One of Father's daughters came to stay with us, I thought we would have enjoyed each other's company, like we did when she came as a visitor. Sadly, that did not happen. Her attitude had changed, she became an unpleasant lady. What had caused her to become so unpleasant? Well, I never knew. Even her brother's ways towards us had changed; he no longer spoke with us. Possibly they were grieving at the knowledge that their dad was dying. They were not Christians so perhaps they did not know about the hope of resurrection. The atmosphere was tense. Poor Dear Aunt seemed scared, she spent a lot of time in her room and always kept it locked. Also, she no longer spied on me through the hedges when I was sent to the shop. As a matter of fact, I was no longer sent to Father's son's shop but to another one closer to our house.

One day, we were moved by fear when a solicitor and his assistant came to our home and demanded that everything in the house be checked. It was believed that the counting was ordered by Father's son in light of the estate being bequeathed to him and his children. I was called upon to show the assistant where things were kept. I was pleased that Selda and Christa were spending a few days with me at the time. Christa, the eldest, was always wise; she suggested that I put some things aside. We heard that Dear Aunt had brought all that was in the house from the States before she was married. We did not believe it would be right for her to have to declare all the things she had bought for herself, so I hid the lovely boxes of silver cutlery before taking the solicitor's assistant around.

It was awful watching everything being counted. Dear Aunt became afraid of Father's son and daughter, she kept out of their way.

Father passed quietly. He was placed in his long awaiting coffin and laid to rest in a plain cemetery not far from the sea. The graves there were unmarked, the significance being that those who die believing in Christ have gone to be with Him in heaven so there is no need to fuss about the body's resting place. Wildflowers grew there in abundance.

The changes that followed a few months after Father's death was just too much. First of all, our kind maid, who still came to help us whenever she was asked, left St Vincent to work on another island. I was delighted when she returned once just for a visit, bringing me a lovely gift and staying with us for a few days. Dear Aunt was left to manage the home with the help of Franado. We looked forward to cousin Dorawa's home coming on her days off. Every day I was late for school, our next two neighbours felt sorry for me and would often say, "Ah! Sheva you late again?" When they stopped saying this, Laurette the parrot that belonged to our closest neighbour, continued the comment but she never stopped until I was out of sight. I bent low as I walked past the tree she perched in, praying that she would not see me but even when her eyes seemed closed, she saw me and called out, "Sheva, you late again! Late again! Late again!" Often when I got to Carmody's house she was gone. I was usually the last one on the road to school.

One day on my way home from school, I spotted Franado's books at the gate, but there was no sight of him. I took the books in and gave them to Dear Aunt. After some time with no sight of Franado Dear Aunt sent me to call our friendly neighbour. She came along with her son who was Franado's friend, but no one knew where Franado was. We were all very worried. When Franado's bike was found later that evening at the foot of our garden pasture, it became obvious that he took the track which led past the cemetery where Father was buried, a rough road but shorter than the highway. It was the same passage he took after he no longer needed to walk with me. So that was the day that my cousin Franado, at about the age of eighteen, made his final escape from Dear Aunt's home in Stubbs Village. He never even returned to visit, but I saw him when I was taken to Lowmans. His dad enrolled him into the police cadets, and he worked his way up to police chief until he retired.

However, we were blessed to have had cousin Dorawa's mum, Dear Aunt's sister and also my great aunt. She visited with her two grandsons and stayed for long periods. Other family members also visited more often which was good, but most of the time it was just Dear Aunt and me. We did everything in and around the house together. Those days were tough times because we lost the luxuries we had been accustomed to. Even church life diminished rapidly after Father's death. Some other elders had also passed, and some were no longer able to travel out. Some members in their late teens moved away to build a future for themselves. The church building was then closed, but after a couple of years it reopened on weekdays as a teacher training centre.

I continued to help Dear Aunt with what needed to be done, such as finding wood for the fire when we were out of coal and gas. I always looked forward to cousin Dorawa's home coming on her days off, she brought groceries and all the necessities and allowed me time for rest. Her presence brought me comfort, joy and peace, but two days were the longest she had to spend with us, and I was back to my normal duties.

While searching for firewood I sometimes found mangoes and would eat too many, causing boils to appear on my legs, the very reason why Dear Aunt never wanted me to eat between meals, especially mangoes. Those boils were painless at first and most of them disappeared but there were three that grew bigger, and their heads got scratched by twigs as I walked through the garden. They became infected and very painful. Dear Aunt did her best to keep them from getting worse, but she seemed to have lost her skill in nursing and eventually she sent me to the nearby clinic to receive treatment. Each morning before school, I had to queue for a long while and when it came to my turn the nurse simply applied an ointment. My sores were not healing, instead they got worse. After being treated at the clinic, I went directly to school, arriving even later than before, and my pain made it difficult to concentrate. At that time I was twelve years old, and still managed to pass my exam for entry to standard six, although my pass grade was below my usual achievement. Most pupils got to standard six, at the age of fourteen but Carmody and I got there two years earlier because we were quick learners. However, I never went to standard six in Stubbs School.

At the end of that term when Selda came to visit I told her how painful my leg was and that I was very unhappy. She said, "Ok, I will ask Mammatee to take you back home." Well, I never expected that to happen as I had given up on ever living in Lowmans again. Surprisingly, within a week Mammatee requested my return. I got to know later that my return was against Pappahen's wish. When the day came for me to leave, my sister Karen arrived to collect me. I was sad to leave Dear Aunt, but I wanted to go. I knew I had to go. I consoled myself in knowing that her sister and her nephews were with her when I left. As I walked to the gate, I saw the unbelievable, Dear Aunt shed a tear or two, and so did I as we hugged and kissed goodbye. Her departing words to me were, "Visit me soon." I had no time to say farewell to my dear friend Carmody, and I had no idea if the school was notified, that chapter I left behind. We boarded the bus and my dreams of living in Lowmans was about to become reality.

MEMOIRS OF A SMALL ISLAND GIRL

CHAPTER 11

RETURN 1954

At last, I was back in my original home with Mammatee, Pappahen and nine beautiful siblings. There would have been fourteen but two no longer lived at home and, as I said before, three had died. We had the occasional drop-in visit from Pappahen's first son, Tony. Everyone in the home and village made a big fuss of me. They greeted me by different names; it was either Windward girl, Stubbs girl, or Dear Aunt's girl. And just when I thought that was the lot, came the question, "Miss Dalby girl, you come back? How you doing?" I accepted all the names with a smile followed by the compulsory mannerly words from respectable children, "Yes, I am back thank you! I am fine, thank you!"

Many were fascinated by my accent especially my sister Christa, "Sheva, come and count to us," she would say, "and recite one of your poems, or tell us a Bible story." I happily did and give my best presentation but was limited due to my painful leg sores, nevertheless, Christa loved the way I pronounced words and numbers. I was trained to speak slowly so that the end of every word and number was clear to the listener, but to be truthful people on the Windward side of the island had a different dialect to those from the Leeward. At times I had to listen closely to understand what was being said to me, and I often delivered messages incorrectly, which landed me with more nicknames, which I'll come to later.

My siblings did their best to make me comfortable in my new surroundings. They were accustomed to sitting wherever they wanted to eat their meals, mostly it was in the kitchen. I wanted to join them. I tried desperately to do as they did but I struggled, and they noticed my difficulty. Christa laid the dining table for me as if I were back with my Dear Aunt, and said, "Come on Sheva, sit in the dining room to eat your meals." I was grateful to her but felt separated, so after some time I made myself fit in.

One day I did the most awful thing, thinking it would be fun. I sprinkled water on Manda's face as she lay peacefully on the floor of the dining room having a quick nap. But this was no joke for her. She jumped up in a rage.

"Why did you do that? What possessed you to do that you stupid girl!" and she immediately reported me to Mammatee.

Well, Mammatee's telling off went on and on. They could not comprehend how sorry I was. I instantly regretted what I did.

"I'm so, so sorry" I said to Manda and to Mammatee I said, "I will not do that again."

From then, I began to see the strict side Mammatee, and I became very cautious, realising that I could not be playful with my more senior siblings.

Within weeks of my return grandma Georgi, Pappahen's mum, became ill and was taken to bed. Everyone said that she was a kind, generous and gentle lady, always had something ready to give to her very many grandchildren as they walked past her home. Even when they had no intention of stopping, she called them, which I discovered myself on my many visits to her. Mammatee sent us all up to say goodbye just in case she was living her last days, so we went in turns. When it was my turn to go Mammatee said to me, "Tell her to ask God to heal your sores." It felt strange asking a dying old lady for help, but I did as I was told. Grandma died peacefully two days later. Every Da Silva child was dressed alike in the same black and white cotton print for the funeral. Mammatee told us that grandma provided for this, it was her wish.

I soon discovered that I belonged to a regimental household. Although there was only one clock, everyone moved to the right time. The cocks began with their, "Cock O doodle doo!" That was at three am. Then the birds sang their sweet songs, that sounded like, "You Monkey Eric, You Monkey Eric, You Wake Me Up! You Wake Me Up! You Wake Me Up!" And on that sound Mammatee opened the door between her bedroom and ours, "Children, come on wake up!" she said, and the door was closed again behind her. On the second opening of the door, Mammatee asked, "You lots still sleeping? Come on now, wake up!" And again, she closed the door behind her. If the door was opened a third time, the whip came down on us. Whip, whip, whip! Those who were still in bed scrambled up, legs and arms swiftly moved out of that room.

Pappahen was already up. We sometimes heard him reciting his Roman Catholic prayer, "Hail Mary, full of grace, the Lord is with thee, blessed art thou amongst women and blessed is the fruit of thy womb Jesus." To him that was enough prayer, and it was all he needed, especially as he had to be out early. He was always the first to leave the house for the mountain to milk his many cows. Mammatee was Anglican. I believe she had a deeper sense of spiritual need and did her best to pass her spirituality on to her children. Her first act of the day was to lead us through a short Bible reading and prayer, regardless of what else had to be done. If for some good reason Mammatee overslept, then the milkmaid, who at that time was my sister Karen, was allowed to skip the prayers, but she told us that she prayed on her way up to the mountain.

Karen had to be on time to fetch the milk and take it to Shop Rock in time for Pappahen's customer, Mrs Summer, when she walked past. If Karen was late with the milk, Mrs Summer would not wait, so Mammatee would then use the milk to make a rich carrot porridge. Going back to morning devotion, after prayers were said everyone went off to do their usual chores. Sometimes Mammatee joined Pappahen in the mountain or stayed at home and did her sewing. Other times she went to Town to sell her produce. When she had a lot to sell, at least three of my sisters carried a basket each. Often, I would not see Pappahen and some of the others again until nightfall.

Evenings were delightful, especially watching our dear little Pappahen enter the yard after a long, hard day's work. I joined Selda in taking water to him and washed his legs and feet. There was a short man in the village, shorter than Pappahen. Whenever he passed our house going to his home from the mountain and saw Pappahen he would call out, "Hi little man!" Pappahen would shout back to him, "Know your damn place, I am no little man with you." After everyone had washed up, we had dinner which was prepared either by Mammatee or one of my older sisters.

After we had eaten, on moonlight nights we would play games in the yard, sometimes the neighbour's children joined in. When the nights were dark, we would play on the veranda or sing songs in the living room. Pappahen loved to hear his children sing, he gave coins to the two best singers. I was always second, Manda was first. Whenever I sang to Pappahen, I sat on his lap just as I did during my years in Stubbs when he visited.

Just before bedtime every child in the house entered into prayer. Liturgical prayers flowed fluently from my siblings lips, they all prayed together as one. I was lost for words because I knew no prayers, I only knew how to pray with words from my heart. Mammatee asked me, "Sheva why aren't you praying?"

"I do not know any prayers," I replied,

"What!" exclaimed Mammatee, "You don't know any prayers?"

"No Mammatee." I answered.

"Don't tell me Dear Aunt did not teach you the Lord's prayer!" Mammatee went on to say.

"No Mammatee," I answered again.

"Well, from tonight you are going to learn and sharp. Come on girls," she called to my older sisters, "each of you see to it that Sheva learns the prayers, beginning with the Lord's prayer."

I learned fast. After mastering the Lord's prayer, I was taught another: *Now I lay me down to sleep, I pray the Lord my soul to keep, if I should die before I wake, I pray the Lord my soul to take.* And there was another: *Now I wake and see the light, God has kept me safely through the night, make me good O Lord I pray, keep and guide me through this day.* In no time I knew them all and it was good to be able to join in with my siblings at prayer times and feel the oneness.

CATHEDRAL

Church life was brilliant. There were three services on Sunday mornings at the cathedral in Kingstown, at five, seven, and nine. Mammatee often went to the first service, I guess because she was an early riser. When she went for the second at seven which most members preferred, she took us younger ones with her. One morning on the way home from a 7 a.m. service, we were met by Christa heading for the 9 a.m. We quickly and discreetly exchanged hats, as the one I was wearing was a better match for her outfit. That's the way it was with us sisters and even with very good friends. We happily shared things when necessary.

We did not go back to Kingstown for Sunday school because one was held at Lowmans Hill by an elderly lady whom everyone called Dear Aunt. Dear Aunt, was a caring woman loved by all. As time went by, she entered me into the stage concerts that was attended by almost everyone in the village and beyond. Attendees praised me for my skill in singing and acting, they always shouted for repeats. There were also other excellent actors and actresses. After Sunday school my sisters took me with them for leisurely walks along the highway, usually towards the Lower Leeward. Sometimes we stopped for a short break at the home of Mrs Spring, a relative on Mammatee's side of the family. Mrs Spring had two sons who were teachers, but they were never there when we passed; I got to know them when I started school.

SCHOOL

Just before Grandma Georgi died, I started my first day at Lowmans Hill Government School, where I was rejected when I was four. This was same building I went to for Sunday school. I later learned that it was an Anglican Church, used by the Government as a school. It was where my siblings went, Christa, Selda, Victor and Harran. This was a tough time for me as I had no friends there, and worst of all, the class teacher, Mr Spring, who seemed to be in charge of a few classes, treated me as if I was a dunce. Would you believe that he did not accept the fact that I was a standard five pupil and passed my exam for entry to standard six? To prove his point, he took Victor, my younger brother by two years, from his class which was standard four and gave us both a test. My brother finished first. Can you imagine how shameful that was for me? Mr Spring looked at me and said, "Standard five for you!" I must admit that the class work in Lowmans Hill school was more advanced than in Stubbs school. Yes I struggled, especially as I could not concentrate due to my painful ankle, but my emotional pain was even harder to bear than the physical. I have never had a teacher treat me as this teacher did. He was also my cousin, one of Mrs Spring's sons as I mentioned earlier. He even ate his lunch prepared by my mother in our home!

There were times when Mr Spring sent me home saying my hair was untidy. *Why did he single me out? Only God knew the answer*. When Mammatee saw me returning to the house she called out, "Sheva what's wrong?"

"Mr Spring said my hair was not combed," I replied.

Mammatee simply brushed it with the palm of her hands and sent me back. To my surprise Mr Spring had nothing to say when I returned to my seat. Mammatee was quite fond of him, she never questioned him or explained that my hair was combed each morning for school and that there was no need to send me home. I met with him about fifty years later and asked him what was his reason for treating me the way he did but he made no reply. If only he knew how difficult it was for me walking back and forth on a painful ankle. Thank God, I believe Mammatee sensed my deep sadness mainly due to pain. She arranged with my brother-in-law, who was a pharmacist, to give me a course of peninsulin injections. Within a month my sores were healed. Free from pain, I was better able to concentrate and was moved to standard six. Once again, as in Stubbs, I was the youngest pupil in my class. I had a lot to grasp, and it was not easy.

LEARNING ABOUT MY FAMILY

I was slowly learning more and more about my family. I discovered that Mammatee loved horse racing and that she sometimes went to watch the races. She always went dressed in her best, as if she were going to church. I also got to know that she owned a dance hall just past Shop Rock, and that she loved the sound of brass bands, so she hired a group to play whenever she organised a dance. This was just another of her past times but with an income. I was not allowed at these dances; I went just once as a special treat, and I had to leave early. We had occasional dance parties on our veranda which was attended by some family, friends and neighbours. It was at these times that Pappahen taught us a Portuguese dance which he called, Pankiba. Mammatee and Pappahen both loved to dance and enjoyed watching our dance moves. My parents were real fun loving. Some neighbours also held occasional parties and we were allowed to join them. There was also a group of young men with steel pans; they played calypso and had open air dances just across the road from our house, we all went.

THE MOUNTAIN

Pappahen had a large farm high up the mountain called Calvary, about a mile and a half from home. He went up at the dawn of each day and often returned at dusk unless he asked someone to cover for him. Mammatee sometimes joined him later in the day. My siblings all had their own chores either at home or on the mountain. Those who were still at school had many chores to do before and after school. I was not given any jobs at the beginning apart from keeping an eye on our youngest sister who was four, which I enjoyed, and when I was asked to do things, they were trivial. I loved it when Mammatee said, "Sheva, you are coming to the mountain with us today," but getting up there was a task by itself. I found it difficult to keep pace with those I was walking with. Although I was a good runner, the uphill was not easy. Besides, I was unaccustomed to such a journey. Eventually Mammatee said, "Sheva take your time, we will walk on, and you can catch up. Perhaps you have too much fat around your heart." She said this because I was chubbier than my sisters.

One man in the village called me 'mother bouff', slang for being fat, which I detested and the more intolerance I showed, the more he loved to tease me. I tried to hide whenever I saw him.

Well, I did not lag behind the party going up the mountain for long. I hated the idea of walking alone, especially when meeting people with their cattle and dogs, but worst of all was the fear of stepping on to steep gravelled tracks and dirt roads that were washed away by heavy rain. One could actually see the river far below, "Oh no, I am not crossing," I cried. At first, I was helped across but as days went by it seemed that Mammatee thought it was time, I learned to be tough, so each time we went I persevered harder until I was in line with their steps.

However, one day after a rainstorm, Mammatee, Selda and I went to a place in the mountain called Briggarn to gather produce. While we were there the rain poured harder and the road back had washed away down into the river far below. It was almost dark when Mammatee said, "It's time to go." Mammatee took the lead, and Selda followed. I took one look, ran back sat down. Mammatee said to Selda, "Leave her, she will soon follow," but I had no intentions of following. I thought about going to my brother PJ's watch house that was just one minute walk behind me and staying there. Thankfully, Selda came back took my hand and said, "Come with me and wherever I put my foot I will make a hole, you put one foot after the other into my footsteps." That I did, well what a relief when we got to the end of that break away on safer track.

I was still petrified of facing dangers and had another bad experience. After another rainstorm, the river overflowed its banks and every steppingstone that was used for crossing was covered. Those who were accustomed to the crossing, knew just where the stones were, however, some people got themselves a stick and felt for them. I stood on the bank trembling with fear of crossing. Mammatee went across in seconds, my dearest sister Selda, once again rescued me. She said, "Come take my hand and we'll step together." How I loved her and still do.

I never had to walk such dangerous places when I lived in Stubbs. My siblings were all very strong and brave, especially Thelma, she was tough and hardworking even my younger brothers put me to shame. Victor was only twelve when he helped Pappahen with milking and tending to the cows. Selda had a goat which she cared for.

HOME

Mammatee soon closed the dance hall and turned it into apartments for rent. There was a plum tree on the grounds. Once a month she sent me to collect the rent and to pick the plums when in season. Although I was afraid of many things, I loved to climb and was fairly good at it. I always managed to reach the far branches to pick the ripe plumbs.

BUSY LIFE

Mammatee reared pigs and chickens in our back garden, everyone looked after them. Life was busy, the family was always going and coming. It took me a while to put the names to the faces of a couple of my senior siblings, the ones I saw little of because, one by one, they left home. PJ went to live with Mamma El, Mammatee's mum. I believe Sonday moved to be with his partner. Manda left for the island of Grenada. Thelma went to work in Kingstown and then moved in with sister Dorada who by then had moved from Mamma El, into her own home with her husband and four children. Prince, sister Dorada's eldest, remained in the care of Mamma El. It was about this time that Karen got married and moved into her own apartment, one that was converted from the dance hall.

KAREN'S WEDDING

On the day of Karen's wedding a fowl hen crowed. It is not normal for hens to crow. Our neighbour shouted, "Kill it! It's a bad omen!" I tried to catch it, but it flew away. After Karen's wedding, the guests were driven to the apartment. When Mammatee stepped out of the car she accidently fell into a concrete gutter because the car pulled up too close to the edge. She was rushed to hospital with blood gushing from her head, her hair had to be shaved for the wound to be treated. She was hospitalised for a few weeks. Our neighbour was convinced that the crowing fowl should have been killed, then the accident would not have happened.

CHAPTER 12

LEARNING TO ADJUST

Christa was sent to secondary school, followed by Selda and later, Victor. I would have loved to have attended a secondary school. Mammatee said I was bright and could win a scholarship to secondary school. She did not know that pupils for scholarship were chosen from standard three and I was in standard six. During this time, I actually felt like an outsider, and referred to myself as no body's child. When I met with cousin Dorawa she said that if I had stayed in Stubbs, I would have gone to secondary school. I began to wish that I had not left and wondered how I might go back but I dared not ask.

HELPING OUT

Life was so different from what I was used to, but I was gradually getting into the swing of things. I became a good all-round helper. Some early mornings I went to the mountain with Mammatee to collect produce and occasionally accompanied her to Kingstown to sell to the early shoppers. I had to be home in time to put the family lunch on the fire and left it with just enough firewood to slow cook before heading off to school. Mammatee said that I had to ask my head teacher to let me out fifteen minutes before the lunch hour to make the gravy as I was the only one left to help. Selda and Christa had to leave home early for school in Kingstown and they did not return home for lunch, also our older sisters were no longer at home to do the cooking. I really missed them, especially Karen, although I was happy to escape her whip. She loved to whip me when I was not quick enough in doing what she asked of me. I was always late for school and had to explain to my head teacher, Mr Glencoe, the reason why. Thankfully, he accepted what I said. Those mornings passed quickly, just as I got into my class work it was time to go home to finish the lunch. I would nervously go to Mr Glencoe asking, "Please sir, Mammatee said "Can you kindly let me leave now to finish off the lunch?"" He simply lifted his eyes towards me, raised his hand and nodded his head affirmatively. I would run all the way home to make the gravy. Lucky for me, sometimes Mammatee got home early and had started it.

Mamma El, my grandmother, requested for me to accompany her to Kingstown on Saturday Mornings, to help her sell her fruits and vegetables. I loved being with her, she was special, and she treated me like a princess. The first time I went with her she spent all her takings on me. She bought me a hat and a pair of shoes. When we got back to Mammatee's house, I said bye to Mamma El, thinking she would walk up to her house without me, but she said, "No, you are coming up with me." I was very happy indeed. When we got up to her house, she said, "Now hang that hat on the peg and put those shoes under the settee, they are for whenever you go to town with me. Thank you for today, now you can go back to Tina." Tina was Mammatee's name. I was a little sad to leave my gifts but was happy to know that they were there for me.

SCHOOL OUTINGS

By this time, I had settled in at school and made many friends. We went on three educational trips. The first was up to St Andrew's Mountain. We walked the Lowmans Hill road all the way up, then followed the track to the peak. At the top we saw mountains with some plantations on the lower Leeward, and across the strait, known as the St Vincent Passage, the island of St Lucia came into view. It was a clear day and our headmaster said to us, "You are now looking at View Fort, the nearest point of St Lucia to St Vincent." We actually saw clothes lines with people's washing blowing in the wind.

Our second outing was to the Old Sandy Bay, High Windward, the northern part of the island. We climbed the high rocks that extended into the sea, from where we should have had a better view of the bay and the towns of Owia and Fancy, but I was too scared to look. We held one another's hands and formed a chain for safety.

Our final outing was to the volcano, La Soufriere. The bus took us to Georgetown, also on the Windward, from there we walked up to the crater. This was another amazing experience. Our headmaster was extremely brave; he went down the crater to the lake and brought up a bottle of water and some seaweed. These three trips involved very dangerous climbs, but teacher Glencoe wanted us to learn as much as possible about the island through nature and to make us strong, brave men and women for the future. His thoughts on children's bravery was the same as Mammatee's.

MAMMATEE'S CHANGING MOODS

At times Mammatee was so sweet, and when she was in this mood, I loved to be near her. But when she was fierce, I steered well clear. I found out that her beatings were worse than Dear Aunt's. Mammatee was much younger and stronger, besides, she used a leather strap that did not fall to pieces like the whip. She also permitted older siblings to beat the younger ones whenever they thought it necessary. Pappahen was different. He could not watch his children being beaten. His question to her was always, "Tina, why are you beating up the children?" Then he would go out of sight. One afternoon Christa, Selda and myself were off to the mountain. We were playing along the way, when suddenly, out of nowhere, we felt, whop! When we looked it was none other but brother PJ. We legged it so fast he did not have time to throw the second whop.

At the end of one school term children were asked to stay behind and help with cleaning benches. I happily joined the team without Mammatee's permission and stayed too long. As I approached the corner where our house could be seen, I saw Mammatee waiting at the gate with her belt in hand. The look on her face made me afraid, I stood at a distance hoping and praying that she would ask, *Sheva, why are you so late?* but those words did not come. One by one spectators gathered, unexpectedly one of my cousins, picked me up and took me to Mammatee. I think she was pleased with him. She beat me on my bare bottom so hard that it hurt when I tried to walk, yet she said,

"Now come on with me to the mountain." That was my second beating from Mammatee, my first came after she found my practise letter writings. Although I wrote many kinds of letters, Mammatee picked out a love letter and without a word she grabbed me and down came the belt. In tears, I asked, "Mammatee, why are you beating me?"

"Why?" She replied, "That letter you wrote to that boy. You are not to write letters to boys!" Lash, Lash, lash. "Do you hear me?"

"Yes Mammatee, I hear you," I replied. There was no point explaining that the letter was not meant to be sent to anyone. Mammatee was still furious when she said, "Now go!" I had often watched her flog my siblings and silently wept for them and wondered how my siblings took all those lashes. I knew I had to find a way out, which you will hear about later.

THE STORM

Not long after Karen was married, her husband went to work in the USA. Mammatee sent Selda and me, in turn, to stay with her at nights. By then, she had given birth to her first son. One night in 1955 there was a storm named, Janet. Janet was fierce, so bad that one Calypsonian composed a song, *'Janet blow with the whole of the army'*. I had never been out in a hurricane before, let alone one as bad as Janet. I got to Shop Rock and there she was in the sky coming down in full force like a rocket circling down right in front of me, a hapless thirteen-year-old. I took to the ground on natural instinct and crawled on my belly like a worm. I wiggled my way along the high road and tried to keep as close as possible to the sidewalk, luckily no vehicles passed at the time. When I got to Karen's house, I was breathless, and panic stricken. Still on my belly I lifted my hand and banged on the door. Karen opened and quickly pulled me in asking," What's wrong? What's wrong?"

"Look it there! There! There!" Was all that I was able to say.

Karen gave me a drink and said, "OK! OK! Go to bed." Next day, the calm was as if nothing happened, but Janet left her story. Plantations were uprooted. Large trees blocked roads. Many house roofs were blown off they had to be recovered and restored. Some houses were rebuilt. Oh what a night that was! Janet was all the talk and for many years after.

EVENTS FOLLOWING THE STORM

About a month after the storm there was a shortage of teachers. In response to this dilemma Mr Glencoe sent me and a couple others from my class to help teach the infants. I loved it, but my education suffered. It was at this time that Christa left secondary school and began teaching at my school. I also think that this was when Victor joined Selda in secondary school. I was still helping Mamma El with the selling of her produce and doing my many other chores. Sadly, Mamma El became ill and bedridden. My sisters and I took turns in staying at her house to keep company with her and those who were living with her. Thankfully, she lived to see some of her great grandchildren. She died September of that same year 1955. PJ returned home, and sister Dorada took her son, Prince. I missed Mamma El a lot, and found myself worrying more about Dear Aunt, because they were about the same age. Mammatee allowed me to visit her regularly. I always made sure cousin Dorawa would be there before going. She still lived at the nurses home in Kingstown, easy reach from Lowmans Hill, so I saw her often, usually on my way to or from the market. Sometimes when she was in her room I stopped by. When she was free, she styled my hair and gave me manicure. She was always pleased to hear that I wanted to visit Dear Aunt.

It was Christa's delight to accompany me to Stubbs until I was capable of going alone or with a cousin. Going with Christa was fun, the first time we went she said, "Stubbs is not far, let's walk and buy snacks with the bus fare," which we did, but we had to stop in every village wherever we found a place to sit, rest and enjoy our snacks. When we reached Stubbs and turned towards the gate, things were different from the way they used to be. Gates were unlocked and no dogs rushed to them. We just opened, went in and searched for Dear Aunt until we found her. Her face always lit up when she saw us, which was welcoming. Most times cousin Dorawa came while we were there and left us there. Dear Aunt enjoyed our company and we loved to be with her. Leaving was always sad and Dear Aunt wore a solemn look except for the times when her sister, cousin Dorawa's mum and her grandsons were with her.

On one of my visits Dear Aunt gave me a tiny piglet, hoping that she would grow, mate and be productive to help us both. I held her in my arms all the way back to Lowmans. She got so attached to me that every day she followed me around like a little puppy; sometimes she hid under my dress and refused to leave. My family named her Frock-tail. One year later she only grew by just a few inches. Mammatee, who knew all about pigs, said that Frock-tail was not from a good breed and needed to be put down. Frock-tail was slaughtered very early one morning while I was still asleep to spare me the pain of seeing and hearing her cries. Her meat was sold but because she was small no profit was made. Dear Aunt was rather surprised when I informed her about the growth of the pig because that was unusual.

I guess you might be wondering was I still at school. Yes, I was, and during the school holidays I helped more on the mountain, especially when Pappahen was harvesting. I had two close friends Stycie and Preccy. Pappahen loved Stycie and was happy to know that she was my friend as he did not approve of all my friends. When he was reaping, he would say, "Sheva, why don't you ask that nice friend of yours to come to the mountain with you? She would be a good helper." Stycie lived with her grandmother, whose permission I had to request. She always said yes, and Stycie was happy to join me and my family. At the end of each day, Pappahen gave her a good helping from his reaping for her to present to her grandmother.

Pappahen did not like that I had returned home from Stubbs although he said little about it, everyone noticed the way his attitude changed towards me. When he was sweet on his Sunset rum, he often said, "I don't know why you leave Miss Dalby and come back here to mix with the crowd." He only called her aunt when they were face to face, he often went on to say, "You were alright where you were." At no time did I reply. Sometimes when he said those words, he made as if he was going to hit me. I hid, mostly under the bed. He sometimes wabbled a stick trying to feel for me, "Where is she?" There were times when Mammatee became worried and sent me to sleep at a neighbour. Stycie's grandmother was just one of those who welcomed me, and I enjoyed my sleep overs. It was good fun wherever I stayed.

My other dear school friend, Preccy, was one year older than me. One day when we were about to go home for lunch, as usual we stood up to recite the prayer: *Grace before meals- Be present at our table Lord, be here and everywhere adore, bless these thy gifts and grant that we may feast in Paradise with Thee. Amen.* While praying, Preccy spotted that I had started my monthly cycle. I had no idea, I felt nothing and knew nothing, no one told me that this was to be expected. Preccy kindly diverted from her way home and walked behind me to my home so that no one else would notice my stained skirt. When we got to our house, she said, "I am not leaving until you tell your Mammatee what's happening with you." I had to quickly tell Mammatee so that Preccy could go home and have her lunch. As I did, she smiled and left. I got the impression that Mammatee seemed to think that everyone knew all about the facts of life as she simply showed me where diapers were kept and how to fold and apply it. With so many older sisters I ought to have known all that there was to know, but I was kept completely in the dark. I still wonder why on earth did they keep such important matters under cover, but perhaps that's the way it was with some families. However I believe, had I remained in Stubbs, Dear Aunt or cousin Dorawa would have enlightened me. I learned every lesson on the reproduction of life the hard way.

We entered the year of 1956 and my sister, Manda, returned from Grenada with a beautiful baby boy.

Throughout her stay, she took over the cooking, which afforded me a welcomed break. She also kept a watchful and protective eye out for us, her younger siblings. At that time there was a girl in my class called Precious, from Montrose. It seems she came to our school for the purpose of bringing teacher Glencoe's lunch, which was prepared by her mother, and she would stay on in my class. She turned out to be a real troublemaker. She told Mr Glencoe many false tales about myself and others. I can't even remember what her stories were. We figured that she was hoping to get him to like her more and dislike us. One afternoon when we left school, I confronted her about her lies. She denied and threatened to beat me up. I quickly ran home and told Manda the full story and that I was afraid of Precious. Manda became furious and asked, "Where is she? I'll soon stop her." I explained to Manda that every day she followed me closely on the way home to lunch. The next day Manda unexpectedly appeared at the gateway as we left school and asked, "Sheva, where is this girl who is giving you trouble?" As soon as Precious spotted Manda and heard her voice she ran for her life and never returned to Lowmans school. Her sister, Blessing, was sent in her place. Blessing was a kind and gentle girl, loved by all. One of the good things about living in Lowmans, almost everyone was family or friend, so no outsider was able to take advantage.

Mammatee no longer needed to wake us in the mornings, we were up in time to pray and do our chores before school. Some days, when she wanted to set out really early for Kingstown, she would wake me to plait her hair. Due to the head injury she suffered, her hair was growing but still too short for her to manage. I also did Selda's for school, hers was very long, I watched as she tried her best to plait it, but she had difficulty getting nice smooth plaits, so I offered my help and she gratefully accepted. I was good at plaiting hair. Mammatee told me that one day while she was in Kingstown one of her tenants, Mrs Grimshaw, noticed her hair and commented on how lovely it looked. Mammatee then said to me, "I told her that you're the one who does it for me." I smiled. Mammatee went on to say, "She asked me, if I can let you plait hers once a month, she will be happy to pay you." Again, I smiled, and Mammatee asked, "Would you like to do it for her?" As it was just monthly, I agreed and decided to do it when I collect the rent. Mammatee discussed the arrangement with Mrs Grimshaw, and she was pleased.

Mrs Grimshaw had beautiful hair, I loved to comb and plait it and I admired it when I was finished. At first, I refused to take her money and ran off when she handed it to me, then she called out, "Sheva, if you cannot take the money, I don't want you to do it again." I turned back and accepted with thanks. Like Mammatee and Selda, Mrs Grimshaw was always happy with her hair styles.

CHAPTER 13

MANY LEFT

1956 was the year that made history. The mother country opened its doors for people to enter, live, work and stay, now known as the Windrush. Many people took up the offer and left the island. Each month they sailed off in boatloads, mainly to St. Lucia where they boarded the ship to Britain. My brother, Sonday, was one of the first to leave, even though he no longer lived at home he was greatly missed. Next was PJ. Then Karen and Christa. Thelma did not join them, she sailed south to the island of Trinidad leaving just Manda, Selda, Victor, Harran, Winnie and me. All too soon the numbers in our home shrank. About a year later Manda gave birth to another son, Follu, but she soon returned to Grenada with her first son, and left Follu in the care of his aunt, Preccy's mum.

SCHOOL CLOSURE

At the end of that year came another blow for me. News began spreading that Lowmans school was going to close. "What, no more school!" I began asking around, but no one seemed to know much. Some people said that a new one was being built in the new village and it would be ready for opening in the new year. More awful news, teacher Glencoe said, "Those who are fourteen will not be accepted in the new school." Most pupils were allowed to stay to fifteen even though the leaving age was fourteen. My friend Preccy turned a deaf ear and went to the new school; perhaps her true age was never revealed. She was accepted but she did not stay there long. I guess if I had joined her, I would have been accepted also. Stycie left her grandma and moved to her aunt nearer to Kingstown. Some others passed their school leaving exams and became teachers in the new school.

GOODBYE SCHOOL

Mammatee said, "Sheva, you might as well stay with me, no point in going back to school." I felt dejected because my brain was just ready for learning. Selda was still going to secondary school and Victor was sent to join her. Harran and Winnie went to the new school, how strange things turned out? At that time, I was the only one on the spot for Mammatee. My workload was doubled; washing, ironing, cooking and mountain jobs were all part of my duties. Pappahen also asked me to wash and iron for his best friend, as his family no longer took care of him. I happily obliged and he paid me generously. Meanwhile, I used every opportunity to plant lettuce and aniseed for sale, to help myself financially. I also joined a family in going to lower Leeward once a week to buy plumrose, sapodilla or whatever fruit was in season, which we then sold in Kingstown to make a profit, although we lost money when the fruits were not sweet.

Selda did the cooking and cleaning at weekends, she also gathered wood for the fire. When she started secondary school, Mammatee no longer let her carry goods to town unless we had large quantities and when she did, it was just to drop off. Selda did not want to be seen by her school friends carrying and selling produce for fear they would look down on her. Mammatee understood and agreed that Selda was not to hang around the market. Mammatee was lovely when she wanted to be. I discovered that her worse fault was favouritism, and she was not good at hiding it. Selda was given shoes to wear to town to maintain her dignity. I had to go bare feet. One morning, the three of us went into town, they both wore hats and shoes I was without and felt uncomfortable. I lagged behind feeling and looking sad. They entered the gate of a customer and walked up to the house. As I stood at the gate, the customer spotted me and asked, "Who is that girl? I wonder what she's selling?"

"Oh she belongs to me!" Mammatee replied.

"Call her," the customer said, so they did.

"Come, come, forward!" they called, so I went.

"What a pretty girl!" said the lady.

"Do you think so?" Mammatee replied.

"Yes, she has a beautiful round face."

"I never thought round face was beautiful," Mammatee said, "I see this one," pointing to Selda "as beautiful. She has a nice long face." Mammatee had always loved best, the ones she thought were most beautiful, which was her reason for never letting me be bridesmaid at family weddings. Yet I loved Mammatee with all my heart. Whenever we out together, and I sensed that she was tired or not feeling too well, I walked behind her as I did with Father when I lived in Stubbs.

DRESSMAKING

Mammatee sent me to learn dressmaking with her elderly cousin up in the village. She was paid with provisions for which she was grateful, and I felt pleased to be a student. I was never shown how to cut dresses. I spent much time basing seams together before I was sent on the sewing machine. Thankfully, it gave me the general idea of cutting. Two of my older sisters were sent to learn with a well-known seamstress in Kingstown who had to be paid with cash. I saw this as Mammatee not wanting me to excel but, bless the Lord, I was soon able to make my own dresses and Mammatee was surprised.

FREDRICK CAME AND WENT

Around this time one of our nephews, Fredrick, who was about six years younger than me, came from lower Leeward to live with us. He was the son of our eldest brother who died when I lived in Stubbs. Our nephew was so much fun, he had the most beautiful smile and infectious laughter. His jokes rolled out one after another and kept us in stitches of laughter. We all wondered where he learnt the tales he told. Sadly, one day his stepdad whom he referred to as a horrible man came looking for him. We hid him well so that he was not found, but unfortunately his mum requested that he be sent back. We believed that it was due to pressure from her husband; he needed Fredrick to work with him. That was the end of our great fairy tale nights.

CONFIRMATION

One Sunday morning in the year of 1957, it was announced in church that confirmation classes were to begin the next week. I felt ready to start lessons, so I asked Mammatee, "Please can I start confirmation lessons?"

"Yes." she said.

I went in the company of my eldest nephew, Prince, along with one of our friends, and also our neighbour's second daughter; they had also expressed their desire to be confirmed. I worked harder growing and selling herbs as well as selling bottles that I collected from wherever to buy my outfit. I had some savings, but I wanted to be sure I had enough, as I did not want to put extra burden on Mammatee. I was always willing to help myself. When I knew that I had an adequate amount of money saved, I bought some white material for my dress which Mammatee made. She already had a veil handed down from my older sisters, so I saved on that. I went to every shoe shop in town until I found a nice white shoe that was my perfect fit. On the day of my confirmation, Prince and I got dressed in town in a room that my brother-in-law rented, which I believe he used as his work's office.

I felt very pure in heart especially when I walked to and from the alter. Everyone who attended commented that I looked like an angel. My brother-in-Law took photos, they were lovely, but I do not know what became of them. From then, I helped with teaching in our Sunday school and also in the Apostolic Faith Church Sunday school, they loved having me. When I visited Dear Aunt and told her what I was doing she was very pleased to hear of my spiritual growth, especially my union with the Apostolic Faith Pentecostal Church.

FRIENDS IN SALES

During my time selling in town, I made other friends. Phyllis was one of them, although we had attended the same school, we were not friends then. Phyllis seldom went to school but whenever she did, her work was always excellent. It was the same with her siblings. One morning, I was late getting home after selling lettuce. It was a hard morning because many people were selling the same kind of lettuce but my skills in selling paid off. Mammatee had taught me well! I did good even though it took me longer than usual; some people had to take their lettuces back home. Phyllis was with me throughout my endeavour and noticed how hard I pushed to get a sale. It so happened that as we walked towards our gate, Mammatee and Pappahen sat on the veranda.

"Sheva, why are you so late?" Mammatee called.

"Well look at dat!" Phyllis blurted out not waiting for me to speak, "Yo do good, Mamma rass yo, yo do bad, Pappa rass yo, yo might as well do bad and done!"

Pappahen heard and he was fuming, "Who is that you in company with? Keep away from bad company!" he shouted.

From then I was afraid to be seen with Phyllis.

Two weeks before, Phyllis had given birth to a pretty baby girl. Phyllis was not a church goer and she had only one other friend besides me who was. She asked us to be godmothers to her baby, we both said yes. I felt honoured, but how was I to tell this to my parents? I could not, and did not, so I kept it quiet from everyone and prayed that nothing would prevent me from attending church that Sunday for the baptism. Phyllis did not even go to her baby's christening, the baby was carried by the other godmother for which I was grateful, and all went well. I soon became godmother to another child and without fear for Mammatee and Pappahen both approved my friendship with the mother.

CHAPTER 14

BEATING?

Things were beginning to look up for me when out of the blue Mammatee called me for a beating. Going back to what I said earlier about finding a way out of being beaten; the following explains how I escaped.

It began one day in July 1958, Mammatee said, "Sheva, come and let me beat you!"

"Beat me!" I asked, "what for Mammatee?"

"Don't you know that the upholder is worse than the thief?"

"Thief? Upholder? What are you talking about, Mammatee?" She did not explain but I soon realised she was talking about something that was taking place which she thought I had encouraged. How strange? I knew absolutely nothing about the circumstance and refused to take a beating for something that did not even concern me. I began to defend myself against the injustice that was set upon me but then I was seen as being rude. Mammatee left and went to the mountain, but I knew she would not forget about beating me. I was supposed to join her on the mountain but instead I washed and dressed in a new dress I had made the previous day and stepped into my new gun slingers, now called flip flops, and off I went to Mammatee's sister, who lived on a hill overlooking town.

ESCAPE

When I got to my aunt's house the door was shut but not locked. I knocked then pushed. "Good evening aunty," I said, without waiting for her reply, I went on, "Aunty, Mammatee wants to beat me for something I know nothing about. Please can I stay with you?"

"If your Mammatee wants to beat you, go back and take your blows, you can't stay with me." Aunty replied.

"Ok, bye aunty." I said, but I did no such thing, instead I walked on to the tiny house that my cousin Tish rented and lived in alone. I braved every step to the door then nervously I tapped gently and waited, followed by tap, tap. The door opened, "Hi Tish!" I said, and asked, "Please can I stay the night? I am scared of Mammatee, she wants to beat me for nothing."

"Ok" Tish said, "you can stay."

"Thank you, thank you!" O boy, I was relieved! But I was still scared thinking Mammatee would find me. Well, she did not. Morning came, Tish made breakfast for us and left for work.

FEAR

My thoughts began to run wild, *what am I do now? I must do something I need to pay my way!* So off I went down to town in search of a job as a sales assistant, I knew I was good at that. I tried almost every store without success. Sadly, I returned to Tish's house. From there I saw every move made in Mammatee's yard. I watched and wondered whether Mammatee would come for me and not give me a beating. I knew she needed help to carry Saturday morning's load to the market in town for sale, but instead that morning Mammatee took my sister, Selda, whom she had not taken for a while. Tish returned from work at dusk and brought me supper. I had no time to eat when I heard *knock! knock! knock!* "Open up!" came Pappahen's voice, "Is my daughter here?"

"Yes, she is." Tish answered.

"Come on out Sheva!" shouted Pappahen, "out now!"

Out I went relieved but scared. As soon as I got to the door Pappahen grabbed me by my arm, he was not alone, he had one of his strong male friends with him; He grabbed my other arm and without a word they carried me. My legs dangled above ground as they walked briskly.

"Oh, Pappahen!" I cried "Mammatee is going to kill me now! Please Pappahen don't let Mammatee kill me!"

"She won't," Pappahen said, but I did not believe him.

As we neared the house Pappahen and his friend let go of me and Pappahen said, "Now go and hide yourself somewhere out of your Mammatee's way." I quickly ran and hid under Mammatee and Pappahen's bed. I said to myself Mammatee would never find me here. Morning came and Pappahen dragged me out by my feet. *How on earth did he know that I was there?* No time to ponder, Pappahen gently whispered, "I am taking you to the mountain with me." Once more I was relieved, Pappahen repeated that action for two weeks. Each morning I made breakfast for us in his cosy watch house on the mountain.

During that time not a word was spoken by Mammatee to me or about me. When we met for supper, she acted as if I was not there. After the two weeks Pappahen said, "Sheva, it's time for you to get close to your Mammatee, I am going to give you a basket with all that she will need for tonight's supper." The basket contained a variety of provisions and wood for the fire. As he lifted it onto my head, his instructions were, "Whenever you notice that your Mammatee need something, jump quickly and get it for her, do not allow Selda do get to her before you, and when you see that the fire is dying down, put some more wood and keep it going." I did everything as Pappahen said. Mammatee relaxed her tension. When I saw a wee smile on her face, I felt good. Pappahen was right, he knew just what would please Mammatee. I no longer slept under their bed, and he no longer gave me that daily call, but some days I got ready and went with him. I enjoyed being with him on the mountain. I knew that Mammatee was pleased to have me helping her again especially when she had a lot to take to town for sale. On the days she ignored me, she would pack two head baskets, one for her and one for Selda, she would also pack a large hand basket which she carried. The day that Mammatee relaxed, I noticed that she had packed three head baskets and just a small hand basket. My heart sang for joy because I knew one was for me. Mammatee did not beat me for running away and I was never beaten again. Hallelujah!

Well, although things became better at home, I still felt like an outsider. I never understood Mammatee's attitude towards me, her moods were so changeable. For this reason, whenever it was possible, I continued to spend time with Pappahen on the mountain.

TAKING CHARGE

February 1959 Selda went into hospital and gave birth to a beautiful baby boy, Gerald. While she was there, Mammatee was admitted for an operation. I did my best to take care of them both by replenishing daily their night dresses and other necessities. Mammatee loved the food I took for her. The other patients sometimes commented that I was nice girl and Mammatee would reply, "Yes, she is my daughter." After a couple of days she said, "Sheva you do not need to cook for me, I get food in here, you have enough to do." Mammatee knew well that all the responsibilities at home was left to me but I enjoyed looking after them both, as well as doing the other chores.

That same week Pappahen's crop of cucumbers was ready to be picked and sold. Victor and Harran helped with the picking and brought them down from the mountain. I took them into town for sale but before I reached the market they sold like hot cakes, and the takings were good. I did exactly what Mammatee would have done with the takings; I bought the weekly groceries and gave the remainder of the money to Pappahen. Pappahen was very pleased until one interfering neighbour came and told him that I made loads of money. In the presence of the neighbour Pappahen asked, "Sheva, why have you brought me so little money when you made loads?"

"Pappahen, it's because I bought the groceries just as Mammatee would have done."

Our neighbour walked away looking despondent, and Pappahen left it at that.

Selda left hospital after one week and Mammatee a few days later. I still continued to be a good manager of the home. Mammatee and

Selda needed to rest and time to recuperate. But how can I explain the joy I felt in having them all home. Selda with my gorgeous baby nephew also Mammatee relieved from pain and beginning to look well again. It was all worth the hard work.

DECISIONS

From then, I began thinking that it was high time to leave home and make my headway in life. Getting married seemed to be one way out. My days of learning to be a seamstress was reduced to almost nil. I still spent few days with Pappahen on the mountain, sometimes we were joined by Tony, Pappahen's first son, who came from his land nearby that was given to him by Pappahen. We had lunch together and enjoyed a chat after. A number of times I brought up the subject of marriage to Pappahen, "Pappahen, I would like to get married." He tried to ignore me.

"Pappahen, Sheva is talking to you." Tony said.

"What?" Pappahen asked,

"Pappahen, I would like to get married." I repeated.

Still Pappahen made no reply. I believe I had good reasons for wanting to get married. The first being I continued to feel unloved and unwanted, by Mammatee. Although we were much closer, I still struggled to understand her changing moods. I was unhappy at home and thought that marriage would be a way out; second, boys had become a nuisance, everywhere I went there would be one whistling, sending messages or following me. I even had to ask Victor to have a word with one of them, it seemed as though they were immune to my words, *get lost!* However, there was one, Cleo. Cleo worked as a driver at a garage in town owned by three brothers related to Pappahen. It was the only garage Pappahen used to hire cars, but he did not know Cleo. Cleo was from lower Leeward and offered me a lift whenever he passed me on the road to Lowmans.

One day Cleo asked me, "Where do you live?"

As he drove to where our house came into view, I pointed it out to him.

"You live in a beautiful house! Can I come and visit? I would like to meet your parents," he said.

"I am not sure what they would say about that," I replied.

"Leave that to me," he said.

The day Cleo came, Pappahen was not in, he introduced himself to Mammatee, and handed her a letter signed by a lawyer asking for my hand in marriage. I believe that that was the correct way of proposing in those days. The next time Cleo visited Pappahen came and saw him in the sitting room.

"Who is this?" asked Pappahen.

"He is Cleo, the young man I told you that asked for Sheva's hand." Mammatee replied.

Pappahen was in a rage and said, "Man get out of my house I have enough sweet potato, yam and dasheen on my mountain to mind my girl children I do not need help."

Poor Cleo ran so fast out of the house and down the steps I thought he would have tripped. From then Pappahen began to keep a close eye on what I wore. When we walked down from the mountain, if I wore a pair of shorts, he would say, "Pass yourself in front of me." Once he asked, "Did your Mammatee see you in those shorts?"

"Yes Pappahen, she made them for me," I answered.

I did not relent from my request to Pappahen about my wish to get married. I still saw Cleo whenever he drove past, but he no longer stopped, I guess he was too afraid of Pappahen. I felt broken hearted as I believed we might have had a good relationship.

MEMOIRS OF A SMALL ISLAND GIRL

CHAPTER 15

DEAR AUNT

One day we received a message from Stubbs that Dear Aunt urgently wanted to see me. Mammatee said, "Sheva you need to go right away." I packed a few things and went to meet Cousin Dorawa at the nurses home. We took the bus from town to Stubbs together. On our arrival at the house, cousin Dorawa's mum and her grandsons were there along with her niece Tish. Tish was sent by cousin Dorawa to help with Dear Aunt's care. Dear Aunt was in bed in her room that was often locked when I lived there. I stood outstood the door feeling a little apprehensive. She knew that I was there and called for me to enter. I went in and looked at her sadly. With eyes fixed on me her hand beckoned, "Come, come to me Sheva," she said.

I moved forward ever so slowly and quietly, when I got to her, she held her hand out for mine. I placed my hand in hers. Eventually I was lying beside her, our arms around each other. She held me close until she fell asleep, then cousin Dorawa separated us. The next morning, I returned to Lowmans. That evening news came that Dear Aunt had passed. I was told that she died of a broken heart and that she was never the same after I left but I think her sadness came about from a number of worries. I was not sent to her funeral, but others went. I was left to take care of the young ones. I was very unhappy at not being able to attend Dear Aunt's funeral. Mammatee had decided that Selda would go to the funeral because I went to see Dear Aunt the day before, so that was that. Thankfully, they did not stay overnight as a vehicle was hired to take attendees from Lowmans to the funeral in Stubbs and back. It was not long after Dear Aunt's passing that her relatives had to vacate the house. The land, house and everything in it was left for Father's children. It was only then it became clear to me the reason for all the checks by the lawyer while Father was on his death bed. Cousin Dorawa presented me with a five dollar note, she said it was my gift from Dear Aunt but I believe it was from her own pocket, nevertheless I was thankful and with it I bought myself a hat for church.

PAPPAHEN LEFT

In the same year of 1959 Mammatee and Pappahen had some disagreement. Mammatee moved into her apartment house and took Winnie and myself with her. I believe she also took Harran I can't fully recall. Selda and Victor were left to help Pappahen. One day when I went into the house Pappahen was in pain and he asked me to assist him. It was personal, but I was pleased to be there to help him. Those days there was very little for me to do although occasionally we went to the mountain to gather crops. I presumed that Pappahen felt unhappy with the situation with Mammatee and, as soon as he was better, he left the island and went to Trinidad. He did not make plans, just up and went, and that was the last I saw of my dearest Pappahen. Mammatee said, "Sheva, let's pack up and move back to the house." And that we did. Around that time Tony also left the island to join our siblings in Britain; he took with him PJ's two children, Dingi and Donna.

TRIPS

My visits around the island did not end when I left school. I went on trips that were organised by a family friend. It was good that she did this because it was the best way to explore the island as well as to socialise. On one of these trips, I met with a chap called Reggie, he was from the same village as Cleo. I told him about Cleo, and he became a shoulder to cry on. We developed a mutual attraction and he asked Mammatee's permission to take me out. With Mammatee's consent we started dating, including visits to his family.

SETBACKS AND DISAPPOINTMENTS

After some time, Mammatee decided it was time I left the island and joined my siblings in Britain. Everything was set in place for my travel when my body began showing signs and the little voice within said, *sorry no travel for you, you are going to have a baby.* Selda was chosen to go in my place. I was shocked when I was told by Reggie's younger brother that his mom was sending Reggie to Britain on the same ship as Selda. My shoulder to cry on became my downfall, a lesson I learned the hard way. Mammatee and I watched as the boat sailed off into the sunset. I guess one can imagine how I felt, I had no words, tears just flowed. Mammatee never wanted to part with Selda, she loved her deeply. We both returned home with sombre faces.

One day, I was on the veranda with the younger ones. Mammatee was also there. She stood by the rail looking at the road, I do not think she realised that I was at the other end. A cousin passed by, and they entered into conversation. Mammatee said to him, "I never wanted to send Selda away she was supposed to stay with me. She, Karen and Sonday have always been my favourites." I don't know what caused Mammatee to look around, but when our eyes met, I saw the look on her face, and I knew that she regretted her words. But nothing stopped me from loving Mammatee. As a matter of fact, I tried hard to get her to love me more than she did. I feel strongly that I was born to love others regardless of their attitudes towards me. I knew that Mammatee noticed my caring actions, especially when others pointed out to her how lucky she was to have such a loving daughter.

PRECCY

Preccy and I were still good friends. I made brief visits to her home. On one of my visits, I heard a faint whimper and, being an inquisitive person, I asked Preccy "What's that?" She tried to ignore me, but I followed the sound and she followed me. As I got closer, I spotted something on a blanket, I asked, "Is that a baby?"

"Yes, it's Follu," replied Preccy.

"Follu! He's, my nephew." I said.

When we got to the spot where he lay, I was surprised at his tiny body and big starring eyes. He looked like a one-year-old child but in fact he was almost three. I did not hang around. On my return home I reported my discovery to Mammatee. She said, "Go back tomorrow and tell whoever is there to send Follu to me, I would like to have him."

When I returned to Preccy's home Follu was no longer there, I was told that he was in hospital. I went back to Mammatee with the news. On hearing she said, "Go to the hospital and tell whoever is in charge that Follu's Grandmother wants him home with her." I went immediately and took my little sister with me. When we got there, we looked around the children's ward until we saw Follu. I said to the nurse, "Follu is our nephew. Our Mammatee, his grandmother, has sent us to take him home." She looked at Follu, spoke with the doctor, then she said to us, "You can take him." And that we did. When we got home Mammatee said, "Now Sheva you look after him." I began to wonder, *how am I going to manage?* I was already taking care of Gerald, but Follu was so sweet. He was never any trouble. He ate whatever he was given. Within six months he was smiling happily and growing nicely. My childhood dreams, prayers and my father's words of me having many children was coming to fruition. Although I was not their birth mother, I loved and cared for them, they were my babies.

CARMODY

One day while in town I bumped into my best friend, Carmody, from school days in Stubbs. Most times when I visited Dear Aunt, Carmody was not in the village. That day she was with her teacher friends and, seemingly, in a hurry. When our eyes met, we were both lost for words, we screamed in surprise and, in shock, she asked, "Where did you get that belly from?" We both ended up in laughter as in the old days. Carmody was still good at turning everything into a joke, but we were really happy to see each other.

ANDY

30th April 1960 my own beautiful, bouncing baby boy was born. He weighed eight pounds. At last, I had someone of my own. I pondered, *what shall I name him?* I recalled a lovely young man, who became a teacher and was still studying to further his education. He was the only child for his mother who was also a teacher, so I thought, *yes! I shall give him a name as close as possible to that young man's name.* I then thought of another young who was also a teacher. I used both names with a little twist to them to name my son. When my friend Murl saw him, she took him in her arms and said, "He's gorgeous, what will you name him?" I told her the names that I had in mind. She replied, "Nice names, but he needs another. He looks like an Andy." His dad had sent money with which I bought his christening outfit. I chose members from his family as well as mine to be his god parents. The nickname Andy remained with him, so that very few people knew his official name and he grew to love that name best.

COUSIN DORAWA

1960 was also the year that cousin Dorawa left the island to further her nursing career in the USA. She wrote to me often wanting to know how things were with me and sent me gifts. The first parcel contained a lovely outfit, which I wore for best, but after some time I decided to wear it to walk along the high road in order to get to Casagrant. Casagrant was across the hill from our house, where I surveyed dried tree branches ready for the taking. I did not want to walk that road in my scruffy mountain dress, so I took it with me. Just before I got to where the wood was, I changed and left my nice outfit in a spot that I thought would have been a safe place, when out of the blue, a woman called Dede who lived in a little hut not far away, came running towards me, hands waving. I ran like mad because she often went off her mind and did crazy things. For this reason, she was nicknamed, crazy Dede. Well, she found my outfit and ran off with it! One Saturday I saw her in town, nicely dressed in it. Although she seemed to be in her right mind, I dared not confront her. The only good thing that came out of my hour in Casagrant was the wood I collected.

TOUGH TIMES

Times became harder physically, financially and emotionally. There was always much to be done. Winnie did her best, but she was only nine and so little and skinny, I did not want her to do too much. Victor and Harran did most of the heavy mountain work even though they were both still in school. I admired their strength and enthusiasm. When I had to go to up to the mountain, if Mammatee was not at home, I left Andy sleeping and asked a neighbour to keep an eye on him. I took Gerard to his other grandmother on my way up, and I left Follu with sister Dorada, who lived just below us. After a while I could no longer take the financial strain and decided to find a job. Reggie had stopped sending regular maintenance, and word came to me that he was going out with someone else, so I decided to forget him.

I found a few hours work each day in Montrose, not far from home. I left Andy with one of my friends, and Mammatee saw to it that the other two boys were cared for. After a few weeks of my boss and me getting acquainted, he said, "Why don't you bring Andy with you?" And that I did, he was very kind and generous. I soon discovered that I was going to be a mother again; my first thought was *no way am I going to tell Mammatee!* I was too afraid. It would be my secret, but I knew that I had to get away. I could have braved it, stayed and got married but no. I began arranging to go to Trinidad. I wrote to my friend who had been there for some time. She replied saying that she would be happy to receive me. Pappahen was also there, whenever one of my relatives came back from holiday, they said that Pappahen always enquired about me.

TRINIDAD OR NOT

I was about to book my fare when, low and behold, Thelma returned from Trinidad because life there had become rough, with the intention of moving on to the UK within a month. Mammatee turned to me and said, "You cannot go to Trinidad, I am sending you to the UK, but I do not want you to join your siblings in London, where Reggie lives. You must stay away from him. I will write to my niece in Reading. You can join her there and apply to study for nursing."

Thelma sailed for the UK, and I began preparing for my trip. I was still working but one afternoon I went to see Mammatee at her market stall in Kingstown. She sent me to buy her lunch on the opposite side of the market. As I walked along the stalls, a rather dishy looking guy, smartly dressed in a crisp white shirt came walking towards me. Our eyes met, there was a glint in his eye and I felt a powerful spiritual connection. I shook my head, *what's going on*! I wondered as I walked on. Neither of us spoke, which was unusual in those days. When I returned to Mammatee with her lunch, I was faced with the same guy chatting away to Mammatee. More thoughts flooded my mind. *What is he doing chatting with Mammatee? He can't be buying.* Then out came his question to Mammatee, "Is she one of yours?"

"Yes."

"I love her! I think I am going to marry her."

Well, I was so embarrassed I immediately ducked under the counter of Mammatee's stall for cover. Mammatee said to him, "Well you are going to England, and she will be on the next boat up so you can meet up there and chat."

When he left, Mammatee said, "Sheva, you can come out now he's gone." When I came out Mammatee repeated what I already heard, "He said, he loves you and he might marry you". To me that was definitely impossible, and I never thought of him again.

CHAPTER 16

AT SEA

As the days drew nearer for me to leave the island, I desperately wanted to take my baby with me, but Mammatee said, "No!" I pondered the thought of leaving him with his grandmother in Layou, because I knew it would have been hard on Mammatee with the other children to care for. Mammatee was adamant, "I will not let any more of my grandchildren live with anyone, I will manage."

The day came for me to leave. Friends came to bid me farewell. I clutched my one-year-old son tightly and rocked him to and fro. Tears streamed down my face. My godson's mother took him from me and promised to help Mammatee care for him, which she did. Parting was hard. I cried all the way on the boat to St Lucia. There were five of us from St Vincent, of which one was a classmate from standard six who took her baby with her. I wished Mammatee had allowed me to take Andy, but I knew she had my best interest at heart. We were taken to a guest house where we met with people from various islands also on their way to the UK. We stayed in the guest house for two days while we waited for the arrival of the Spanish ship, Biancaci, to take us to the Mother Land. On my first day in St Lucia, I enquired about my sister Dorada's brother-in-law, Mr Robbi. He was easy to locate because he owned a drug store not far from the guest house. Three others accompanied me to his store. He warmly welcomed us and said that he would love me to meet his family and invited us to lunch the following day.

We were well entertained by his lovely wife and their two daughters. That was the first time I tasted flying fish. It was delicious! The Robbi's wished we could have stayed longer. The feeling was mutual. They were a wonderful family, but our ship had arrived, so we needed to make haste. The pain of leaving my son began to ease when we got settled on the ship. There was always entertainment, I took part in some of the games, and I enjoyed the dances; I even won second prize in a limbo dance competition. Those fun times kept my mind occupied and made me forget my troubles, at least for a while.

The ship docked in Tenerife, and we were allowed to disembark, but gosh it was so scary getting out of the ship into the tiny boat that took us to shore. We had to climb from the stern onto a rope ladder that extended across deep water to a sailor in the tiny boat. Thank God a strong man from Lowmans was with us. He held my hand, also the hand of some of the other ladies, and supported us as we climbed in and out of the ship. We went shopping, I bought a nice lacey half-slip, called a cane cane slip in those days. The slip is now sixty years old, but I still have it. From Tenerife we sailed to Genoa in Italy and were put onto a train to Barcelona, then a ferry to Southampton, and finally a train to London Victoria. Our entire journey took two weeks. It was a great experience.

ARRIVAL

At Victoria station I was met by Thelma. I wondered how she knew the way. She had only arrived two months previous. My first question to her was, "Is this really London?"

"Yes." She replied.

I was surprised. I had expected to see beautifully painted houses, like in St Vincent, but every building looked ancient. The sky was dark, the atmosphere was damp and gloomy as the cold breeze enveloped me. Everyone wore big ugly coats. Thank God Thelma brought me a green jacket that fitted nicely and kept me warm. We took the train to Tottenham to Karen's home. It still puzzled me how Thelma knew her way around so well, she was brilliant, which I told her, and she simply smiled. I spent two weeks with Karen and her husband Larry, then Karen took me to Reading to be with my cousins Pam and Cena as was arranged by Mammatee.

READING, BERKSHIRE

In Reading, I shared a room with Cena. Her friend got me a job where she worked as a Hoffman presser. Out of my first wage I bought a little outfit for Andy and posted it to Mammatee. She said it was the perfect fit and he loved it. I made friends quickly. I got to know some Vincentians who lived in Caversham. One day I was on my way home from visiting them when a car with two men stopped and one said, "Your cousin Cena sent us to pick you up and drive you home."

I had no idea about the scams some men got up to, but my inner voice said *run*, I ran and shouted, "Go away!" They drove off. I am sure God protected me.

Another day when I was home alone, I heard knock, knock, knock, on the door.

"Whose there?" I asked, as was instructed by Cena.

"It's me!" came the voice.

"Me who?"

"Reggie!"

"What are you doing here? And how did you find me?" I asked through the letter box.

"Got your address from my brother."

I ought to have known, because not long after Selda had arrived in London she married his brother. Mammatee predicted that Reggie would try to contact me which was the very reason why she sent me to stay outside London.

"He had no right to give you my address, how dare he. I will not open, so go away! I am not having anything to do with you!"

Eventually he left. I guess he spent the night with friends before going back to London.

STREATHAM

I was no longer able to hide the growth within me and because the landlord refused to have babies in the house, against Mammatee's wish, I moved to London. I stayed with Selda and her husband, Doug, in Streatham. Their landlady took care of two small children, a brother and sister, brought by their mother each morning. Soon after she left, the landlady went to work and returned about one hour before their mother came for them. The youngest, the girl, was left strapped in the pram in the passageway and her little brother stood beside the pram. At times, the baby cried especially when her bottle fell, I took the liberty of attending to her. One day their mother came early, just before the landlady. I opened the door to her, and she realised that her children were left unattended. She took her children and never brought them again. The landlady was cross with me for opening the door and from then she became inconsiderate towards me. Thankfully, I met with Mr James, who remembered me from my time in Stubbs. When I explained my situation to him, he said, "I will tell my wife about you. I am sure you will be able to stay with us and our children."

That weekend Thelma came to visit and with her was, Fitz, the young man I crossed paths with back in St Vincent at the market. He also had his brother with him. My mind reeled. *What are they doing here*? As it happened, they went to see Thelma as she knew Fitz when they both lived in Trinidad. He told her that he would like to meet me. We did not have much time to talk and, besides, I was quite nervous, but we agreed to stay in touch.

MY MOVE TO BALAAM

Well now, guess what happened? The following week Mr James returned on his big motor bike to get me. My case went in the carrier that was attached to his bike. When we arrived at his home in Balaam I met with his family, they were incredibly kind, and so were his tenants. We all became one big happy family. One of the tenants decided to buy a house and she offered me a small room in return for my help with her children which I accepted gladly. I told Thelma what I was about to do, and she wanted to see the room, so I took her. It was just a short walk, two streets from where I was staying, Thelma saw the room I was being offered then she asked to see the other room that was available. When she saw it, she said, "Why don't we share this room, it would be better for us and your baby," which we did.

FITZ AND I

Fitz visited us at our new home a couple of times. It felt as if something beyond our control kept drawing us together, but I cannot honestly say it was love, although I sensed that he felt it too. He could have seen that I was about to have a baby, and we talked about Andy, but nothing deterred him. He was convinced that we would make a good life together, with my baby, provided I was prepared to drop all ties from the past. I contacted Mammatee as being underage I needed her permission to be married. She loved the idea of Fitz and me seeing each other.

"Yes, you would be good together, he loves you!" Mammatee said, "I knew his family well. His mum and I were best friends when we were little girls. We even dressed alike."

My sister, Dorada, also said in a letter to me that I should accept him, he would be like a father to me. *I didn't want a father!* Karren was not sure about Fitz, she thought he looked too bossy. Thelma who knew him best said that I should marry him, he's a good guy. PJ said that I should marry Reggie. But for me, Reggie was out of the question, and I knew that Fitz and I had a connection. We corresponded by letters.

SNOW

One morning in November 1961, I had a dentist appointment, and as I opened the front door, I beheld snow for the first time. Yes, I had seen it on post cards, but this was different. I was so scared, I quickly closed the door and ran upstairs to one of the other tenants, a couple, whose room was closest to mine. I knocked hard and sharp on the door and when it opened, I ran in stammering, "There's something out there, like it wants to swallow me!"

They burst into laughter and looked out of their window. "It's snowing!"

"Oh! so that's how it looks?"

"Yes! and it won't hurt you!" one said.

"Well, no way am I going out in that!"

I went back to bed. After a few days I got accustomed to it and decided to go to the dentist. The dentist was not a happy man and told me off something rotten. He did not turn me away, but I felt his anger when he began drilling into my tooth without a local anaesthetic. I screamed, jumped out of the chair, and made for the door.

"What's wrong?"

Holding my jaw, I moaned, "Uhm, uhm, uhm!" in pain.

"Come sit down, " he said. Then he proceeded with an injection in my gum. It felt better, but that was the last time I went to him. I told my story to every dentist in fear of that happening again, they all smiled as they listened and promised to be gentle. I am no longer afraid of dentists because since then they have all been kind.

PATSY'S BIRTH

My contractions began and I knew that my baby was ready to enter the world. Because I was alone in the house, I walked over to Mrs James, and she walked with me to Nightingale Lane hospital. She could not stay with me as she had to get back to her small children. Thelma was meant to be with me, but she was at work. One of the nurses kindly signed for my admission and delivery on my sister's behalf, as I was still underage. Thelma came as soon as she was able, which was just after the birth of my absolutely beautiful baby girl. I thought to myself that although the circumstance of her conception was beyond my control God allowed her to be for my joy. The following day Fitz came bearing gifts, a watch and a bunch of flowers. When asked by the nurse in charge, "Are you related?"

"Yes, I am her fiancé," Fitz replied.

Only close family were allowed in. After nine days I was discharged from hospital. Mrs James came to meet me, I stayed at her house until we knew that Thelma was on her way to our home from work. Mrs James then walked me home to be with Thelma.

PATSY'S CHRISTENING

Within a month I christened my baby, Patsy, at St Mary's Church in Balaam, a short walk from our home. I chose Thelma and Christa for godmothers and one of the tenants who later married Thelma to be godfather. He loved the name Patsy, and so did I. Patsy's father sent enough money to cover the cost. He wanted to support her, but Fitz said, "No!" We had a lovely party in my landlady's large front room. It was attended by Fitz and his brother, Thomas, my siblings, their partners and all the occupants in our house. From that day, in keeping with Fitz's request, I no longer corresponded with Patsy's father, and we began to plan for our wedding.

CHAPTER 17

OUR WEDDING

Fitz invited me to meet his relations whom he lived with in Brick Lane, East London. They liked me at first sight and said to us to get married as soon as possible as there was no point in waiting. We agreed and decided on a date. Fitz moved from their home to Canning Town, to a room he rented from my sister Karen and her husband Larry in their newly purchased house. Fitz was a good saver. In just one year he managed to accumulate one hundred pounds. He brought it to me and said, "Take this money to get what is needed for our wedding." I went first to Mr & Mrs James for advice. "I will help you. Leave the reception to me," said Mrs James.

I then informed my siblings. Selda took me to Brixton where we bought my outfit. One Saturday Fitz came to me, and we went shopping for my ring. As soon as I looked in the window, I knew which one I wanted. It was nice and neat with inset diamonds all around, I pointed it out to Fitz.

"That's too small! Why are you choosing such a narrow ring? Don't you want people to know that you are married?"

"Off course I do, but I do not like large jewels." This was true but I was also looking to keep the cost down.

"If you are thinking about the price of the others, don't worry I have enough." Fitz said, reading my thoughts.

"No, I really like this one." I replied. And I really did which is why I still wear it today even though the diamonds have worn away. Fitz has bought me others, but they just do not compare to the original.

24th March 1962, the day of my wedding. Just before I got dressed, I sat on the stairs and cried loud cries. It just came naturally. One of my friends in the house asked, "Why are you crying?" I had no answer, I suppose it could have been the thought of leaving them, especially Thelma, and journeying into the unknown, I still have no clear answer.

We had three bridesmaids. The chief was Selda's sister-in-law, Ena, she was my friend back in St Vincent before she left for England to meet her fiancée whom she had told me about. How strange things worked out? At that time, I did not know that her fiancée was one of Reggie's brothers, just as I did not know that Selda would have married another brother. When I stayed at Selda I was told that a relative in Battersea asked if I would like to care for their child a couple days a week. I agreed. When I got to the home, I was shocked to see that the mother of the child was Ena, we had a splendid reunion and from then her husband welcomed me as a member of the family.

My other two bridesmaids were Selda and of course Thelma. Fitz paid for Thelma's dress. My one flower girl was my niece, Sharlene. My two little nephews Dingi and Leon were the only other children at our wedding. PJ, my brother, gave me away and Doug, Selda's husband, was Fitz's best man. There were twenty-five guests at our wedding. Everyone looked lovely. We were married at St Mary's Church, where Patsy was Christened, and where I attended on Sundays. We walked to it, and after the ceremony, most people walked over to Mrs James for the reception. Fitz and I were given a lift with Larry. I could not believe that the room we entered for the reception was rented by Reggie. He had allowed Mrs James to use it to cut our cost, which was good of him, but how awful that he was there! He even came and asked me for a dance. I obliged him to save an argument and any embarrassment. As we danced, I did my best to keep him at bay, but he drew me close and whispered, "This should have been our wedding." I made no reply and was relieved when the music stopped.

After the reception I took my belongings from Mrs James' house which I had dropped off a few days before the wedding. I joined Fitz, PJ and Karen in Larry's car and travelled back to their home in East London to be with my husband. PJ and his family were also living there. I had taken some of my things the day before, and Patsy I took early on our wedding day to be looked after by my sister-in-law, Hilda, PJ's wife who had given birth to a bouncing baby boy, Brandon, the month before my wedding and so was not able to attend.

Life was pleasant, especially with PJ's three children, but the cold was too much. I cried daily for St Vincent and the sun. I was also concerned about Andy's welfare; it troubled me, because I had no money to send to Mammatee for his care. I also knew that Fitz needed help. Thankfully, I found a job in a nearby clothing factory, walking distance from home and Hilda looked after Patsy. I was able to help Fitz financially and contribute towards Andy's care.

Fitz worked in Shoreditch, so he was gone for most of the day. I got in from work and did all my housework before he came home. On nice days, after dinner, we changed into our best clothes and took Patsy to the park in her little pram, sometimes with my young niece Donna. Fitz and I took a while getting to know each other. It required patience and perseverance on both sides. I guess it would be hard for one to believe that I was very shy; Fitz had to wait outside our bedroom door while I washed and dressed, and I turned Mammatee's picture down at bedtimes. Our relationship rocked from the start, but we were determined to make it work. It was difficult to let go of my independence and allow Fitz to be in control, but it was necessary for love, peace and progress. I recalled some words in sister Dorrada's letter, *listen to him and he would be like a father to you*. That was all well and good in words, but it broke my heart when he threw my nice dresses that I told him my Mammatee made for me in the bin, saying, "They are too skimpy! Why did your mother make you those dresses?" I retrieved them from the bin but wore them indoors only.

Fitz was a tailor by trade, but he was employed as a painter. Two days a week after work he went to night school. One night he studied pattern cutting and on the other, painting and decorating, which meant he got home very late. He was also late one more night every fortnight. I once went out hoping to meet him walking towards me, when a man crossed the road to my side and shouted, "Are you looking for your husband?"

I turned around and ran. He followed me but as I opened the gate he turned back. When Fitz came home, I told him what happened, and he was cross with me.

"Don't you ever come looking for me, I can take care of myself."

"So how come you so late and had me worried?"

"Oh, I passed by an old friend, she sent these for you." He held out a bag to me, but I did not take it.

"Oh yes? So, what's her name?"

"Susy. I have known her a long time."

I left it at that. There were sweet potatoes and a yam in the bag. It took a while before I decided to cook them.

June of that same year 1962 I accidently tripped down the stairs in the old factory where I worked and suffered a miscarriage, but I soon recovered and after three months I was expecting again. The old sewing factory had closed but I found work in Bethnal Green, pressing, folding and packing men's shirts.

Patsy walked at nine months which was a surprise to everyone. Hilda continued to care for her while I was at work. Fitz and I left home together, and we took the same bus to Shoreditch, then he got another or walked to where he worked, and I did the same to my workplace in Bethnal Green.

March 1963 Karen gave birth to a son, Delboy. He was so pretty I could not believe he was a boy, I thought someone made a mistake, so I checked to be sure.

GLENDA

Two months later in the month of May, I was blessed with another beautiful baby daughter, Glenda. Fitz was over the moon for he loved babies as much as I did. Glenda was as quiet as a mouse, she never cried, we had to listen closely for her, 'eeee', which often fascinated Patsy, so she tried to communicate by throwing her own soft toy from her cot over to Glenda as she lay on our bed. They made me so happy, I dressed them alike. Everyone in the house was happy, it was wonderful being in a home with my three siblings and their families. We did our best to help each other. When PJ's wife, Hilda, went out to work, I cared for my nephew Brandon.

CHRISTENING OF GLENDA, DELBOY & BRANDON

If I remember well, Glenda, Delboy and Brandon were christened on the same day at St Luke's Church in Canning Town. I was privileged to be godmother to Brandon. My friend from work, who was more like a loving mother to me, was godmother to Glenda along with Fitz's cousin and her husband with whom he lived before we got married. We had a nice little joint reception.

MISUNDERSTANDINGS

Fitz and I fought often over simple things. Patsy would scream, "Mummy and Daddy, stop fighting!" Fitz was mighty strong, and I was always relieved when Larry came to my rescue. One day after an argument I walked out intending to get the bus to my brother, Sonday, who lived in Stoke Newington. It was a good walk to the bus stop. The bus came quickly but as I stepped in, I was grabbed from behind, by none other than Fitz.

"Come on now! Where are you going?" He took my hand. "Come on let's go home."

I went without a word while he held my hand firmly, and we walked home in peace. No matter how much we fought and argued we never went to bed in anger, as a matter of fact, our love grew stronger. We both believed we were meant to be. Our evening walks on nice days continued, with the girls head and tail in the one little pram.

WORK

I felt ready to return to work, I had to keep earning, besides, I needed to get out. Hilda got me a job where she worked. We found a good child minder for our children in our street, but we did not always start and finish at the same time. The atmosphere at work was lovely and it was good to be a part of something different for a change but gosh the going was hard. We needed two buses to get the factory or one bus and a long walk. Some of my white friends thumbed lifts and refused to leave me behind. I lived farthest so that I was the last one to be dropped off but somehow, I never felt in danger as the girls took note of the number plate and always warned the driver, "Make sure you take her safely, we've got your number!"

Lifts were good as I saved on bus fares, because by the time I paid for the girls' care and my bus fare, my wages were gone. Still, I kept going. Fitz and I struggled to make ends meet but we always had the essentials. I made my daughters' dresses from remnants that I bought cheaply on the market stall. Hilda taught me to knit. I made cardigans, jumpers, dress suits, and matching hats and gloves. Once, Claire, Sonday's wife made two beautiful dresses for Patsy. When a photographer knocked saying, he was taking and framing pictures, I dressed Patsy and Glenda in those dresses and cardigans that I had just knitted, the pictures I still have. I also knitted jumpers for Fitz and the occasional hat and jumper for myself.

After a while, the factory where I was working closed. I got another job nearer home making Union Jacks. The stitches had to be very neat with no puckering, even neater than sewing dresses. I wondered why did they made such a fuss on flags just to fly in the air. Many times, I had to unpick and redo. I hated it, so I left, anyway, another baby was on the way, so it did not matter. Karen was also expecting another child and needed more space in her house before the arrival.

CHANGES

PJ bought a house in Poplar and moved with his family. I moved into the two small rooms that they had occupied, but I did not find them as comfortable as the one large room that I had. Patsy suffered from nightmares in the bedroom, even when she was awake, she saw shadows moving along the wall. We were all kept awake with the worry. Hilda told us, that when she was there Brandon kept seeing a cat and one neighbour said that previous occupants had similar problems with their child who slept in the same room.

Apart from that problem, the girls got up to doing things they thought were helpful when they were alone in the sitting room. One morning I left them and went shopping for small groceries as I already had most things in the cupboard. Karen was downstairs, so they were not alone in the house. She heard no sound from them, usually they played together quietly. When I returned and entered the room, they had mixed in a bucket the flour, sugar and water that we kept in the room.

"We were just making a cake," said Patsy.

Bless them, they were trying to make me happy, but I was cross. After cleaning up I had to go right back to the supermarket to replace the sugar and flour.

We badly missed PJ and his family, but we visited them often. During my visits Hilda taught me to crochet. I admired her, she was ever so patient and skilled in many things.

CHAPTER 18

MOVE TO BURRARD ROAD

I looked in the mirror and asked myself, how did I get to be this big? I was never this big with my other babies, I can't even walk up the stairs. I had to work out how to get around doing my chores without venturing the stairs unless Fitz was in to help me when going up. One evening I decided to sit on the stair and wait for him to come home. While there I began to wonder where will we put our new baby? When Fitz came, I shared my thoughts; we both knew that our two rooms would not be adequate.

"Yeah, you are right," said Fitz, "no space for a cot, keep your eyes open for somewhere for us to move to."

Well, what do you know! The next day, on my way to the corner shop, I looked across the next road and ever so bold was the huge advert, flats to let, with the number to call. I wrote it down and when I got home, I sat on the step again, anxiously waiting for Fitz to get in from work.

At 6 p.m. when the door opened, I spoke first, "Hi Fitz, you ok?"

"Yeah, I am fine. I see you're in your favourite spot."

"Yes, waiting to tell you the good news."

"Uhm, what's that?"

"Flats to let in the next road."

"How much do they cost?"

"Don't know. But I have the phone number."

"Well give them a call tomorrow."

"OK." I replied and that I did while he was at work.

"Hello, I see you have flats for rent. How much per week?"

A male voice at the other of the phone quoted the price. I could not believe the price was within our budget.

"When can I see it?" I asked.

"Do you have children?"

"Yes, two and one on the way."

"Then the ground floor would be just right for you. You can move in today, pick up the keys from the corner shop."

When Fitz got home, we checked it out, it was perfect, and we agreed that the price was just right. Because it was unfurnished, it was less that what we had been paying, so we were able to get what we needed for the flat on credit. We shared the front door of the house with the tenants upstairs. The door to our flat opened into a big sitting room, another door led to the large kitchen. One step down from the kitchen and we were in the bedroom, from there a door opened into the bathroom and another door led to the toilet. We also had a large enclosed paved garden, accessed from the kitchen. In the kitchen we put a double folding bed for the girls and a cot in our bedroom for our new baby.

SECOND SON

The following day I made what seemed to be like endless trips carrying our belongings from one road to the other. Where did my strength come from? Only God knew. The very next day, three weeks before Christmas, I went into labour. Karen cared for my daughters during my week stay in hospital. I had bought them dolls for Christmas but when I went into hospital, I allowed them to play with the dolls to keep them happy. Within one hour of admission my second bouncing baby boy, Dudley, was born weighing seven pounds ten ounces. Fitz was so happy. "I've actually got a son," he said, "I did not think I could make a son. I'll make all his clothes!"

When I got home from the hospital the girls were over the moon with their baby brother and they were also still full of the joys of our lovely new home. After one month Dudley was christened at St Luke's Church where I attended; we had a small gathering. His godparents were one of my cousins, his wife and one of Fitz's friends. Everyone was happy, it was nice to be able to welcome family and friends into our lovely new home.

SURPRISE

Fitz had good taste in everything and did his best to keep our home to a high standard. He still attended evening classes and became very skilled in painting and decorating; one only had to step into our front door and the fresh smell of paint told the tale. Fitz also made me some lovely clothing, but I often wondered where he get the extra cash from? I knew he loved to put a little bet on the horses; how much he spent and lost I had no idea. One day he came in with his shirt tail out holding lots of money, with much excitement he said, "Gal, come help me check money a yo rass!"

That week we bought all sorts of nice things for the flat and of course he saved some, he was still good at saving. Fitz always dreamed of buying a house. His bible was his bank account, even when we struggled, unbeknown to me, he managed to put a little in it. One day he revealed to me that each time he thought he had enough to deposit on a house, the deposit for the house went up so he turned to his family for help but without luck.

Seeing Fitz's winnings on the horses I decided to have a go. The betting shop was close to our house. Fitz taught me how to place singles, doubles, trebles and syndicates. Syndicates I could not afford, so I went for trebles - six pence each way. I quite enjoyed it and I often won but my winnings just covered my bet. One afternoon, I ran to the shop with my bet in hand ready to be placed after I had watched the form of the horses on TV. On entering, the man in the queue in front of me whom I had seen and spoken with days before said, "Let's see what you've got." When I showed it to him, he continued, "That's a sure looser. Got no form, change to a favourite."

I took his advice but the horse I had intended to bet on came first at twenty to one. The real reason I had chosen it was because it had Patsy's middle name. I would have received twenty pounds to my one. I looked at the man and said, "Why on earth did I listen to you?" But I knew it served me right and that was last time that I took advice from anyone about horses, as a matter of fact I only went back to the shop once after that. I stopped when another man's question was out of line.

SUNDAY SCHOOL

Patsy and Glenda were now Sunday school age. From birth I had sang to them all the little songs that I was taught when I was a child and sang when I was alone in Dear Aunt's garden. Here are just two of them: *'The birds upon the tree top sing their song, the angels chant their chorus all day long, the flowers in the garden bend their hue; so why shouldn't I, why shouldn't you praise God too?';* and *'Jesus loves me this I know, for the Bible tells me so, little ones to Him belong, they are weak, but He is strong.'* I also told them the stories of Jesus, and, like me, they loved to hear them.

HEALTH VISITOR

During those times, our elderly health visitor came by without notifying me. I did not mind her dropping in as she was nice, and I welcomed her company. She always commented on my well-kept home and lovely children. She somehow sensed that I struggled financially. One day she said, "You will do well looking after another child. You are very good with them, and the income will help you. Think about it." I thanked her and, after discussing it with Fitz, I decided to accept her offer. On her next visit I told her that I was ready. She said that she had a child in mind for me and explained that because of his background the church would be involved. Well, that was fine by me. She went on to tell me more about the child. "His name is Stephen, his mother is Arabic, and he is six months old, the same as your Dudley."

We arranged to meet with all who were responsible for the upbringing of Stephen. When the day came, Stephen was brought to me by Miss Jessup, a member of staff from the Mayflower Church Centre, we connected instantly. Stephen was a beautiful boy with a sad face. Miss Jessup said, "Sheva, from what I have heard about you, I know he will be happy here with you and your family, you will be his temporary foster family."

FOSTER MOTHER

The following week Miss Jessup brought Stephen to stay, and the health visitor's visits increased but we did fine. Glenda decided that Stephen was hers, she fed him with his bottle and gently tapped him when he cried. Patsy claimed Dudley and did likewise, they were elated having their own babies to love and care for. One month later we were privileged to be introduced to Stephen's mother, Molly, a lovely lady. We became close friends and I introduced her to Karen and her family. Molly occasionally sat with the children while I ran errands. Meanwhile, Miss Jessup introduced me to the Mayflower Church - it was great to be part of a church family again. I went to the Sunday morning services and to the Bible study group on Thursday evenings, which was held at the home of Reverend Adams. It was there that I was blessed to meet his father-in-law, his wife, and their young daughter, who was the same age as Patsy, and some other church members. His wife and I sometimes met along the road while taking our daughters to school and we nattered about our delights in bread making and church events.

One day Miss Jessup said, "It would be good for you and Fitz to have some time out." Fitz and I both smiled at the idea, when she told us her plan, we looked forward to the day. When the day came, Miss Jessup brought someone from the Centre to care for the children, then she drove us to the Royal Albert Hall where we were delightfully surprised to join in Billy Graham's Crusade. It was a real treat, our first time to something that was very special and fulfilling; she even treated us to refreshments, I was part of an extraordinary family.

BYE, STEPHEN.

Within weeks, Stephen no longer wore a sad face but was a happy smiling boy. He was just one year old when a permanent foster home was found for him. We all cried when he left. We never saw or heard any more about him. Molly still visited for a while, and I continued to go to the Mayflower.

CHAPTER 19

DILAPIDATED CHURCH

I discovered that the dilapidated Anglican Church across the road, that was always closed, was used occasionally. One evening, I happened to have been looking out of my front room window and spotted a young man opening the church door. I thought about catching him to find out more about that place, so I quickly ran out and got over to him just as he was about to shut the door.

"Good evening, I have not seen you before", I said,

"I do not live around here, but I grew up in this road. My mum lives a few doors down. I am Terry, an Anglican Church Army Captain. I come Sundays at three p.m. to take Sunday school but today I am here to meet the scouts."

"That's great, I shall be bringing my girls aged three and four to Sunday school. I always thought this place was closed to be demolished."

"It will be eventually. It's a branch of St. Luke's Church not far away."

"Yes, I know where it is, that's where my daughter and my son also some of their cousins were Christened, and a few times I have been to the service on Sunday mornings but now I mostly go to the Mayflower."

"That's fine, we are all one. I can collect the girls on Sunday and bring them back."

"That would be nice of you," I said. But I knew that I had to be there to listen to his teaching also to see inside the church. On the Sunday we got there just as Terry was opening the door. Inside was old, dark and musty but Teddy was very good with the children; they called him uncle, Ted. There were just six including my two, they all enjoyed it. Patsy and Glenda looked forward to going back. Most times I dropped them off and Terry brought them home. One by one I was introduced to the parents of the other children and one day I met with Terry's mum. I gradually became involved in the community but going out late or staying out late was risky, we were constantly on the lookout for Teddy boys, Skin heads and Black haters.

DANGERS

Fitz was very protective whenever we were out together. He always walked behind to shield us, he kept a little pen knife opened in his pocket in case we met with the bad boys, but we never met with any. It was unusual for people with young families to be attacked, they were more out to get lone men. One late evening Fitz was on his way home from evening class when he met with a group of Teddy boys. He told me that one of them said to the others, "Black man! let's get him!"

"I had to get brave," Fitz recounted to me, "I kept my hand on my knife in readiness, then another one said, "Leave the man alone!" I could not believe my luck, and God's great care and protection over me."

DECISIONS ABOUT CHOICE OF SCHOOL

Patsy was excited about starting school, there were three nearby. I pondered which one to choose then I thought check them all, which I did. The first one I went to I did not think too highly of; the second was good and closest to home, it was also where Jackie from the Mayflower went; but just a few yards ahead was St Luke's school. My heart leaped for joy as my spirit said, *yes, that's the one!* So off I went to speak to the headmaster, but before I could speak, he said, "Sorry this school is full. What's your address?" When I told him, he replied, "There is one nearer to you that would be much better for you."

I was not prepared to give in, and protested, "I am an Anglican. I was a Sunday school teacher. My children were Christened at St Luke's Church. They go to the Sunday school across the road, run by the army captain. Sir, can't you kindly make room for one more child?"

His eyes pierced me. "Alright, take a seat."

Relieved, I smiled and said, "Thank you, Sir."

Patsy started three months before her fifth birthday. She loved school and was quick at learning. She also made an excellent choice of friends. Her best friend's mother occasionally asked me if I would allow Patsy to go home with them and stay to dinner. Sometimes I said yes and collected Patsy before dark.

PROTECTIVE

Fitz was becoming more protective. He checked out all who I became involved with. Patsy and I walked to and from school in the company of another friend, Angie and her parents, Mr and Mrs Darcy. After a few weeks, one evening Mrs Darcy offered to take Patsy to school as they had to pass our door. This was good for me because I was always rushing to dress Glenda and Dudley. The next day I waited with Patsy at our gate for Mrs Darcy, but she did not turn up. Instead, Mr Darcy came without her holding Angie's hand, he took Patsy's left hand and off they went. Glenda missed Patsy while she was at school and looked forward to meeting her at home time. She walked beside me holding Dudley's pram - they were such good children. On Fitz's arrival home that evening I blurted out in excitement, "Guess what? Mr Darcy, whose daughter goes to the same school with Patsy, took her to school today, so I stayed in. He and his wife has offered to take her every morning."

"Mr Darcy? Who is he? Where does he live?"

"Up the next road," I replied.

"Okay we'll see!" said Fitz. Next morning, Fitz did not get up for work.

"What's wrong, are you not well?"

"I'm fine, I'm taking my daughter to school today, I want to see this Mr Darcy who's so generous!" Fitz took Patsy's hand and off they went to school, from there he went to work. The following day Fitz said to me, "Make sure you take Patsy to school yourself and do so from now on".

Following my husband's instructions, I took Patsy to school. On the way I came across Mrs Darcy who, with a little smile, said to me, "Your husband really had a go at my husband yesterday for taking Patsy to school. We thought we were doing you a favour and that we could be friends."

"What! I am so sorry! Please tell Mr Darcy I am sorry."

"You can pass by this evening and tell him because he feels so cut up."

That I did. When Fitz came home, I asked him, "Why didn't you tell me that you told off Mr Darcy for taking Patsy to school?"

"You do not need to know everything!" was his reply.

"Well, I've apologised to him."

"Apologised? Have you undone what I have done?"

"I don't know what you mean. To me, he was just being kind by giving me a break from having to rush out with the little ones every morning. Mrs Darcy was the one who told me how badly her husband felt after you told him off."

"Okay but don't ever do that again, we don't need help."

I hardly saw the Darcy's after that. Perhaps they found another route to school, or they went earlier than I did. Other events followed that showed Fitz was becoming possessive. He would bravely tell off any man who looked at me too hard. I sometimes felt like I was a child again back in Dear Aunt's care. There were things I shared with him which I ought to have kept to myself, it would have prevented the unexpected blow, but did I learn? No. I tried, but I so loved to share my thoughts and still do, hence the reason I am writing.

GLENDA STARTED SCHOOL

September 1968 Glenda happily joined Patsy in school and made friends with Patsy's best friend's younger sister, who started the same day. I felt at ease knowing that my girls were in a good school with nice friends.

OUT TO WORK

Money was still tight. Thank God for the children's allowance and my little temporary jobs. I also bless the Lord that He led me to answer an advertisement in the Daily Mirror, which said, *Machinist wanted in Aldgate for sewing flags*. I was a bit nervous as I dialled the number but the voice at the other end was warm and gentle. "Hello, I am Miss Price, I suppose you are calling about the job advertised in the paper?"

"Yes please."

After we discussed all that was involved, Miss Price asked, "Can you start on Monday?"

"Oh yes, thank you, but I can only work from 10 a.m. to 2 p.m. as I have two daughters to take to school for 9 a.m. and collect at 3 p.m."

"That would be lovely, four hours a day, five days a week is just what I need," replied Miss Price.

Karen kindly offered to care for Dudley at no cost, which was excellent, and he was on cloud nine because he saw more of her boys, and Fitz was pleased with my arrangements.

The ladies in the sewing room were very nice to me, perhaps because I was so young. They were not accustomed to being around black people. They kept looking at me, one day the lady who sat next to me asked, "Can I touch you?"

"Yes, off course," I said.

She passed her hand gently down my bare arm and said, "My God, your skin is so soft. Feel mine." I did and was surprised how hard and leathery hers was. Having said that, Christa often said that I had the softest and smoothest skin of all my siblings.

Well now, not only did my wages help, going out to work and being with good adult company was brilliant. I had started having nagging headaches and going out to work seemed to ease the tension. My church life also began to bloom, and I believed that my spirituality showed, bless the Lord!

OVERWEIGHT

We were better off financially. When Fitz got paid on Fridays, he came bearing sweets for the children and Cadbury's chocolates for me. I began to increase in size, I was surprised to discover that I was thirteen stones. When we got married, I weighed ten stones, ten ounces. In desperation to lose the extra weight I kept myself busy. Although I cleaned the flat daily, every Saturday morning, I scrubbed and polished it. When it shined to my satisfaction, we all dressed and went shopping in Rathbone market; we looked forward to it, it was like a special treat. One Saturday I heard a faint sound behind me, each time I looked back it stopped. Eventually the girls laughed and said, "Mummy when you walk, daddy is behind you moving his hands up and down and saying, "wigs, wags, wigs, wags", in line with the movements of your bottom and whenever you look around, he stops."

"Right! that's it," I said, "I am going on a crash diet. No more chocolates, please!" My diet was a foolish one, all I ate was Slimcier, a slimming bread. I thought that the more I ate, the faster I would lose the weight. I did lose a little weight but after a fortnight I became very ill. My doctor had to be called in. She gave me a prescription for lecithin tonic and counselled me on healthy eating. The weight that I had lost went right on again.

BABY ON BOARD

I soon realised that I was three months pregnant, so I no longer bothered about my weight. I began reflecting on my life and had accepted that God does not make mistakes. I explained earlier that because of my loneliness as a child, I prayed to have babies to care for. Father had predicted that I would have many children like my mother.

My godmother had also said that I would be the one to follow my mother's footsteps and have many children, in reply to my godmother I said, "Only God knows." All I knew, was that my children were my pride and joy, they still are.

GOOD MOVES

I continued working in the sewing room at Aldgate until the journey became too much for me. I explained this to Miss Price, and she made me an offer to work from home and said that she would pay me hourly and extra for my electricity. To me that was a wonderful idea, and I thanked her, but instantly I knew that I would have to get myself an industrial sewing machine. On my way home I passed in at Singer sewing machine shop in Rathbone market and had a quick look around, the manager came to me and said that I could get one on easy instalments.

With Fitz's approval I went ahead with the purchase. The following day I accepted Miss Price's generous offer. My machine was delivered, followed by my flags. I was much better off financially by working at home as I saved on bus fare. My work was delivered and collected weekly. Miss Price found it hard to believe the hours I claimed. "You are not totalling your hours correctly, the hours you put down is not enough." She always paid me more. I was so happy. It was good to be able to send a bit more money to Mammatee for Andy and Fitz started driving lessons in the hope of taking us out, but that took a few years.

MAMMATEE'S VISIT

Pappahen became ill and returned to Mammatee from Trinidad. Mammatee cared for him with the help of sister Dorada but after some time, Sonday decided that Mammatee needed a break. Sister Dorada took over Pappahen's care so that Mammatee was able to come to us in England. We were all excited when she came over from St Vincent. Although she stayed with Sonday and his family she spent some time with me and each of my siblings. The time she spent at me was heavenly. She adored our children and they loved her. Her and

Glenda made what Mammatee called sweet eyes to each other. Mammatee was a regular church goer she had always looked forward to going with me to the Sunday morning services at the Mayflower family Centre. There was just one other black lady in the congregation, she seemed to know all the members.

Although Mammatee knew no one, she bravely went forward for communion just as she did in the Cathedral back in St Vincent, I was reluctant. “Come on, Sheva, let's go up.”

I had not taken communion there before, but I was not prepared explain to Mammatee, I simply followed. At the end of the service, someone came to Mammatee and said, “You were brave going up for communion.”

Mammatee with her bossy look, replied “Why should I fear? I am accustomed to taking communion.” And with that the conversation ended. I missed Mammatee when she returned to St Vincent.

One time, I was alone in the church garden when a young man sneaked up to me and whispered in my ear. “Don't you think you don't belong here?”

Taken by surprise, I shook my head and turned to look at him, but he briskly walked away. I reported this to Reverend Adams, who apologised to me for the young man’s behaviour and asked me to describe him. I did, and the Reverend said, “Don't worry it will not happen again.” That was the first and last time I saw that young man. The team at the Mayflower were excellent.

CHAPTER 20

TRACY'S BIRTH

April 1968 was the hottest Easter on record. I left Forest Gate hospital with another beautiful baby girl, Tracy. Weighing six pounds thirteen ounces, she was the biggest of our three girls at birth. Although I was worshipping at the Mayflower, we still Christened Tracy at St. Luke's Church. Her godparents were our friends, Jeana, her husband Lennard, and one of Fitz's friends. Jeana was one of my good friends back in St Vincent. She came to England a few months before me and married Lennard. Since Jeana's arrival in England we had not corresponded, however, the year after I arrived, one day while in conversation with Hilda's brother he gave me her phone number and address. I rang her that very day and arranged to meet. Fitz and Lennard also became great friends, that was why we decided to choose them both to be Tracy's god parents. And when they had their second child Fitz was honoured to be his godfather.

Five weeks after Tracy was born, we were all in bed when we heard the most awful sound as if the heavens were coming down on our house. We ran out in our night wear as did everyone nearby and before our very eyes the newly built Ronan Point, a block of flats twenty stories high that towered above our house had crashed to the ground like a pack of cards and killed four people. Everyone was badly shaken, but we had to go back into our homes and get on with our lives.

Patsy and Glenda were very helpful as always, they looked after Dudley and Tracy while I did the family washing. Most times my hands bled, finally I decided to go to the launderette in the early hours to avoid the long queue. Meanwhile I saved all my six pence's in a jar towards a deposit on a washing machine. Each week I kept my eye on the one I wanted and prayed that no one else bought it and hoped that the price would remain unchanged. At last, my jar was full, I checked it, it totalled two pounds fifty pence, the exact amount needed for the deposit. I jumped for joy and praised God. "Thank you, Jesus, thank you, thank you!"

Off I went to Curries Domestic Appliance and placed my deposit on that long awaited Indesit twin tub. It was delivered same day. Life just got better and better, although there was one downfall, sadly the sewing shop that I worked for closed, so our income decreased, but God had other plans. One day Patsy said, "Mummy one of my friend's mum, Melda, asked me where do you buy our dresses? I told her you make them. She wants to know if you will make for her girls." I spoke with Melda and agreed to sew for her girls, especially as they were the same age and size as Patsy and Glenda. Melda brought the material, I supplied everything else. Her payments to me were always delayed and in part. Most times Melda paid me with sausages and meat which her husband got from the factory where he worked as a butcher and that was fine because we became friends and helped each other out. Later, Melda found work and I cared for her girls after school for a small fee, my health visitor still visited occasionally, and she approved.

PAPPAHEN'S DEATH

When all seemed to be going well, we received a call from Mammatee, saying Pappahen had died. I was very sad because I had hoped that I would visit him one day and we would have caught up on long lost times. My sadness was made worse by the knowledge that at the time it was not possible for me or any of my siblings in England to go to his funeral. Sister Dorada and Mammatee did their best for him. He was buried in the grave with his dear mother.

THE CHILDREN'S CHARACTERS

Patsy was slowly becoming an artist. I failed to believe that the drawing I saw of a horse on the pavement in our garden was done by her, although she said, "It was me, Mummy!"

"No way!" I said, "So, tell me the truth, who did this?"

"Patsy did it mummy, I saw her," said Glenda.

I still remained unconvinced, so I went in, got a drawing book and said to Patsy, "Draw one here for me." She did and yes it was nice but not as perfect as the one she drew on the ground from her own inspiration. I was slowly learning my children's character and discovered that they were all unique in their own little ways. Glenda was like a second mum, always wanted to help with everything.

Dudley was into racing and fast-moving vehicles. He had to be watched closely so much so that I kept a rein on him and sometimes tied it to the settee when I was working in the back. He often stood on the settee and fiddled with the bolt on the door until he worked out how to shift it and open the door. He once opened it and ran into the road. Tim, our friendly shop keeper across the road spotted him, ran out, brought him in and called to me. Dudley's aim was to stand in the road when fast vehicles were coming, do a dance until they got close then make a run for the sidewalk. I was always afraid to take him off the rein. Had we lived in the Caribbean he would not have been on a rein because there, everyone enjoyed the freedom of being outdoors and neighbours looked out for each other. People said, "Hello, good morning, good evening, etc." Londoner's kept to themselves, especially in my street. Thank God for Tim! Most people looked the other way the moment they saw you, but if you looked back you would be sure to catch their eyes on you. It became a joke and sometimes I turned my head just for a laugh to see their sharp reaction and if you happened to be walking past their gate, they would quickly run in and close their door.

DEALING WITH HEADACHES

Headaches had become a daily occurrence. It had started with, thump, thump, before I moved to Burrard Road, so I did not pay much attention to it. However, my thumping head turned to pain and gradually grew worse. I found some relief by banging it lightly to the wall. Eventually I went to the doctor who diagnosed migraine and said that I should go out more and have some fun. I agreed that I was too cooped up. However, the daily news reported that many women who were on the contraceptive pill were suffering from migraine and thrombosis. I returned to my doctor and told her what I was hearing on the news, concerning the effects that the pill had on many women. She convinced me that I was safe. But Fitz became so worried that one day, he threw all my pills in the outside bin. We then decided to do some sight-seeing because the children also needed to see some of London. When we told them about our plans to take them out, they were over the moon.

We began with days out on the buses. Two adult day passes, or one pass to cover the week was all that we needed to get us around London. Children went for free. We packed a picnic and hopped off to eat and for a walkabout when the bus came to a nice park. We often returned home by another route. One bank holiday we took the train to Southend. Our trip went well, until we walked down the steps to the beach to picnic on the sand. I was shocked when a teenage white boy in a group of about six, stood at the top and deliberately spat down on my baby. I shouted, "Oh my God! Look! Look! Someone has just spat on my baby!" I looked up and there they stood laughing, but when they noticed Fitz's brisk move up the stairs, they all scampered. Luckily, the spit fell on our baby's hat which we immediately discarded and bought her another. We were not discouraged by the incident, we enjoyed our outing and the next time we went there we used the slope, so much to learn. My migraines continued but to a lesser degree.

CHAPTER 21

BIG MOVE

In May 1970, a letter came from the council stating that our house would be examined to see what condition it was in because homes in our area were going to be demolished, but not to worry as we would be rehoused. Two weeks later surveyors came, looked around and said that our house was the best kept in the street. After one week we received another letter saying that our house has been passed as fit for living and that we will be rehoused in a brand-new house in Stratford. *How on earth would we be able to afford the rent?* I thought. There was a number to call, I immediately dialled it. The officer on the other end of the phone listened carefully as I voiced my thoughts to him. He kept reassuring me not to worry, all will be well.

"Your new house will have a bedroom for your daughters, one for your son, a box room for your baby, and one for you and your husband. You will need to view it to see if you like it, although it's not yet completed. We will send a taxi for you. What time would you like to come?"

"Well, my husband should be home in the next two hours, so any time after that would be fine." Perfectly timed, the taxi arrived as Fitz entered the door and we were all taken to see the house. The cab pulled up at a beautiful gate where an officer stood waiting.

"Come in and look around," said the officer.

I could not believe my eyes, end terrace, with garden on every side. The children burst into excitement. They ran around the garden then into the house, calling to each other; "Come! Come! see this room! Look, here's another one!" Fascinated by the sound of the echo of their voices, they sang and shouted and laughed. The officer who sat at the table waiting to interview us said, "I don't need to ask if you lot are happy with what you have seen."

"Yes! Yes! We are happy, we love it in this house can we have it please?"

"Let's hear what your mummy and daddy has to say first."

They ran to us, "Mummy, Daddy, please, please, can we have this house?" It was as if they were conditioned to speak the same words together.

"We'll see," we said, still concerned about the cost of the rent. We sat and discussed the implications with the officer.

"All you have to say is yes you would like to have the house; a price can be arranged to suit your budget."

I do not need to say what our answer was. The cost of the rent was reduced to what we were able to afford. When the house was completed, we received the date for moving in. Packing was not too difficult as we did not have much. A removal van was sent to take us and our belongings. Some of us squashed in at the back. The scene created good free fun for onlookers, we joined in their fun by waving and laughing. We did not care how we got to the house as all long as we got there safely. When our van entered the road that became our road, removal vans were everywhere, some other people also travelled on their removal van. Ten other families moved into their homes that same day and a community began. Everyone was seen as equal, some of us borrowed and shared garden tools. There was much to be done in everyone's garden; one neighbour helped us, and Fitz returned the favour, from then we became friends.

CARPENTERS SCHOOL

Our children and most of the neighbours' children attended the same Carpenters school. It was an old upstairs, downstairs building. The stairs were outside, I feared for the children's safety. I was also concerned about the busy Carpenters Road that they had to cross to get to school. It was good that all the children in our street played together after school and on weekends. Back in those days I disliked

Stratford, with its busy traffic and foul air from the nearby sausage factory. My beautiful home was my attraction. My inner voice kept saying, *have you forgotten that in Matthew's gospel Jesus says, "Ask and it will be given, seek and you will find, knock and the door will be opened unto you?" Yes, I know it's up to me! OK!* From that moment on I prayed without ceasing about everything I thought needed changing and improving in Stratford.

PRAYER FOR CHANGES

"Please Father God, let a bridge be built across Carpenters Road so that children can cross safely to and from school, also please provide a shortcut to Stratford. Lord, we could also do with a cinema to take our children for enjoyment and, last but not least, help me find a welcoming church nearby." One by one God answered every prayer and granted me so much more than I could have ever imagined. Stratford has now become a city. I now look back and say, "Thank you God, you are truly great and marvellous in all your ways."

DUDLEY

Patsy and Glenda walked to school with their friends, but I took Dudley to pre-school at the age of four. He was very smart and full of pride. I learned not to kiss him goodbye if his friends were within eye view, yet when we were alone, he loved a kiss and a cuddle and enjoyed playing with my arm. One Saturday we went to the supermarket, after we emptied our shopping onto the checkout belt, Dudley said, "Mum I need to wee."

"Hold on darling, we won't be long." But then I noticed that Dudley was desperate, so I said, "Go out and do it on the side." Well, that was what all children did back then. He went but did not return. Panic stricken I looked from side to side asking, "Has anyone seen a little boy about four years old wearing an Arsenal tee-shirt?" Some people showed concern, some said no, some others gazed at me and went on their way.

Finally, one lady said, "Yes, I saw him, he went that way towards the crossing."

"Oh thank you! Thank you" I replied.

Oh my God he's heading for home! but how would he know the way? And how would he cross that busy road? I walked and ran as I pushed the pram with the girls either side. We got home to find Dudley sitting comfortably watching football. Luckily, his dad was in to open the door for him, that was a giant relief. Dudley felt good knowing that he was capable of looking after himself and, even as a young boy, envisaged taking care of us. He often sat and composed songs about the things he hoped to do for each of us when he grew up, and he named them one by one. It brought us pleasure just by looking and listening to him. At times he would be annoyed with the girls when they did not give him a chance to watch football, I had to laugh when one day he said, "I am the man." He continued to be very independent and when he was about twelve, he played football five a side, then moved to bigger teams in the under 18's league, later he became a coach to young ones on the field.

FITZ CHANGED HIS JOB

With a big house and garden to keep we entered again into financial difficulty. For this reason, Fitz changed his day job as a spray painter to working three different shifts at Fords Motor Company in Dagenham. This was good, financially, but I hated being alone at nights with my small children, especially as I was aware of frequent fires from oil heaters and gas cookers. My mind was forever on the go. I measured the distance from the window to the ground, tied sheets together, and kept them in readiness. I thought if there were a fire while we were in bed, I would lower the children to the ground one by one in the sheets.

EXTRA CASH

I had lots of work to keep me busy, but I gladly made time to earn extra cash. I saw an advert in the paper, *Indoor machinist wanted for men's jackets.* I had no experience in sewing men's clothing, but I called the number. "Hello, I am calling about the job advertised in the paper."

"Can you sew?" the voice replied.

"Yes."

"Ok, come in and we'll see what you can do."

Our lovely neighbour, Mrs Brown, looked after Tracy for one week in which time I mastered the art of sewing jackets. My work was delivered and collected. I worked in the dining room which was under my bedroom. The constant Brom, Brom, Brom, from the singer sewing machine made it difficult for Fitz to sleep. The trouble was, the more jackets I made, the more they sent. "No increase please, I need some time to take care of my family," but they took no heed. The girls helped as much as they could with little jobs about the house.

TRACY'S SUFFERING

About a year later there was a terrible accident. Dear little Tracy was rushed to hospital where she spent a week recovering from a badly scalded arm. Two days after I was also admitted to the same hospital for high blood pressure. I was allowed to visit Tracy and the nurses also brought her to me, this was a terrible time for everyone. Poor Tracy who was always a happy, smiling child and wanted to assist in everything, sadly, lost her joy, and it tore my heart. Her arm healed with a permanent scar but thankfully she slowly regained her cheerfulness and I never returned to paid work at home on the sewing machine.

CHILD CARE

Our new health visitor brought a lady to meet me. She needed someone to care for her two boys, Chinny and Fatchy. Chinny the eldest was Dudley's age and Fatchy was Tracy's age. I agreed to care for them during her working hours but that was short lived. Fatchy never stopped crying, he stood at the front door constantly banging and calling for his mum. He refused to eat or be comforted by anyone, not even his brother. One day Sonday came to visit and seeing the commotion of the child, he asked. "Sheva why are you looking after these children?" Pointing to Fatchy, "That one is too highly strung! It's all too much for you, you have enough of your own." He pulled some money from his pocket and handed it to me. "Take this, if it's money you need." From then he and his wife Claire occasionally brought me gifts. I stopped caring for the boys but saw them occasionally.

MY SIXTH CHILD

I was now two months pregnant with my sixth child and my battle with high blood pressure continued. My new doctor kept saying that I must rest and come off the salt; to boil fish and eat it unsalted.

"But doctor I can't eat fish without salt. I will vomit."

"I do not care if you vomit from here to kingdom come. Leave out the salt!"

Her strictness and harsh words often brought tears to my eyes, but I followed her instructions and became accustomed to eating every kind of food unsalted. Fitz had to stop working overtime hours to help out more at home. I spent most days of my pregnancy in bed due to my high blood pressure. The midwife at clinic said, "Well done you have lost weight and your blood pressure has dropped." Up to the day of delivery my weight remained the same as when I was seven months, but the midwife still said that no increase in my weight was great. Well yes, the loss in weight was good for me but not for my baby! No one realised that my baby had stopped feeding from seven months, so there was no growth - the real reason why my weight did not increase. This was the only baby I carried with such small stomach, I just looked plump.

On the twenty fourth July 1972 the ambulance drove me to Forest Gate Maternity hospital. I looked forward to the arrival of my new baby with no fear of anything going wrong. My other babies were all born in the early hours of the morning. I expected the same for the sixth time, but I was wrong. I gave birth the following day at 11 a.m. I glimpsed something. I was not sure what conclusion to make of what I saw, but it was as white as a baby lamb. Not a sound was heard and immediately it was removed and one by one, doctors came and pressed on my tummy. They pressed with jumping movements as if they were trying to revive someone whose heart had stopped. Eventually they stopped, and I asked, "Did I have a baby? Where is my baby? What is it?"

"Just you rest" was the answer, "You need to rest."

"But where is my baby?"

"Just rest now," and with that they left me to rest.

Later that day I was moved to a ward and Fitz came to see me. "Fitz, I don't know if I had a baby. No one seems to want to tell me anything."

"You need rest. Don't worry about anything," Fitz said.

"But I need to know if I had a baby. I saw something white like a lamb but there was no cry."

"Sheva go to sleep," urged Fitz, and he sat watching me until it was time for him to leave. That silence went on for four days. Everyone seemed to think that keeping things from me was the best way to reduce my blood pressure, but I am sure the worry of not knowing merely aggravated the situation.

On the fifth day a doctor came to me. "Hello, Mrs Williams, your baby is not very well."

"Baby! So I have a baby?"

"Yes, you have a beautiful baby girl, but she needs your help. She has lost blood whilst in your womb. Can we take some from you for her? Yours will be the best as you are of the same blood group."

"Yes, please do! Take whatever she needs. But where is she?" I asked.

"She is in an incubator, being looked after by special care nurses. She is very tiny, she weighed four pounds fifteen ounces at birth. Her weight is now four pounds eleven ounces," said the doctor.

I was relieved at the knowledge that I had a baby and that she was going to be alright. Next came a nurse with a breast pump. "Can I have some of your milk for your baby?" she asked. Well, my blood pressure must have plummeted. The knowledge that my baby was about to be fed was music to my ears. I was also relieved to pump the milk from my enormous and painful breasts.

On the seventh day I was taken to see my baby. Gosh! She was so tiny I did not know how I would hold her. I was then told that I would be discharged on the nineth day without my baby, and that I would have had to return each day with milk for her because she had to stay until she gained sufficient weight to be discharged. On the nineth day my little fighter weighed five pounds and together we went home. I thanked God.

It was difficult to decide on a name for our new baby because she was so tiny. Her dad called her Peenie number two. He had also called Glenda, Peenie, although she was almost three pounds heavier at birth. Peenie number two needed to be fed every half hour. She was only able to take one ounce of milk at a time then sleep. When she was a bit stronger, Patsy and Glenda held the bottle for her, and she suckled slowly, sleeping in between. It was difficult to understand why she was the only one who preferred the bottle to the breast, I then realised that her first stage of feeding was from a bottle by the nurses in the hospital. However, I thanked God that she continued to gain weight. I guess she was helped by the daily dose of Abidec drops that I had to give to her which was prescribed by the hospital. She was soon big enough to be held by her dad and her siblings. Our neighbours' children flocked to see her. Patsy and her friend Vera from next door pushed her in the pram along the sidewalk. They often went into Vera's house, and I had to go to fetch them. Whenever I knocked, the door was opened by Vera's dad, who would sometimes say, "Come in, Patsy is just about to have tea with us."

"Thanks, but I can't, I am about to dish up dinner."

Most times Vera's mum would show her face at the door laughing.

"Can Patsy stay for a bit?"

"Ok, but I need to take my baby."

Patsy soon followed.

PEARL'S WEDDING

January 1973 my niece, Pearl, announced her Easter wedding and we were all invited. I made dresses and jackets for the girls and a dress for me. I bought Dudley's suit as Fitz did not have much time to sew for him as he had promised. The wedding day was quite chilly, nonetheless, Pearl looked beautiful and so did all of us. We had a lovely time.

CHURCH LIFE IN STRATFORD

One fine Sunday morning I went into each of our children's rooms and said, "Time to get up! Today we are going to find a church." I laid out smart clothes for everyone, then I quickly made breakfast. It was nice to see how swiftly they got ready, and we were off. We walked up to Stratford until we got to the Romford Road where we saw a sign showing Highway Church. We went in and were made to feel welcome. It was nice there and the children loved it, but I did not go back because some people prayed in tongues - a language that I believed required an interpreter. The next Sunday we went out again with my hope to find an Anglican Church. As we walked, I heard church bells. Why did I not hear them before? Perhaps I never passed when they were ringing. We followed the sound to St John's Church along the Broadway, that big church in the middle of the road. We had walked past it many times but failed to see it, although a war memorial stands tall in the yard, I guess too many trees surrounded it.

"Come, let's go in," I said.

"Mummy, why can't we go back to the one we went before?" asked Patsy.

"Well darling, it's a bit far." I did not say to her that it was also because some people prayed in tongues, a language that I believed only God understood, and which at the time made me feel uneasy.

We entered the lovely church. There were many empty seats. I checked fifteen white people and three black families. Most were very welcoming, others appeared to be shy. The Reverend Canon Moss, the church leader, reached out to us and within a week he paid us a visit at our home. He explained many things to us about St John's Church and Christ Church, the sister church, which was on Stratford High Road, much closer to us. No services were held at Christ Church, nonetheless, it was where the guides and brownies met. I took Patsy and Glenda along to be admitted and they thoroughly enjoyed being brownies but when the time came for them to progress to the guides, they had no wish to join.

CHRISTENING & CONFIRMATION

After trying out many names on Peenie number two, we settled for Vilna. She was four months when she was christened, at St John's Church. Her godparents were PJ and my nieces, Pearl and Donna. We had a lovely little family celebration. From then, St John's Church became our regular church for Sunday morning worship. Patsy and Glenda joined the choir. They went back at six thirty for Songs of Praise, they enjoyed singing and were delighted to know that they would even be paid. When they received their first pay Patsy said, "Ooh, Mummy! we've got our own money."

"Wow! that's good" I said.

Going out kept them busy and the money added to their excitement. They were up and out in time for practice and, if memory serves me well, in November 1973 they were confirmed together - another family celebration. I made their dresses, designed by Patsy, they looked beautiful.

CHURCH OUTINGS

I was pleasantly surprised when in the summer of 1974 Cannon Moss invited us on a coach outing to the seaside. He kindly paid for us and gave us money for lunch, and this he continued until he left. I later learned that for many years he had paid for the elderly and people with young families and gave two pounds fifty pence to each person for spending. That was a lot of spending money in those days, and we had some good times. Dudley never joined us, as football was his thing, he practised on Saturdays and played five-a-side on Sundays.

SECONDARY SCHOOL

In September of that same year Patsy started at Sarah Bonnell, Secondary School. Uniform time and less dressmaking for me. Patsy travelled with her friends, and all went well. A year later Glenda joined her, she also went with her friends, they were good girls, I had no cause to worry about anything.

Four months after Vilna's birth I was expecting my seventh child. Blood pressure checks reminded me, that it still had its grip on me. My doctor said, "It's too risky! You'll have to terminate and shut the shop." My seventh child, the number of children which someone had predicted for me was no more because of ill health. Strange how I had always thought that six children would have been a nice round number. Both Father and my godmother had said that I would be like my Mammatee, but I never wanted to have fifteen children like my Mammatee. I believe that God knew best.

CHAPTER 22

BREAK DOWN

About a week after Pearl's wedding, I began to get strange, weird feelings. *What is this all about*? *Why can I not sleep? Ten days with no sleep.* My mind had become alert like never before. I saw everything in a new light. It was as if I had suddenly entered into a new dimension and it made me think of the man in John's gospel chapter 9:25 who was born blind, and Jesus gave him sight. In answer to those who questioned him about the sight he received, he replied, "One thing I know. I was blind but now I see." For me, things that I never understood before started to become clear. W*here did the sudden wisdom come from?* I saw a war between good and evil. My mind said*, you need help.* I listened and called PJ. "You've got to come now. Something is not right with me," I said.

"Why what's wrong?"

"I don't know just come."

PJ came without hesitation. I explained what was happening to me.

"You need to rest, and all will be well in a day or two," said PJ.

I tried to rest but that did not work so I called Mrs Brown, my lovely neighbour. She came and said, "Perhaps you need prayer for healing. My pastor can help you."

The following day Mrs Brown drove my children and me to her church, what I experienced there was scary. The pastor prayed for me then he touched my forehead. I fell backwards. Someone caught me and lowered me to the floor then covered my legs with a large towel. I was not aware that Fitz came to meet us. When he saw me laying on the floor after being prayed for, he was very upset with the pastor. On my return home that night I lay on my bed unable to comprehend what was happening to me, I just knew that something was not right. Fitz was mad with me for going to another church. He believed that whatever went on at that church had had a bad effect on me and had caused my anxiety. His words were, "I am not sleeping with a mad woman," and with that he slept downstairs, but I knew that no one was to blame for the way I was feeling. Patsy called on her siblings, "Come let's stay in the bed with mummy." I was not prepared to put my babies through my turmoil. I dialled 999. "Ambulance please!" I have no recollection of what I told them was wrong, they obviously thought that I was in labour as I was taken to the labour ward at White Chapel Hospital. The doctors later discovered that I was having a nervous breakdown brought on by the termination of my pregnancy, postnatal depression and anxiety.

That day in the hospital I prayed like never before. Fitz and some of my siblings came to see me, I don't know how they knew where I was because I told no one. I had left my children sleeping. "How did you find me?" I asked Fitz.

"The hospital called me," he replied.

PJ hugged me tight, and I fell into a sweet, deep sleep. When I awoke a lovely nurse, called Cyndy, was at my bedside. She became afraid when she heard a voice coming from me that was not mine but that of a man. The voice said, "Be still my soul, I am the true Christ." Cyndy ran for the doctor, she must have told him what she heard. He came and asked me to repeat what I said the way I had said it. I explained that the voice which spoke through me was not me. From that moment my healing began, it was as if I was given a new lease of life. However, Fitz had to take time off to care for our children.

It was great having visits from my siblings and their grown-up children. Christa visited regularly and took me for long walks and shopping along the White Chapel Street market. Whatever I saw and liked she bought for me, then walked me back to the hospital. One day while I lay in bed a strange thing happened: Two white ladies came visiting, one wore a beautiful broach of many colours, my eyes dazzled at the sight. "Your broach is so pretty," I said.

"Do you like it?" she asked.

"It's nice," I replied.

She removed it from her dress and pinned it on mine, saying. "Well now it's yours, it will help to make you better." Then quickly they left. I got up to find them, but they were nowhere to be seen. When I asked around the ward, the answers were the same. "We have not seen them." I concluded that they were my guardian angels sent from heaven above.

After that encounter, my healing was rapid and I was drawn closer to Jesus, deep in my heart I knew that one day I would teach and preach the gospel. My experience of good and evil was phenomenal, I had a lot to share and still have. I believe people need to know that Satan is real but thank God he had no lasting hold on me. Jesus brought me through. I always knew that Jesus was ready, willing and able to save and to heal all who believe and trust in him. I also thank God for the doctors, nurses, psychiatrists and all who faithfully worked to aid my healing. I see them as God's instruments. I spent three months living between home and the psychiatric ward at White Chapel Hospital. My life was changed for the better, but there still remained a small problem - Fitz never got used to the advice he was given by the psychiatrist, "Your wife is like a bird in a cage she needs to be set free, she will not fly away she loves you."

"Ok if that's what it takes, I will stand back." Fitz replied.

From then I noted Fitz's distance and the loss of some comforts from him.

ST ANDREWS

1974. *Come on girl, it's time you pursue the career that your Mammatee had hoped for you when you left St Vincent*. I answered an advertisement for auxiliary nurses at St Andrews hospital, nearby. I was interviewed and accepted. It was my intention of moving up to becoming a qualified nurse. The nursing officer who was present at my interview said, "You would be excellent working with our dear oldies." There were different shifts available, I took the 5 to 9:30 evening shift as it suited me best and worked well with Fitz's shift. I was based on the female geriatric ward. I loved caring for the old dears, it felt as though I was looking after my own mum, a privilege I had lost, even though they were all white. When I worked on the male ward, some patients showed utter contempt. "Take your black hands off me! I fought in the war." etc. etc. Some who had mild dementia threw their faeces or spat at me, but it did not deter me from giving them my best. It saddened me when one passed but I slowly accepted that that was the way it had to be, and my colleagues were all wonderful. My worst experience was one day in 1975, we had seven deaths from a flu virus. I got home that night and played my gospel music loud in the hope of easing my own pain after comforting grieving relatives. I had no intention of upsetting my dear neighbours. When they called from across the fence, "Sheva turn that music down our boy has just gone to bed!" I apologised, turned off my music, had a hot bath and retired to bed. The next morning the death of our patients made headlines in the newspaper.

CHAPTER 23

HOLIDAY IN 1976

Things began to look up, financially, so I started saving for a holiday back home. I longed to see my son, Andy, my Mammatee and numerous relatives. I had planned to go alone, and Fitz was prepared to stay behind and care for our children, but big brother Sonday stepped in and suggested that it would be better for Fitz to accompany me. "Don't worry about the children I will sort out who will take care of them," he said. After discussions with his wife and our siblings he returned with a plan. "Claire and I will have Patsy, Glenda and Vilna. Dudley will go to Karen so that he can be with her boys and Tracy will go to Selda and I will come and take care of your plants." My other siblings were happy to help they also thought that both Fitz and I needed a break, especially following my breakdown. This was an offer too good to refuse. Although I had already booked my flight, Fitz managed to book the same flight but unfortunately his seat was in the row behind me.

We packed our cases long in advance, then I packed the children's. The day before our flight, Sonday came and took the children to the different homes. The next day he returned and drove us to the airport for our first ever flight. We were both nervous but excited to get home. After eight hours in the sky, we landed in Barbados and boarded the Liat, a small plane that took us to St Vincent. When the plane touched down half an hour later and we stepped out, I knelt down and kissed the ground three times. It was a wonderful feeling to be back on the beautiful island of my birth after fifteen long years. Our taxi driver, a family friend, was on the spot to collect us and within thirty minutes we were in Lowmans Hill. Mammatee had spread the word about the date and time we were due to arrive. Many villagers gathered at Mammatee's gate to welcome us, even Mammatee's dog, known for chasing people away, greeted me with a wag from his tail.

Mammatee was shocked, "Look at that, she knows you, she can smell your blood, she knows that you are mine," she said, the onlookers were also surprised because they dared not enter the gate.

It was great to hug and kiss all who were there, but when I looked at Mammatee I was moved to tears of joy and those little boys that I had left and longed to hold were all out. Victor had emigrated to Canada while Harran and Winnie had made their homes on nearby Islands. When Andy came in from his day at secondary school our eyes met and the expression on our faces were like the sun on a glorious day at high noon. Then suddenly Andy became shy. "Come to me," I said, and he came. We embraced and kissed until we were both satisfied. Each time he looked into my eyes he smiled, went shy and shook his head.

"At last, I get to meet my mother," he said. I knew just how he felt.

"Darling I am sorry. I wish things had been different, but I am here now I am with you for five weeks."

"Five weeks! So where are your clothes?"

"There," pointing to my suitcase.

"Let me have a look at what you brought."

When I opened my case the first thing that popped up was a white fluffy rug forty-eight by forty-eight inches.

"What are you going to do with this?"

"It's a gift that someone asked me for."

Next came a bedspread.

"And that one?"

"Oh just another gift."

"So, mummy where are your clothes? You can't be going around in the same outfit we don't do that down here."

"It will be OK" I said.

"Well next time you come make sure you bring your clothes not giant size gifts for people."

"OK" I said.

I thought gosh he was smart and masterful. Gone was the shyness. Follu and Gerald came home later. Like me, they also wore broad smiles in our joys at seeing each other. Follu spoke first, "Hello auntie, welcome home, so nice to have you. You resemble aunty Winnie and Mammatee." I thanked him and we greeted with hug and kisses.

"You have grown into a very cool, handsome young man," I complimented "I'm so happy to be here with you all."

Gerrard just stood smiling shyly. With my arms opened wide I beaconed him into my embrace. To every question I presented him, his answer was "yo, yo, yo," whilst maintaining a smiling face.

Meanwhile Fitz renewed his acquaintance with Mammatee, then he exchanged greetings and made small talk with the others who were there. We spent our five weeks between Mammatee and Fitz's dad in Evesham Village. Fitz's mum had passed the year after we were married. His dad shared his home with his daughter Lorraine and her children, they were all kind and entertained us well. Fitz proudly introduced me to all of his relatives in the village and beyond. After one week in Evesham, Andy wanted me with him, and to be honest, I longed to be with him, Mammatee and the other boys, so I left Fitz with his family and returned to mine, however every two days we visited each other.

Whenever Gerrard and Andy were free, they accompanied me through Lowmans Hill. Everyone was happy to see me, just as I was at seeing them. Some presented me with gifts of fruits, vegetables and coconut water, one of my favourite drinks. All too soon our five weeks were up, time came for farewells but not goodbyes. We exchanged hugs and kisses. With each hug, voices echoed, "Don't leave it so long to come back."

"By the grace of God, I will," was my reply.

Andy lowered his face and smiled but his eyes revealed a saddened heart. For certain we shared the same sentiment.

Check-in from St Vincent to Barbados was good as was the Liat flight, however, when we checked in at Barbados to London, we were overweight, and we had no money to pay for the extra weight. One kind attendant looked at Fitz then turned to his colleague, beckoning his hand he said, "Man leh deh man go long."

Fitz and I smiled with relief, I bowed and said, "Thank you!"

"Bless you brother!" said Fitz.

"No problem man," replied the attendant.

ARRIVAL BACK IN LONDON

Sonday was already at the airport to collect us. When we got home, he took us straight to our garden. "Look how well your garden has done, your cabbages are big, your spinach are thick and green." We were pleased, our tomato trees were laden with red and green tomatoes and when we dug up a carrot it was a nice size. Sonday was so excited with the growth of what we had planted, and we were grateful to him for taking care of them for us. "I reaped some and took them home," he said. Good job he did, he saved them from rotting. The following day he brought Patsy, Glenda and Vilna back to us. Doug brought Tracy, and Larry returned Dudley. As they entered the door their voices were like music to my ear, "Mummy, Mummy, Daddy, Daddy, you're back!" We were all up in air with excitement, kisses and cuddles flowed freely. We had four glorious days together then it was back to school and work. I had never made any real plans for my future except for that holiday, but from then I began to put some in motion.

PLANS

I took myself off to West Ham college and enrolled to study English and Human Biology. Both classes amounted to just four hours a week.

I went during our children's school time and while Vilna was at nursery.

A year later, praise the Lord, Fitz bought a blue Vauxhall Viva. Occasionally, we packed ourselves in it with our picnic and he drove us around. During school holidays we went to Chessington Zoo, London Zoo and Southend on sea. We also visited family and friends, and depending on his shift work, he picked me up after my work. Having the car also relieved the strain of carrying the heavy shopping.

CHAPTER 24

CANNON MOSS RETIRED

I attended church more regularly. When dear Reverend Cannon Moss retired, he was greatly missed, and in January 1979 he was replaced by Reverend Daley. Daley and I got on like hands in gloves, perhaps because we were the same age. His wife, Fiona, was also a very lovely lady, their love was felt by all. Fiona was very helpful, they both worked well with church members and encouraged social activities. They organised scenic route coach tours in the evenings so that people who worked during the day were able to join in. We went to Thaxted in Essex and followed along with Morris dancers, in their annual event, as they danced through the streets and stopped at pubs along the way. On one trip we were in the middle of the highway when, after a couple pints, nature called. “Driver,” when is the next stop?” I called out politely.

“Stop? I wasn't planning on stopping but if I must it will be in half an hour.”

“Half an hour! You've got to stop now!” I said desperately.

Daley looked at me, saw my agony and called out, “Driver pull up at the bank!” and with that the driver did. “Sheva just go quickly and stay by the side.” Off I went.

“Stay right there go no further!” shouted Daley. *No way am I staying here where they can all see me!* So I made one step up the bank, and one step down. *Oh my God! I'm rolling, rolling, rolling! Oh dear will I stop? How can I stop?* By then my undergarment was torn to shreds by the bushes but thank God I had stopped rolling.

”Sheva where are you? I can't see you. Come back now!” Daley called.

“I'm coming, I’m coming!”

Luckily, it was easier going up. My step back on the coach aided by Daley, ended in fits of laughter by everyone, including me as I told my rolling story.

Later that year I was invited by the Church Council to join the Mothers' Union. I found it rather interesting and became a member.

Also in 1979 Tracy was confirmed. I made her a white dress, like I did for her sisters before, and she looked beautiful. While we were at church for the confirmation service two of my nursing colleagues came to my home and decorated the table in readiness for the celebration on our return. It was a joy to have lovely colleagues. We had a nice little party with family and friends. Tracy later joined the choir with her older sisters.

Our church also had a lady Curate. She was based at St James, our sister church, but came to St John's whenever she was needed. I joined her on a number of occasions. One memory that stands out was our weekend stay in Norfolk, I think we travelled in four full cars. I took Vilna with me. The hall where we stayed was on a farm, where lambs were reared. Our dinner that night was roasted lamb and two vegetables. The lamb was taken from the farm and freshly killed. Everyone ate and commented how fresh and delicious the meat was. I could not pay the same compliment because as a Caribbean girl I believe in well-seasoned and marinated meat, hence to me it was ghastly. However, I made no comment but decided that one taste was enough. Vilna and I had settled for vegetables and lots of ice cream for dessert. On our way home the sky opened, and the rain bucketed. Vilna and I were in the curates car, she too had also taken her youngest son; he was about seven the same age as Vilna, he sang choruses and prayed, asking Jesus to stop the rain. His favourite prayer was "Gentle Jesus meek and mild look upon a little child..." We joined him in singing until sleep got the better of him. We continued singing and had fun driving home even though the rain slowed us down.

This was also the year that Glenda started fulltime work. Before then, she and Patsy were in part time jobs after school. Dudley had also found himself a little paper round, and after a few weeks he got a better job as an evening manager in a supermarket petrol station. It was almost three years since my holiday, and I was determined to have more.

I began thinking, *the children are doing well, and apart from Vilna, they can take care of themselves, they are good children. I can take Vilna with me so that Fitz won't have to worry, but where would we go?* Then one day the thought came to me, *why not write to cousin Dorawa and tell her you would like to pay her a visit.* WIth no hesitation I wrote.

> "Hi cousin Dorawa,
>
> How are you? I Pray all is well. I would love to visit you and bring Vilna with me would you be able to have us? If yes, when would be the best time for us to come?
>
> Your loving cousin
>
> Sheva"

I was amazed at her quick reply.

> "Hi Sheva,
>
> Yes, I would love to have you both. Just book your fare, let me know when you will come, and I will take the time off work. Franado stays in the house next to me, but he may not be around, he's planning to go back home to see his family, so you might miss out on seeing him, but the good thing is you and Vilna would be able to stay in his apartment and be with me during the day. I look forward to seeing you both.
>
> Love cousin
>
> Dorawa"

NEW YORK

Wow! New York we're on our way! I paid the fare for Vilna and myself then organised my home. Fitz was happy for us to go. Cousin Dorawa met us at LaGuardia Airport. I had heard so much about the dangers in New York, that our ten minutes of waiting for her to arrive was scary. But at the sight of her all fears disappeared. She reassured me that I was not to worry because things were not as bad as they sounded. She came with Karl, her nephew-in-law, and he drove us to their home in the Bronx, where we met his wife and an elderly cousin whom I had never heard of. She, however, knew all about my family's history, it was a treat to listen to her stories. Karl also drove us to different places with Cousin Dorawa. When he was at work, cousin Dorawa took us by public transport to places of interest. We visited the Bronx Zoo, the Statue of Liberty, the Statue of Abraham Lincoln and Davis at Mount Pulaski Street.

In the second week of our holiday we flew to Toronto, thanks again to cousin Dorawa for her generosity in purchasing our tickets. We stayed with my niece, Esther and her family, it was good to spend time with them. Vilna enjoyed being with her cousins especially as they were close in age. Sister Dorada, Esther's mother, lived close by with her husband and a niece. Two more of Esther's younger siblings had made their homes in the nearby towns. We spent a couple nights with sister Dorada, and while we were with her, the other family members came to visit and together we went to Lake Ontario and had a lovely day swimming. During our time at Esther's home, besides going on shopping sprees, she took us to CN Tower, Stratford and Niagara Falls. We had an eventful and exciting time in Canada. When we returned to New York, Vilna was tired, but she tried not to show it, and thankfully we had a few days to rest before our flight back to London. Holidays are brilliant, especially when spent with lovely caring families whom we had not seen in years, but it was always good to be home where the heart is. Patsy, Glenda and Dudley were still at work when we got home.

Fitz and Tracy met us at the door, we were so happy to see each other, we hugged and kissed, “Tracy you’ve grown so much,” I said,

“Do you think so Mummy?”

“Yes, it seems so.” When the others got home, one by one we greeted. It was wonderful to be back with them, it was then that I noticed how right I was that Tracy had grown; as she stood beside Glenda, they were the same in height.

“Look Tracy you are as tall as Glenda,” I said,

Tracy just smiled with her big beautiful talking eyes.

DRIVING LESSONS

The year of 1979 continued to be an eventful year. I started driving lessons with Kim’s school. On my first day behind the wheel there was an unexpected bang on the back of the car. “What’s that?” I asked, Dave my instructor.

“Oh, it’s not you, you have done well! It’s that idiot behind!” I remained in my seat until the incident was sorted then I carried on as if nothing had happened. Dave looked at me smiled and said, “You are amazing, carry on.” I enjoyed driving but the examiner failed me on my first test, which I thought was perfect driving. Dave was not happy because he said, “You were on top form. He failed you because they had had enough passes for that day.” That afternoon I went home and made bread. I took my revenge out on the dough, it helped to let the tension out.

My second test followed a few weeks after but, unlike the first, I was nervous thinking, *what do I have to do to pass*? I did not hold out much hope. What a surprise when the inspector said, “I am pleased to tell you, you have passed your test.” Wow! I felt great. Dave and everyone was happy for me. That Thursday night I celebrated and by the weekend I was behind the wheel of my red Ford Escort; it was a wonderful feeling being able to drive myself to and from work and to take my family out and about.

ACCIDENT AT ST ANDREWS

Just when all was going brilliant, I suffered a back injury at work. One never knows what can happen from one minute to the next. One evening while putting a patient back to bed with my ward sister the phone rang and without thinking, she let go of the patient and went to answer the phone, leaving the full strain on me. I tried to save the patient who had left hemiplegia, from falling but within seconds my back pulled and resulted in a slip disc. *Why on earth did sister just let go of our patient and dash to answer the phone at the first ring.* Instantly it dawned on me that she was not yet her true self. Sister had shared her problem with me. She was being treated at the psychiatric hospital, following a breakdown so I sympathised, having walked that same path, I tried to exercise patience. When she returned after about a minute, she noticed my distress, and together we put the patient back to bed. Luckily, I recorded the incident because it became useful for my future statement.

The following day my back was so painful, I could not straighten up, I had to visit my doctor and I was given time off work. I struggled to keep up with daily chores. After six months of being off work and visiting doctors, I was given a course of treatment at the hospital which included traction. The treatment helped but I was still not well enough to return to work, so I went privately for further treatment with the same Orthopaedic consultant Dr Fenn, who was treating me at the hospital. Thank heavens for my little escort as walking became difficult especially up and down curbs. Dr Fenn had reassured me that, because I was young and having the extended treatment, with rest, my back would get better. And yes, I felt the improvement. However, I received a letter from Miss Paddy, the senior nursing officer stating that, Dr Fenn requested to see me at the hospital for a check up to return to work. I rang Miss Paddy and explained my condition and that I was still undergoing private treatment.

Miss Paddy replied, "Well, you have to keep the appointment, our Orthopaedic Consultant, Doctor Fenn, wants to see you as stated in my letter.

"Ok thank you," I replied and with that Miss Paddy hung up.

I went to see the consultant on the date I was given. "Hello," I said to the receptionist, and presented my letter. "I am here to see Doctor Fenn."

"Doctor Fenn is off duty," she replied.

"Off duty? My letter says I am to see him."

"There has been a change. You are now assigned to Dr Chung in room four. He's waiting, I'll take you through."

"Hello Dr Chung, I have not met you before. Are you new here?" I asked.

Doctor Chung made no reply but simply said, "Get on the couch let me examine you."

I obeyed. Dr Chung gently tapped my back then said, "Ok you can go now." It was unbelievable all that way for a tap, tap on my back. Seven days later came another letter from Miss Paddy, it stated return to work on Monday your report shows that you are fit for work. I knew I was not fit enough for work, so I went to my GP, his report confirmed that I was unfit for work for a further two weeks.

It was still hard keeping up with my housework, I just did what I could. When my two weeks sick leave was up, I went back to work but after three days my legs became weak and shaky. I had to go off work again. On my next private appointment with Doctor Fenn while we were in conversation, I mentioned the letter I had received from Miss Paddy at the hospital the previous week with his request to see me. Dr Fenn looked surprised and said, "I requested no such thing, nothing to do with me." I explained to Dr Fenn what had happened. I further informed Dr Fenn that I felt a lot better after the two weeks sick leave and went back to work but after two days of lifting my legs became weak again, so it was not possible for me to carry on. Dr Fenn suggested that I see a solicitor and recommended Darren and Sons. I took his advice. After briefing Darren about the incident at work, he said, "You have a very good case, would you like to pursue?"

"Yes." I replied,

"Ok leave it with me, I will call you when I'm ready." During that time, I was sent to see an Occupational Health Advisor, who advised that I do light work only. In 1980 I was made redundant.

COLLEGE

Back at college, exam time was announced. *Oh dear,* I said to myself, *I am so not ready for this*. My Tutor had suggested that myself and some others who had left school many years before ought to study for another term before taking the exams. I ignored my tutor's advice and went forward. On the day of my exams my back pain added to my worry and the pain was worsened by sitting for long hours. I was a bag of nerves. I knew the paperwork, but I could not write and before one could say 'Jack', time was up. I knew that I had failed. I could have returned to my studies and resit the exam, but I thought, *what's the point when my nursing career was over?* After one year off work my back felt healed but my doctor still advised me to stick to light work. My case was fought, I won and was compensated.

CHAPTER 25

GOOD NEWS

Still in the year of 1979, we received a letter from the council it stated: You now have the right to buy your home. The following year we took up the offer and discovered that we were better off buying than when we paid rent. I looked forward to receiving my compensation from the hospital with the hope of doing some renovations on our home and also having a holiday. I did not receive the compensation until about a year later. Meanwhile, I began thinking about a new kitchen, after ten years it needed a facelift, but my vision was not achieved until 1984.

GRANDCHILDREN

In the year of 1982 my first grandchild, Gaylene was born to Andy and his partner Gloria. I would have loved to have been there for them, but I was not yet strong enough to travel alone following my accident at work. One month after Gaylene's birth another fish was frying - Patsy was expecting. I decided to put all my plans on hold until the birth of Patsy's baby. August bank holiday, while West London was alive with the sound of Caribbean music and splendid displays of carnival costumes, I sat at Whipps Cross Maternity hospital outside the delivery ward anxiously awaiting the birth of my second grandchild. Yes, Patsy was in labour. "It's a boy!" exclaimed his dad, I went in and joined them. "Oh Praise God, you've done it my girl, well done! He's so lovely," I said. I picked him up, lifted him above my head and thanked God the giver of life for His blessings to us.

I lowered him and then, thanked God for Patsy's safe delivery and for the midwife's skill, they both joined me in prayer. "What will you name him?" I asked Patsy, "Lee," she replied, his dad seemed pleased with the name. After a week Patsy and Lee returned home from the hospital, and because I was out of work, I visited them regularly. Lee was baptised a few months later, on Patsy's birthday. Everyone was doing well. Glenda learned to drive and shared my car for her work. Dudley was happy in his job and with his football. Tracy got herself a part time job and Vilna was settled in Sarah Bonell Secondary School. I said to myself, time to visit the family back in St Vincent and when I get back, I am going to get that new kitchen.

ST VINCENT

I landed safely in St Vincent after spending a night in transit at the airport in Barbados. It was good to be back on my beautiful homeland.

My dear nephew, Prince, stood at ET Joshua Airport awaiting my arrival. As our eyes met, we greeted each other with lovely smiles and waves. He took my case from the attendant who was helping me and tucked it in the boot of his car then opened the door for me, I sat beside him. We chatted all the way to Lowmans Hill. As Prince turned the corner where Mammatee's house came into view, I spotted her and said to Prince, "Look there's Mammatee sitting in her favourite spot on her veranda waiting for me." As quickly as I was out of the car I shouted, "Hi Mammatee, you look good!" It was wonderful to see Mammatee's pretty broad smile.

"Welcome back, you look like a star girl!" Mammatee said.

We hugged and kissed to our hearts content. Prince greeted Mammatee then he took my case to the bedroom. He stayed with us for about one hour and we updated each other on the latest happenings. Meanwhile, Mammatee poured us refreshing coconut water that she had prepared and kept refrigerated, it was delicious. Then she brought me a nice juicy mango, gosh, it was so good to be home.

The air was cool, I must have dozed off in the recliner when I heard voices. I opened my eyes and before me stood my nephew Follu, who I cared for when he was a baby, looking rather dashing. "There you are Follu! Boy you are more charming than when I last saw you," I said.

"Aunty I could say the same for you, you have taken off a few years," Follu returned the compliment. We laughed, hugged and kissed. Next came my other nephew, Gerrard.

"Hi my darling you've grown so tall," I said.

Gerrard laughed deeply from his belly, "He he he heee." His eyes were full of love as we hugged and kissed.

Andy was the last to come in from work. He came on his big black and yellow motorcycle. He spoke while parking up and did not wait for me to speak first. "Hi mummy, you reach!"

"Yes babe, quite a while now," I replied.

"How was your trip?"

"Really good, no problems."

"But Mummy, you look like a young girl!"

"Really?"

"Yes, you do!"

"Well, I remember when I came before you said, when I come back you want to see me looking the part."

"Good on you Mummy! You've done it!" We hugged kissed and stared at each other with smiles. Smiles were our fixed features each time we gazed on each other.

The following day Andy's lovely partner Gloria visited with their beautiful two-year-old daughter, my granddaughter, Gaylene. I welcomed Gloria with open arms, then I opened my hands to receive Gaylene, she came to me as if she knew me. As I held her, I felt lost in love and joy. I took her to my bedroom and tried on her dresses I had bought for her. Each dress I put on her I took her into the sitting room for her parents and Mammatee to see. They commented that the dresses fitted her perfectly. I was very pleased at how nicely they fitted. Gaylene was happy, however, Gloria changed her back into what she was wearing and packed the new dresses away, saying, they would be her going out dresses. It was impossible to miss the love and care this little family shared and their happiness granted me peace. My first born was looking up.

Andy took me many places on his motorcycle, I made sure I held him tightly. My first ride was to the police barracks in Kingstown where Andy was a constable. After Andy parked his bike, we walked up the steps to the tiny reception. Andy was ahead of me. An officer at the door looked down at us and asked, "Constable who is that lady? Is she your new girlfriend?" Andy smiled but said nothing until we were both at the door, then he said, "Meet my mum." The officer dropped his head to one side and lifted his eyes in disbelief, "You joking man!" he said. Andy made no reply but led me inside and proudly introduced me to the officer who was sitting at the desk. "Superintendent, please meet my mum."

"Your mum, incredible!" replied the superintendent, then we greeted.

"You have a brilliant son, he's going places," he said.

"Yes, I know," I said, looking at Andy.

From there Andy took me to Layou where we met with some of his family and friends. One lady said, "Andy, your mum looks as young as you." Andy just kept smiling. We stopped at the home of a relative, there we changed into swimwear and went for a quick dip in the sea. Gosh, Andy swam like a fish; at one point I did not see him, he dived for what seemed like ages and scared me. When he swam back to where I was, I scolded, "Don't do that again!"

"Mummy, you worry too much. I learnt to swim when I was training for the police force in Barbados." Andy reassured me with smiles.

After about half an hour in the sea we returned to the house and changed out of our swimming costumes. Andy's cousin treated us to light refreshment. More compliments were paid to me about my youthful look, I believe Andy had heard enough, "Come on mummy time to go, he got on his bike, I seated myself at the back and firmly held around his waist. When we got back to Lowmans he stopped and knocked on my godmother's door. When she opened, "Hi Andy, you got a new girlfriend?"

"Hello Nennen, it's me Sheva," I interrupted, not allowing Andy time to reply.

"Oh my goodness, I'm sorry Andy, your mom looks as young as you!"

Oh dear, poor Andy must be tired of hearing this, but he glanced at me and smiled just as always.

When Andy could not take me around, my nephews Prince and Terence stepped in, so I was very much on the move. On my second week I stayed two days each with close relatives. My first visit was to Fitz's sister Lorraine, their dad had passed in 1977, the year after Fitz and I had visited. Lorraine and I got on really well. Next, I went to Prince and his family; it was good to be with my great-niece and nephews. Then on to Winnie and her children and lastly to Terence. While at Terence, I opened the fridge and my eyes beheld the loveliest mango, the aroma was a knockout, I took it out, turned it around, held it up, took a sniff then replaced it. Later I took it out again, another sniff and returned it again to the fridge. Terence was at work. When he got home, I said, "That mango is temptation."

"It's yours have it," he replied. I still left it, as by then I had had enough to eat.

The next morning after Terence left, I took the mango from the fridge, ate and enjoyed. About an hour after I became quite ill, I thought I was dying. I reached for the phone and called Prince. I was surprised at how quickly he came. "Shall I take you to the hospital?" he asked.

"No, no, I think I would be fine soon," I replied. But I got worse, so Prince called Mammatee, she agreed that I would be better after a day or so.

A call came from my sister Manda in Grenada, "Sheva, why don't you come over and visit me?"

"I would have loved to, but I can't I am not well," I said. Mammatee stepped in saying, "You ought to go, she lives close to the sea, the air and the water will do you a world of good."

"OK Mammatee I will."

Prince's wife, Della, decided to accompany me.

GRENADA

The flight was scary, as the plane was very tiny like a helicopter. It seated only four people, the pilot, his attendant and two passengers. Della and I sat in the centre, with our suitcases behind us. When it took off, all we heard was "chuck chuck chuck" We hovered like we were on a big bird in the sky. Below us was the deep blue sea. Della held on to me for dear life, and hid her face in my shoulder, while repeating the words, "Oh no, oh no, oh no, aunty, aunty, I'm going to be sick!"

"No you will be fine." I tried to comfort her but hid my own fear for her sake. We landed safely in Grenada and had a good laugh at our experience. Manda's friend, Carlos, who I remembered well from when he lived in London, picked us up from the airport. We had a splendid reunion with Manda and her lovely family.

Della did not stay with Manda, she stayed with a friend of hers and returned to St Vincent after a few days. Carlos also drove me, together with Manda, around the beautiful island of spice. The sea was just across the road from Manda's house, much closer than I imagined when Mammatee described it. The water was just how I liked it, warm and shallow. Each day one of my nieces, accompanied me to the sea, and after two days on the island, I was well again. I attended Manda's church a couple of times. It was a treat to be with such an exceptionally warm and welcoming church family. All too soon my time was up, and Carlos drove me back to the airport, Manda came to see me off. I hated goodbyes, I found it easier to say *I'll be back soon, take care now*. We hugged, kissed, then waved until we lost sight of each other.

Within one hour I was back in St Vincent. Lovely families are a treasure. Prince was already at the airport waiting for me. A fifteen-minute drive and I was back with Mammatee and the boys. The sad thing was that Andy was no longer among them. He had grasped the sudden opportunity for better prospects on one of the British Virgin Islands and went almost immediately. I was pleased for him, but it took a while for me to come to terms with not knowing when I would see him again.

As I reached out to greet Mammatee she said, "You are looking much better, I knew the daily sea bath would have helped you." I agreed with her and had even forgotten that I was unwell when I went.

I began to focus on my return to London. Two days later, I went to explore Kingstown and to check out souvenirs for gifts. I passed to see Mammatee at her stall in the market where she sold her herbs and vegetables. She was very happy to see me. One by one she called to the traders around her, and told them, "This is my daughter, the second to last girl. She lives in London." As I greeted Mammatee's colleagues, a young lady came by and hugged Mammatee and instantly Mammatee was in tears.

"What's wrong Mammatee?"

"This is Vivian, Winnie's eldest daughter, I have not seen her for a very long time. I worry about her," Mammatee replied.

"Hello Vivian, nice to see you," I greeted.

"Hello aunty, I heard you came," replied Vivian with a big smile.

All three of us hugged, then Vivian quickly ran off and left us wondering, but within ten minutes she was back with a nice new white handkerchief, with it she wiped Mammatee's face then stuck it in Mammatee's pocket. Seeing the love, I too was in tears, however Vivian did not hang around, she was off again, where to? Only God knew. Mammatee explained to me that whenever Vivian passed to see her, she left giving the impression that she would be back soon but sometimes it was months before she showed up again. I was ready to go when Mammatee said, “No, not yet there is someone I want you to meet.”

“Oh, ok, who is that Mammatee?”

“Wait and you will see,” was her reply.

Within seconds a very pregnant young lady stood before me. She had a beautiful smile that displayed lovely white teeth.

“Meet Flora, Andy’s intended, she’s soon to have his baby,” Mammatee introduced.

I stood speechless for about sixty seconds before I greeted the lovely Flora. I could not prevent my thoughts - *so that’s how Andy got his reputation about the girls, he actually has more than one, no wonder some people thought that I was another*. I did not have much time to chat with Flora and it was not possible for us to meet again before my flight.

I still had a few friends and relatives left to visit, not as many as on my first visit in 1976 because, some had passed, also some had left the island. As I walked through the village, every young person I met, I figured out who their parents were just by looking at them. They were surprised when I looked at them squarely and asked, *are you the son/daughter of Mrs So and So? Yes, but I don’t know you*, was the usual reply, however, they soon connected after I made myself known to them. Those who were my relatives wanted to know more.

On the 2nd of June it was time for me to leave. I reminded myself, no sad farewells, by the grace of God I will be back. Those were my words to everyone that I hugged and kissed, to others I waved. Prince drove me back to the airport. My flights were smooth with no setbacks, and after nine hours I was safely back in London. Dingy picked me up from the airport. I felt very fortunate, and still do, to have lots of loving caring family members in different countries.

The holiday was great but home with Fitz and the children brought renewed fondness so that everything and everyone was seen in a new beautiful light. As I was unemployed at that time, I regularly visited Patsy and Lee, however, I began to think about finding light work. Apart from Vilna, our other children who still lived at home were all working and made small contributions towards the cost of housekeeping, but I had always loved to have an income of my own. I joined my niece Pearl in early morning office cleaning but after just two mornings my back said, *oh no, this work is not for you!*

June 17th, two weeks after my return from holiday, Mammatee called with exciting news. "You have a new grandson, Flora's baby was born today, and she has named him, Ian."

"Oh, Mammatee, thank you, that's so lovely, how are they?"

"They are both fine," replied Mammatee.

"Well look at that, if I had had another three weeks on the island, I would have been there for them, but God always knows best."

"Yes, indeed,"

"Well, bye for now we'll speak soon, give my love to Flora and take care of yourself Mammatee. Love you!"

CHAPTER 26

EMPLOYMENT

I browsed through the Newham Recorder in the hope of finding some suitable work. I spotted an advert - Sales Representative wanted to work in the East End. I looked at it several times before dialling the number. When I did, a soft voice answered, "Hello, I am Jane, supervisor for Valdo. Are you calling about the vacancy?"

"Yes, please." I replied.

Jane asked a few straightforward questions then arranged to meet with me two days later at my home. Jane was punctual, after a one-hour interview, she said, "You are just the person for the job. We shall be sending you for training. You will stay two nights in a hotel in Loughton, all expenses paid. Until then, I will work with you for half an hour, one day each week."

"That's sounds lovely!" I replied excitedly.

Jane and I met every Thursday in the appointed store in Stratford, where she taught me what I needed to know about selling and displaying the company's products. On the day of my training, I took the train to Loughton and was picked up by a company car. The hotel was fabulous, more like being away on a short break. I was the only black person on the course. We all had to do a presentation. I did well and was commended as being gifted for the job. We were all given a tabard embroidered with the name of the company that had to be worn at all times when on duty.

After four months I was still only working half an hour each week. Jane kept promising that the hours would increase, well it did but it meant that I had to work another half an hour on a second day. Meanwhile, other companies were offering me jobs. After some thought I decided to work for another company called, Toss, on the same two days that I worked for Valdo. Toss also expected me to wear their tabard when working for them. I thought, *Ok I can handle this*; I wore Valdo's tabard and did their job first then changed to Toss's tabard and did their job. Jane no longer came to the store, so I had nothing to worry about. One morning, however, I sensed a presence and recognised the perfume. I looked up and there beside me stood Jane with a cross look on her face. "You are betraying our company."

"But Valdo don't sell these products."

"No, but we are expanding and hoping to take over that company." I was not going to argue nor give up Toss, as the hours I worked for Toss were much more than for Valdo, and they paid more an hour. I was pleased to be working at both jobs, especially as my back was holding up well. It seemed that merchandising was just right for me, and perhaps it was because I started with so little work and expanded slowly that my back strengthened. I was grateful to Valdo for the half an hour a week start, and I believed it was also God's way of protecting me from further injury. Jane soon accepted my situation, and I later went on to work for a third company called Nevil on the days that I did not work for the other two companies.

My commute expanded to cover stores in and around East London. I left home at 6 a.m. and returned about 9 p.m. I managed to catch up with housework, family and church on my short days and at weekends. Hotel meetings for all three companies were a must, nevertheless, I managed to fit them all in.

Fitz disliked me leaving home in the early hours of the mornings and returning late in the evenings, but he understood that I was solely in charge of the jobs I did. It was my duty to stay until my work was done to perfection and to leave a good impression, besides, I loved my work. My managers were all pleased with my achievement. The hours with Valdo and Toss gradually decreased until they ended, while my days and hours with Nevil increased. Nevil was divided into regions; my region always received the highest sales, for which we were awarded remarkable gifts such as a coffee percolator and electric lighting.

I was driving home one afternoon. When I got to just past the Bow flyover there was an awful bang on the back of my car. I quickly pulled my handbrake up, my head went whop, whop, backwards and forwards. *What is this!* I looked to my right there was a red mini crashed on to the sidewalk, I looked again and saw two policemen, one walked over to me and asked, "Are you alright?"

"No, my neck hurts," I complained.

"That's probably whiplash."

"Do you know what happened?" I asked him.

"Yes," he answered, "that red mini ran into the third car behind you, and you received the full force from them. Luckily, you were sharp on your hand brake, it saved you from going into the car in front of you."

The policeman took information from everyone that was involved. He then advised me to pull over to the side, leave the car and make my way home. He also advised me to see my doctor as soon as possible, which I did.

My doctor confirmed whiplash. I was summoned to court by the police as a witness to the accident. The case was won, and I was compensated for my injury and for the damage done to my car. I repaired my car and sold it, with the intention of buying another, but lost confidence in driving. A few years later I took two driving lessons, a gift from Vilna to encourage me back on the road. The instructor said, "You are a competent driver, go and buy your car and get behind the wheel." I never did. I made good use of the trains and buses as they were just a five-minute walk from my home, and I decided to have more holidays instead with what I saved from not having a car. So, I travelled from store to store and to everywhere else on the buses.

PREMONITION

On April 16th, 1985, I decided to have an early night to be up in time to face the long day ahead. I was meant to start at 6 a.m. at the store in Beckton.

I woke at 3 a.m. wet with perspiration and had to change my night dress. I went back to sleep but as soon as I dozed off, I felt the presence of someone lying beside me. "Is that you Fitz?" I called, but I realised it could not have been him, he was on night duty. I glanced at the clock it was 3:45 a.m. I dosed off again, and I heard a sweet and tender voice, laughing, *hahaha the clock is playing tricks on you, I bet when you get to the bus stop, you'll miss your bus, and you will be late for your six o'clock start*. To my surprise it happened just as the voice had said. I became scared and told my premonition to a couple of people as I waited at the bus stop and also to the person that I sat next to on the bus. I just had to share the unusual story. When I got to work, I apologised to the Store manager for my lateness; he was ok with it as I was usually on time. I then told him about my premonition, others who were near heard my story and chorused, "That's SOOO spooky." When I got home that evening, Fitz asked, "Sheva have you heard the news?"

"No, what news?"

"My sister, Lorraine, died six o'clock this morning."

My body ran cold as the reflection of my premonition unfolded. I recalled the voice I heard and remembered that it was the sound of Lorraine's voice.

Lorraine and I were very close, in her last letter to me she wrote,

> "I am not feeling too well, however, I am going to have an operation in April, and after that I will be fine."

I believe that Lorraine's operation was on April 4th. She passed on April 17th. Fitz and I hugged, and I was in tears, Fitz was not one for shedding tears. Our children shared our grief although they had never met their aunt as she lived in St Vincent.

The following year Fitz took a trip to St Vincent. He spent the time between his relatives and mine, they all took good care of him and drove him around the island. We had hoped that he might have seen a property for sale, ideal for us to purchase with the possibility of us returning to settle. He tried his best, but it was not to be.

In the same year, 1986, Reverend Daley, his wife and their two sons, born to them whilst serving at St John's Church, went to the Caribbean on a sabbatical. They spent some time in St Vincent with Prince and his family. They got on well together, they also visited Mammatee and was fascinated with her lovely little house, and the colourful skylight window. I believe Daley also gave a sermon in the Cathedral in Kingstown.

ANNIVERSARY PLANS

March 24th, 1986, after 24 years of marriage I said to Fitz, "Next year let's celebrate and dance, give thanks and praise to God for our many years together."

"Yes, why not? Go ahead organise it, you are good at that," he agreed.

I began to set the wheel in motion. Daley was pleased to assist me. I reserved the church hall, sent out invites and booked a musician well in advance. Selda happily agreed to take charge of catering. Cakes and floral arrangements I left in the capable hands of Claire, my sister-in-law, she and Sonday were excited at the idea. I paid in full for a one-week package holiday to Costa Brava. In my wardrobe hung a stunning black and silver dress, a Christmas gift from Glenda not yet worn, ideal outfit for the occasion.

SALES JOB ENDING

Just when everything was going well financially, my sales representative manager called. "Hi Sheva, how are you?"

"I am fine, and yourself?"

"I am OK but it's the others." He went on to say, "I do not have good news for you, by the end of November our jobs will cease to exist. Stores are cutting out the middleman. They will no longer require representatives and merchandisers. You will receive a letter with the date that your contract will be terminated."

"That's a bit of a blow, just before Christmas." I replied.

"We knew it was coming, I think we are the last region to go. I am thinking of getting our team together for coffee, will you be up for it?"

"Yes, of course."

"Great, I'll give you a bell when I've arranged a date."

"Looking forward to it, ok bye for now.

"See you soon," and with that the conversation ended.

I received my letter showing the date of termination and in the letter was a cheque; a bonus for my excellent performance over the years, plus, gifts were left at my door. Unfortunately, the team meeting for coffee did not take place as the other the ladies were not keen on the idea because we lived miles away from each other.

CHAT AT THE BUS STOP

On the evening after my last day at work, I stood at the bus stop waiting for my bus. While I was there a lady came by, she wanted to know how to get to Stratford.

"That's where I'm going, just take the bus that I take, and I will tell you where to get off."

"Thank you, that's kind of you, she replied.

When the bus came, she sat beside me, and we got chatting.

"My car is being serviced, I came here to have a look around the store, and I spotted you there working." she revealed.

"Yes, this is my last day, my job has come to an end."

"Oh why is that?"

I explained, and we carried on conversing about different things. Just before we got to her bus stop, she handed me a card and said that Milsborn supermarket would be interviewing for staff at the job centre in Stratford, and that I could apply. I thanked her and we said goodbye.

THE INTERVIEWER AT THE JOB CENTRE

On the card was the date for interviewing and a number to call to make the appointment. The stores that I had worked in had offered me employment, "Come, work for us, we want you!"; "There's a job here for you!" but I was undecided, thinking it would be better for me to work nearer to home, like I did when I first started, especially as I had no car. With this thought I made the appointment at the job centre in Stratford and turned up for the interview. I could not believe my eyes, coming from behind the curtain, that was there for privacy during the interview, was the very lady on the bus, who handed me the card, we had not even exchanged names. She was smiling, we both ended up laughing quietly. She invited me behind the curtain to her interview space. We got chatting again. "You've tricked me, you didn't tell me you were the one doing the interview."

She smiled and informally presented herself, "I am Syble. I do interviews in London and further afield for Milsborn Supermarket."

"So, what do you need to know about me?"

"Nothing. I have already interviewed you; the job is yours if you want it, just complete and sign this form."

"I would first like to let you know that I have a holiday booked for April, it's my silver wedding anniversary. Will that be ok?"

"Yes, that should be fine. When you start, tell the manager." I took the form from her, filled in my name and address, signed it and handed it back to her.

"When would you like to start?" she asked.

"Well seeing it's Christmas, can I start in the New Year, 6th of January?"

"That would be fine." she replied. We hugged, said goodbye and she wished me well.

WORK BEGINS AT MILSBORN SUPERMARKET

How swiftly the weeks went by. I turned up to work and was taken to the manager, Mr Browne.

"Good morning, Sheva," said Mr Browne, in a very pleasant and welcoming voice.

"Good morning," I replied.

"I have heard a lot of excellent things about you, I have also heard that you have a forthcoming holiday."

With my eyebrows raised and my head slightly tilted, "Oh, have you?"

"Well, Sheva, I have just the job in mind for you, but everyone must first learn the checkouts, so you will be on the checkouts for two weeks."

When the two weeks were up Mr Browne took me to the dairy section to work under the provisions manager, supervising the cabinet. I loved the job. I have always enjoyed whatever God blessed me to do.

ANNIVERSARY HOLIDAY IN VIEW

I kept thinking about my holiday. I wanted to be certain that cover would be provided during my absence from work. I realised that Mr Browne was told about it from Syble, but I was not sure that the office staff had been notified. I spoke with personnel and to my surprise she and the supervisors knew, and arrangements were already in place for when I was away. I smiled at God's goodness.

PREPARATION

March 24th, 1987, the day of our 25th wedding anniversary dawned with a beautiful sky. My family and I were in full excitement. Sonday and Claire came to me quite early in the morning and off we went to decorate the church hall in readiness for the celebration. Sonday was not at all well. For twelve years, he was in and out of hospital suffering from leukaemia, but this day he had a jubilant spring in his step. God had given him strength to be there for me. Sonday and Claire made sure that the hall was decorated to perfection. When everything was done to their satisfaction and we were about to exit, Sonday took one last look then he went back to the table, straightened the white lace tablecloth and adjusted the silver ribbon that decorated the cloth. We then went home, got dressed and returned.

CELEBRATION

Our guests were asked to arrive at 4 p.m. which they did. Fitz and I made our entrance at 4:30 p.m. Reverend Daley opened the event with prayer and blessings, speeches of congratulations from our guests followed. We were presented with many gifts to mark the joyous occasion. I later bought a display cabinet for the silvers and crystals. We also received monetary gifts from Sonday and Tony.

The party was going brilliantly as planned until a minor debate between two of our guests went a step too far and got out of hand. At that point, we ended the party at the church hall and decided on continuing at home with just a few guests. Sadly, after a couple of hours that was also ended because of another dispute. Thank God, it was just twelve days to our holiday, we looked forward to that.

HOLIDAY

We arrived safely in Costa Brava, Spain. "Lovely hotel!" said Fitz.

"Yes, and just a short walk from the beach," I added.

Although I knew that Fitz never liked the sea or the hot sun, I hoped he would have been tempted to join me, but that was not to be. A family of four, with whom we shared a dining table, invited me to join them on the beach; this was good for me, and Fitz happily rested in bed.

We had buffet breakfast, lunch and set dinner. When we were taken out during the day, we were given packed lunches or taken somewhere to eat. One night we were told to dress up because we were going somewhere special. The coach arrived and we were taken to Barcelona to a stage show with dinner and dance. After dinner we thought that was it but then dancers came on stage in beautiful costumes, and halfway through the show all the ladies appeared topless, Fitz's eyes beamed, onlookers screamed in excitement. I was dumfounded. At the end of the show, the host asked the audience what part of the performance you would like to be repeated. Fitz shouted, "The topless girls! Bring back the topless girls!" I could not take my eyes off him; I had a wide smile that almost twisted my face. We got up ready to leave. We had to cross the hall to get to the exit door. On entering the hall the music blasted from a band. "Hold on to your partners!" said a musician. *A dance? Another surprise*! Well, I stood speechless as this huge German woman grabbed my husband and started wheeling him around the floor. I could not believe my eyes, and Fitz did nothing to resist. A chair was nearby, so I sat and watched. *Keep calm! Just keep calm*! I repeated mentally. If it was me with a man, Fitz would have done his nut. The band played three straight sets and then stopped abruptly. "Time to get on the coach," came a shout. The German woman looked at me with a smile and bowed as if to say, thank you! or foolish you! I lowered my head to the left and widened my eyes with a fixed stare into hers, no words between us, within seconds she was lost in the crowd.

"Fitz, what was that all about? You danced all three dances with that woman and left me sitting there."

"Didn't you see how she grabbed me and held me tight. Was I to fight and make a scene?"

"If it was the other way round, what would you have done?"

Fitz made no reply, but his eyes warned be quiet and the subject was closed. Another afternoon we were taken to watch bull fighting, a very scary game. I sat shaking, all I could say was, "Those men fighting with bulls are extremely brave." Our holiday ended with a medieval night out. That was a night of real fun, lots of laughter as we made grab for the roasted baby chickens that were quickly being passed above our heads. It was a lovely holiday, our first in Europe but I had mixed feelings about future holidays with the two of us. I began to envisage the possibility of occasional group holidays.

CHAPTER 27

SADNESS AND JOYS

Two weeks after our return, my first cousin's fiancée, Cathy, died suddenly in bed from a massive heart attack. While we were in the car going to Cathy's funeral, Tony, my half-brother spoke of the sadness he was feeling for Sonday who was undergoing much pain and long-suffering. He predicted that Sonday would be the next to pass.

"Don't you feel sorry for him?" he asked.

"Off course! We all do", I replied, as I fought back tears.

Two weeks later, as fate would have it, Tony also died from a massive heart attack in the lift in his flat. Ironically, Sonday was the one who buried him.

BROTHERS' DEATHS

God never tells us who will be next or when. It makes sense to be always ready to meet with Him. Sonday passed six weeks after Tony. Although we knew that he had little time left and we were prepared, his death was still hard to take in. He was the father figure to the entire family, especially to us living in the UK. I thought of the days when, unexpectedly, he would pull up in his Ford Cortina at my gate, knock on the door and run back into the street to do a dance, just to make us laugh, even when he was sick. Cathy and my brothers were given lovely send offs. The three are buried rows apart at City of London cemetery Manor Park.

Siblings flew in from abroad for Sonday's funeral.

COMPASSIONATE LEAVE

I was given two weeks compassionate leave from work. I cried for the whole two weeks, after which I had no tears left. Moorfields eye hospital prescribed teardrops which relieved my dry eyes. With the monetary anniversary gift from Sonday and Tony, I purchased a painting to their memory. Everyone was kind to me on my return to work. When times are rough God's grace covers.

CRUISE BREAK

The next month, through my firm's holiday club, I went on a weekend cruise break to Denmark, with Patsy, Tracy, Vilna and Lee, Patsy's son; Lee was just four. That was the first time I tasted caviar; it was so delicious, I kept going back to the buffet for more. The ship docked in Copenhagen, and we went off for a stroll, but gosh, it was very snowy, windy and cold. We were delighted to return to the warmth of the ship. The night before we set sail for home there was a party. Patsy stayed most of that night in her cabin with Lee, and people jokingly called the three of us who were left, The Three Degrees, because we sang and danced in harmony.

STACY'S BIRTH

December 1st, 1987, Glenda, my second daughter, gave birth to a beautiful baby girl, Stacy, her first child and my fourth grandchild. I was blessed to be present at her birth, to be the first to hold her and lift her high in thanks and praise to God as I did with Lee her cousin, four years before. Stacy had a look of wisdom in her eyes not at all like a new-born baby. When my sister Selda saw her, she also commented on how wise Stacy looked for a new baby. We were both puzzled especially as it was only six months from the passing of the three, but we harboured no thoughts of reincarnation. Stacy was christened about one month later, followed by a lovely little family party.

REVEREND RICK'S LEAVING

Church life continued to be joyful and strengthening, spiritually and socially, but it was always sad whenever someone had to move on, especially when that someone was loving and caring. It was Reverend Rick's time to move on to another parish. The four years, 1983-1987, seemed like no time at all. He and his wife, Bibby, became our good friends. One month before he was due to leave, he organised a coach trip to go to the seaside two months after his departure. With a big grin on his face he said, "Here you are Sheva, take over!" We were both in fits of laughter as he knew he wouldn't be attending and I had never organised a coach trip before, but it went well on the day and paved the way for many more. Rick and Bibby moved to a nearby parish, so we continued to meet, we are still very good friends and meet for a meal and a chat at least once a year.

HOLIDAY TO YUGOSLAVIA

July 1989, myself, Fitz, sister Karen, her husband Larry and sister Selda set off on holiday to Yugoslavia, as it was called then. It was great that they accepted my invite. I had no intentions of sitting alone on the beach or watching and waiting while some woman danced with my husband. I can't even remember if there were occasions for us to dance in the hotel where we stayed in Yugoslavia, but during our two weeks' stay, we certainly visited many places. We travelled by coach to Slovenia, Croatia and to Lake Bled, the most stunning lake in Europe. After a short boat ride across the lake we stepped off and onto the path where a little walk led us to remarkable sights. Just in case you are wondering, did we go into the lake? Well of course not! but some others did. However, before leaving Croatia we did spend quality time in the lovely Adriatic Sea. We had such a fantastic time that from then holidays became priority.

REVEREND DALEY'S MOVE

That same year of 1989 Reverend Daley announced his moving to another parish. The news was a big blow to all but especially to myself and Cynthia as we were the church wardens. Not only would we miss him and his family, but we were about to enter into interregnum which meant we would be left in charge. When his moving date was confirmed, I hired a coach to take church members and other associates to his induction service at his new parish. I did not know I would have to give a speech, I was momentarily called upon. I believe God spoke through me and gave me the words to speak. Everyone was moved to tears, many hugged and congratulated me afterwards. On the way home we sang the 23rd psalm - The Lord's My Shepherd and the song - God Will Take Care Of You. There was not a dry eye on the coach, but we soon cheered up knowing that our God will never leave us nor forsake us. He would make a way.

INTERREGNUM

God surely made a way. When Reverend Daley knew that he was leaving, he arranged for several priests to take the services covering one year. Only on one Sunday Cynthia and myself had to take the service. That was a year of many changes; we even had a new bishop. Cynthia and I visited him at his home, he was genuinely nice and offered us refreshment. While we ate, he said that he had a couple of prospective candidates in mind for interviewing and he promised to do his best for us so that we would not be too long in interregnum. We thanked him, and as we left, he took my shawl and wrapped it around my neck just as any caring father would. It was a chilly day. Cynthia and I left feeling positive about the future for St John's Church and returned home smiling.

INTERVIEWS FOR CHURCH VACANCY

One evening our bishop telephoned to say he wanted us to meet Reverend Percival, one of the prospective candidates that he had in mind for the priesthood vacancy. We had already received his letter with all the information we needed but I suppose he wanted a chat to help to build my confidence. As the church wardens, Cynthia and I would be the ones required to interview the candidates. At the end of the conversation, the bishop reassured me that I was not to worry if I was not too sure about Percival because the next person whom he had in mind might be better for St John's Church. The following week Percival called and agreed to meet with Cynthia and myself for an interview at my home. The meeting went well but neither of us was completely sure that Percival was the right person for the job. Percival said he would think about it. When we next heard from our bishop, he said that Percival decided against the position. My next letter from the bishop wrote that he believed he had just the man for us, and his wife is very much into the work of the church, so we will be having two for the price of one, but the choice was ours, we had to decide. I immediately informed Cynthia and together we shared in the excitement.

Cynthia came to me early on the day that we had arranged to meet with Reverend Paisley and his wife, Cecilia. We prayed and prepared ourselves with the questions we thought best to ask them. Lastly, we prayed for God's help in making the right decision for the church. When they arrived, we were pleasantly surprised by their youthfulness and how well connected they were. Every question we asked they answered in full agreement with each other, like Siamese twins. We both agreed with the bishop that they were perfect for the role, and we told them so. When they left, we prayed again that they would say yes to us. Praise the Lord they did! Later, on many occasions, Paisley said he did not really want to come to us, but he felt called by God. Well, that was so much the better that he adhered to God's call rather than following his own mind. God's will was done. Hallelujah!

REVEREND PAISLEY'S INDUCTION

Reverend Paisley was inducted into the parish. Many members from his previous parish attended as did others from neighbouring parishes and changes soon began. Some people left for various reasons. A few elderly members left because, the 1662 service on Sunday mornings at 7a.m. which they preferred, was removed. They were given a home communion service, which was much better for them especially in the months of winter. When all was said and done, growth rapidly increased, we experienced new beginnings. Cynthia and I were pleased and thanked God that we made the right decision on behalf of the church.

EMERGENCY FLIGHT TO ST VINCENT

December 1990 was not a holiday to St Vincent but an urgent trip. One morning sister Karen paid me a visit at work. "Please, Sheva, can you come with me to St Vincent? I've just had a call from Prince. Mammatee is in hospital, she is exceptionally low, they do not hold much hope for her."

"Oh my God! So, when do you want us to go?"

"In the morning or as soon as I can get the flights."

"But I am working. I can't just drop everything."

Karen looked so stressed. She had not seen Mammatee for a while.

"OK, let me go and speak with my manager."

I did not need to worry, because as soon as I explained the problem to my manager, his answer was, "You only have one mother. Go now and take as long as you need."

FLIGHT TO ST LUCIA

Karen managed to get us emergency flights for the next day via St Lucia. It was the best deal on offer but when we got to St Lucia we missed the last flight out to St Vincent, due to aircraft delay on leaving London Gatwick airport. We were driven from Hewanorra International Airport in Vieux Fort to a fabulous hotel by the sea for overnight stay. On our arrival at the hotel we were served an exotic dinner. The next morning, the buffet spread, was best I have ever seen. It had far more than one would expect for breakfast. The cakes were more like for a wedding, and they were delicious; we were even allowed to take a lunch pack. We were highly cared for, and the airlines paid the cost. However, throughout the time we prayed that when we got to St Vincent our Mammatee would still be alive.

ST LUCIA TO ST VINCENT

After breakfast, the taxi returned and drove us back to the airport where our flight was awaiting. Twenty minutes and we were in St Vincent. Thank God, our nephew, Prince, was there to collect us and drove us directly to the hospital. When we got there brother PJ was already with Mammatee. He had flown out from London, a few days before us and left before us.

Sadly, Mammatee recognised everyone but me. Even though I was the last to visit her and the most frequent. After sponging her and combing her lovely, long and thick hair which had little grey for someone 80 plus, Mammatee said, “Thank you.”

“You don't need to thank me, Mammatee,” I reassured her.

She looked towards Prince and said, “Thank the nice lady for me.”

I could not believe my ears and turned away in tears. Someone tried to comfort me saying, that perhaps Mammatee has a touch of dementia. Those days I knew little about the effects of dementia and to me Mammatee seemed fine mentally.

MAMMATEE’S HEALTH IMPROVED

Within a couple days of us being on the island, Mammatee's health improved, and we took her home from the hospital to Winnie's house - our youngest sister. Winnie was Mammatee's carer, and she was the only sibling still living on the island. Although this was not a holiday, because Mammatee had improved, we were happy, and this afforded us to have had some real fun. One day, we went for a ride on a speed boat and on other days we simply enjoyed the sun, sea and sand. One evening, Prince drove us to a hotel on the sea for a superb seafood meal.

KAREN AND I LEFT ST VINCENT

When Karen and I left the island Mammatee looked rather well. Winnie took good care of her until she was joined by sister Dorada from Canada, Manda from Grenada and Selda from London.

When I arrived home, the house was nicely decorated. New carpets were laid in readiness for Christmas. Fitz did his best to surprise me, and the children rallied round helping him. I was briefly held in sentiment as they all stood at the door to welcome me in my newly decorated home, I told myself that no matter where I roam it's always good to be home.

Mammatee passed peacefully on 18th January 1991, one month after Karen and I left. We did not return for her funeral; we were happy that we went while we were able to communicate with her. We know that she was given a splendid farewell. Later that year, I organised a service in loving memory of our dear Mammatee at St John's Church. It was well attended and was much appreciated by all our family and friends.

BACK TO WORK AFTER CHRISTMAS

I returned to work at the end of 1990, just after Christmas. I was warmly welcomed by all and to my surprise, Faye, a member of staff from one of the stores where I had previously worked, joined Milsborn. This was excellent and she was followed by my daughter Tracey and one of her friends, although they worked evenings and Saturdays it was nice to bump into them occasionally. One morning while I was busy tiding up the dairy cabinet, which was my department, I became aware that someone was standing beside me. When I looked to my right it was Mr Browne. "Sheva, come with me." *How can I leave the cabinet so untidy?* But I knew better than to point that out to my manager. I immediately followed him. He took me to the office and said, "You will be working here as systems clerk grade one from now on. Netty is the supervisor and Dianne is a grade three clerk, they will both train you. I smiled and thanked him.

OFF THE DAIRY CABINET

Although I loved working on dairy, I was happy to be moved because, the cold cabinet had taken its toll on my hands, and my fingers bled easily from slight scratches without me even realising. Dianne and Netty were easy to get along with. They were incredibly patient and understanding. They did not even mind when I mentioned to them that I had another holiday in view. Mr Browne left the company soon after I moved to the office, he was replaced by another nice manager, but he also moved on about eighteen months later. Our new manager, Mr Cowdry, took over and his method of managing was different from the previous two managers. Dianne and Netty moved to higher grades on other departments. My friend Faye was also moved to office work.

I was moved up to grade three systems clerk with the responsibility of training others. Everyone I worked with was pleasant and quick to learn accept Brenda. Before Brenda started training on systems, a couple of times she had expressed to me that she wanted my job. She was serious. She persuaded Mr Cowdry to put her on systems. Perhaps she thought that my job was simple, and that she would be better at it than me. She had been working in the store for a few years, and she was on a higher grade than me. Mr Cowdry told me that he wanted me to train Brenda on systems. I had trained others and I found it a pleasure. Training Brenda was difficult; she refused to be humble, therefore she found it difficult to learn. Every time she did something wrong, she defended herself in tears, and told Mr Cowdry it was my fault for not showing her properly. She even told him that I was prejudiced. He once called me to his office and scolded me as if I was in the wrong. I was no longer shown respect, and when I was off, those who worked with Brenda found her to be very abrupt; they complained to the manager that she made many errors.

My life at work had become a misery, singing songs in my heart and reading my Bible in my lunch break was my comfort. Sometimes after work on my way home, I passed in to my dear friend, living a few streets from me, to offload my woes. She was an excellent listener, I always left felling soothed. My family also comforted me. When Patsy heard of the things I was going through, she bought me a device so that I could secretly record my conversations with Brenda and Mr Cowdry, just in case I would need the report.

ST PAUL'S CATHEDRAL

Surprisingly, Linda, one of the staff from the cash office, knew about my role in the church, and told the others. They kept the knowledge quiet until one day, in the presence of all the office staff on duty, she asked me, "How do you get on with your area Dean?"

"Um, pardon?" I replied with squinted eyes and head tilted.

"My husband is a church warden, he knows you," Linda continued. "We are both invited to the bishop's inauguration at St Paul's Cathedral."

"I can't remember meeting with your husband, but I am sure we would have had attended some functions at the same time. So, see you later at the Cathedral." I concluded.

I did not see Linda or her husband at the Cathedral, it was very crowded and impossible to find anyone, besides, I was more focussed on being ready to read the lesson that was asked of me by the bishop. I felt highly honoured and a little nervous, but I gave my best and was complimented.

Next day at work in the presence of the office staff Linda said, "Sheva, you're a dark horse! You never mentioned that you were reading a lesson!"

"Well, Linda, some things are best left unsaid."

I hoped they got my meaning that it was not for me to boast about what I was asked to do. From then it somehow seemed that Mr Cowdry and the office staff looked at me in a different light. Their attitude towards me changed and the tension I was under eased.

BACK TO SVG WITH THE GIRLS

Before Mammatee became ill, Tracy and Vilna were hoping I would join them to visit her in St Vincent, and to introduce them to the family there. They also wanted to experience the island's annual carnival. Sadly, they did not get their wish to meet Mammatee. We had already booked our holiday date for July 1991, so we still went and took silk flowers for Mammatee's grave. We spent most of our time with Winnie and her children. A nine-day early morning street festival preceded the carnival, it still takes place and is called 'Nine Mornings'. I did not go to them, too early for me! The carnival commenced with stage shows. I watched the performers in their magnificent costumes and exotic dancing, and after the show they paraded the streets. We joined the crowds following behind the bands, swiftly moving from one band to another in order to try them all and to not miss the best ones. The carnival was much fun, and when it ended, we had more excitement in the days that followed.

We visited the amazing Salt Pond in Owia, in the northern part of the island, enjoyed a meal and a swim. Next, we went with Larry, Karren's husband on his brother's speed boat to the Falls of Baleen, south of the island. Larry was also visiting from the UK and had arrived a week before us. Tracy just doesn't like long holidays, so she only booked for two weeks, while Vilna and I booked for four. Our last night as a threesome was danced away at the island-famous Aquatic Club. Finally, we visited Uncle Pat who was in his ninety's, the last of dear Pappahen's siblings, he was delighted to see us. After Tracy left, Vilna and I visited more relatives and friends, and also explored some more of the island. Our final night was spent with friends at a party. That surely was, what I call, a sensational packed holiday, and that's what you get when you go away with young ones. When we got back to home, sweet home, we shared our delightful adventures with Fitz and others.

RETURN TO WORK

I entered the door at work and before I could speak, I heard, "Well hello, Sheva! You sure caught the sun."

"I surely did!"

"Welcome back!" said another.

"Thank you. It's good to be back!"

I greeted everyone I met with a broad smile. I had no time to stand and chat, that, I left to my lunch break. I needed to get on with my work. Come lunch hour, I met with Netty and Faye, we had a good old chit chat. That evening I rang Hatti, my church sister and dearest friend, to let her know that I was back, and the following week I visited her. As usual, we talked for hours.

FITZ'S 60TH BIRTHDAY

Fitz's 60th birthday was just two months away. My head was doing the organising until I shared my thoughts with our children, and whatever seemed difficult to me, they took in hand. When Fitz heard us whispering, he insisted to know what we were up to, when we told him he sent out some invites. The party was held on 21st October 1991, in our church hall. Fitz thoroughly enjoyed it and so did everyone.

CHAPTER 28

GOOD NEWS

One day my dear friend Hatti came to tell Fitz and myself about a man who she had met, called, Kaleb, and that she would like us to meet him. As Hatti explained her sweet story, her face shone with pleasure and lit ours. When Hatti came a week later with Kaleb, he seemed to have all the qualities that Hatti had told us about. A wedding was in the making. Fitz and I helped where we could. I accompanied Hatti to the stores and assisted her in choosing the outfits and accessories for her and her bridesmaid, her beautiful four-year-old daughter. The dresses were not perfect fits, so I altered them, made her daughter's headdress out of the dress cuttings and matching bouquets for them both. I was lucky to get my dress in the same store on the day we purchased theirs; it was a perfect fit.

HATTI'S NIGHT OUT

A few a days before the wedding Patsy called, “Hi mum, can we take Hatti on a hen night out?”

“Yeah, what do you have in mind?” I asked.

“We'll decide on the day mum.”

“So what would you like me to do?“

“Just invite Hatti to stay with you for the night.”

“Ok! I'll try.”

I called and asked Hatti if she would like to stay with me for one night before her wedding.

Without hesitation and full of excitement, Hatti said, “Yeah! Yippee!”

On the night that Hatti stayed, my daughters and I took her on a pub crawl between Stratford East to Stoke Newington North London. In one of the pubs the bride-to-be was serenaded by a well-known artiste. That was so much fun. How did we get home, you might wonder? I think we called a cab.

HATTI'S WEDDING

The morning of July 25th, 1992, the sun rose early. With a joyful heart I set to work on Hattie's hair, I have to say I did an excellent job. When my sister Karen saw Hatti's hair, she commented that that was the best hair style she had seen Hatti with. At the church everyone looked the part. Larry, Karen's husband, stood in as father of the bride. It was so nice to see the care he showed walking Hattie down the aisle. It was quite moving as he presented her to Kaleb during the ceremony. I was honoured to be called along with two others to sign the register. The wedding was followed by the taking of photographs, then a small reception at Kaleb’s home. Hattie was a fully qualified chef, so she did her own catering in advance. It was a lovely little wedding.

CHURCH GROWTH

Meanwhile, the ball kept rolling at St John’s Church. Social activities and Sunday school no longer took place at the church Institute because the building was sold. The proceeds were used to restore the church and to build an extension to accommodate the activities that had taken place at the institute and much more. The new look of the church became an eye catcher that brought many enquiries and visitors. We soon had a regular flow of new members. Some came for a while and left for good reasons, but the majority stayed and became long standing members. As growth increased new members were voted onto the Parish Church Council to take active roles in leadership. Cynthia and I had overrun our years as church wardens and we were voted off, but God had other plans for us which I will come back to.

MEMOIRS OF A SMALL ISLAND GIRL

TRIP TO ORLANDO

Through my work's holiday club membership I booked a trip to Orlando. This was a vacation for daughters Glenda, Tracy, Vilna, granddaughter Stacey and myself, although the main purpose was to see and to enjoy some of the attractions of Disney World. It was also to include Glenda's birthday towards the end of our stay on 28th May 1992. We were privileged that sister Dorada welcomed us to stay with her and we had planned to visit my sister, Thelma, and her family. When we arrived at Orlando airport and collected our luggage, we made our way to the information desk to enquire about our self-drive seven-seater van that I had booked with the flight. We were directed to where to go and wait for the van. The van pulled up as soon as we got to the stop. The driver stepped out and handed us the keys and a map.

"Where are you heading?" he asked.

"Palm Bay." I said.

"Ok, get in the van drive out, turn left, then right and follow the road all the way, don't stop for anything or anyone. It's a one-and-a-half-hour drive."

We thanked him and took the road.

We were still driving for almost two hours with no sign of Palm Bay. My phone rang, it was sister Dorada.

"Hello Sheva!" her voice trembled as she asked, "Where are you?"

"On the road driving to you."

"Well, you ought to have been here by now. What road are you on?"

"Can't see any signs at that moment but the last one we saw, showed Disney World ahead," I replied.

"Girl, you are going the wrong way, turn around and follow the sign to Kissimmee!"

"Ok! thanks see you soon."

We finally got to sister Dorada's house. She stood waiting outside, not giving us time to speak, she exclaimed, "Girls, you all give me such a fright. You can't mess about on those roads, they are dangerous!"

"Ok, Sis calm down we are here now, and we had fun on the road. We played music, sang and bopped away to the beats."

"Oh well, thank God you got here safely."

"And you know what, Aunty, it'll be easier now for us to find our way to Disney World and to Kissimmee beach, " one of the girls spoke.

"Anyway, you'll be going with us, so we won't get lost, " said Glenda.

"No not me, I'm too old for that! Perhaps Thelma and the girls would go with you."

Sister Dorada's home was nice and spacious, enough room for us all.

After a day's rest and chat with sister Dorada, Thelma came and accompanied us to Disney World. The rides were fantastic, and one was extra scary. Thelma and I sat together on the rides, we screamed like youngsters. Luckily for us the other rides were easier. As we walked from the rides a show was about to begin, we stood at the back waiting to watch. One actor approached me saying, "You look like you have an enquiring mind, please come and help us with the show."

"Who me?" With my hands to my chest in alarm.

"Yes, you, please come!"

"But what would I have to do?"

"Don't think about anything, just be you," he said.

"Go on mum!" the girls encouraged. "You know you love that sort of thing."

I followed him but my mind baffled. Once I got behind the scenes what I was asked to do became fun, ten minutes and the show was over. The actors were pleased with my little performance and the girls said, "You did well mum!", "Good on you!", "You are so brave!"

We had a full day of fun and went back for the second day, having bought two-day passes.

VISIT DORADA'S FRIENDS

After we had rested for a couple of days, sister Dorada invited us to meet some good friends of hers. They had a beautiful home with a lovely big swimming pool. We swam, played pool games and ate. We were treated like royalty, and the host was not in any hurry to see us go. The following day we drove to Kissimmee beach with sister Dorada, she loved it there and it was not too far from her home besides, she wanted to be sure we did not get lost. The beach was spectacular, everything was there to meet our needs but on that day the waves were unkind, nevertheless we tried to made the most of it, and we enjoyed.

GLENDA'S BIRTHDAY CELEBRATED AND FAREWELL

We celebrated Glenda's birthday in a posh restaurant, booked for us by Elmond, Thelma's husband. Stacey who was only four stayed at home with sister Dorada, they adored each other. It was good that Elmond went with us to the dinner, otherwise Tracy would not have been allowed in the restaurant and bar without a document showing her age. She never thought of taking her passport; why would she at the age of 24? Everyone thought she was under the age for drinking, she fools everyone with her girlish looks. Well, that was a laugh as Tracy was the one doing most of the driving. Because the manager knew Elmond, he allowed him to sign Tracy in. We had a delicious meal and two fantastic weeks in Florida. We left on the following day. It was a sad farewell, especially as sister Dorada lived alone but we knew we would meet again soon.

"Love you all! Go safe in the name of Jesus!" she said.

"Bye! Bye!" we waved from the van until we were no longer within her view.

We got home safely. All was well with our folks at home. Church was blooming. I had expected to find my work at the supermarket in chaos, but to my surprise, it was in very good order because a supervisor took control.

MY BIRTHDAY SURPRISE

23rd October 1992 I was given a wonderful birthday surprise. Fitz and I were driven by our son, Dudley, to a west-end theatre, to see a live play. It was so exciting, especially as it was our first time to see such a show, we thoroughly enjoyed it and when it was finished, Dudley was back to collect us. When we got home and opened the door, we heard shouts.

"Surprise! Happy birthday mum! Happy birthday Sheva!"

"Oh my God! When did you lots do all this? Thank you! Thank you!" I kept repeating.

Hugs and kisses flowed like water from a tap. My first ever birthday party at 50, celebrated with family, work friends and friends from church. Fitz knew all about the party but kept it from me, and during the dance, his face lit up as he presented me with a little sewing machine that he knew I would be happy with. I had a wonderful time, we all did. I am grateful to have such a thoughtful and caring family.

COURSE IN CHRISTIAN STUDIES

A three-year part-time course in Christians studies was being prepared at church, starting September 1993 to be held at the vicarage, Reverend Paisley's home. Myself and other church elders were invited to join. This was fantastic. With the growing congregation that the restored church building attracted, a wider knowledge of Christianity and deeper depth into spirituality was required. I believe that this was what Reverend Paisley had hoped for when he started, so to me this was none other than the hand of God on the handle. I joined the course along with Cynthia and others. The study covered the following six subjects - THE BIBLE, CHURCH HISTORY, CHRISTIAN DOCTRINE, LITURGY AND SACRAMENTS, SPIRITUALITY AND DISCIPLESHIP, and COMMUNICATING THE GOSPEL.

I loved everything about the study, and I was deeply drawn to the work of those great fathers in the book, 'History, of Christianity'. If not for the course I don't think I would have read this book, let alone study it. I chose to write on Irenaeus as one of my presentations because his work touched my soul. I also loved reading the book, 'Holy Listening: The Art of Spiritual Direction' by Margaret Guenther, it helped me to examine my life and brought conviction, in that the baptism of Jesus caused me to question my obedience to the word of God.

ST JOHN'S AND PASTOR TOM

Before starting the course in Christian studies, I had an urge to know more about other Christian denominations, and in my quest for learning, I spent some time with a Pentecostal group led by a pastor, named Tom. I liked their down to earth teaching and their method of adult baptism. They worshipped at St John's Church from the time that Reverend Daley was in office. Their service started when ours ended, so it was easy for me to join them. One Sunday as Pastor Tom shook my hand, his words were, "My God! sister Williams, I can feel the power of God in you." Then looking towards the altar, he said, "You will stand behind that alter, and you will be on fire for the Lord, but right now something or someone is blocking you." I shrugged at the thought, not knowing how Pastor Tom's prophecy would come about.

When our church was being restored, Pastor Tom's Pentecostal fellowship moved to our sister church, but he went to another church. I later learned that he had returned to Jamaica, his homeland. Even though I seldom saw anyone from that ministry, I often thought about them and hoped that one day, I would meet Pastor Tom again in the hope that he would baptise me in a pool without expecting me to become a member of his fellowship.

MY DESIRE FOR WATER BAPTISM

My desire to be water baptised and to openly testify God's love, grew stronger daily. I was baptised as a baby. My mother and godparents answered to the statement of faith on my behalf. My confirmation was my decision, and I declared my faith then. Nevertheless, I wanted to do what Jesus did. He was thirty when baptised and began His ministry. I explained this to my bishops in conversation and in writing, they understood and sympathised and hoped that one day changes would come about. I tried hard not to offend my vicar and church members, so I said as little as possible on the subject.

I knew that water baptism was not important for many Christians. I was also certain that it would not have made me perfect or be the answer for me getting to heaven. However, it was something I wanted to do from when I lived with Dear Aunt and witnessed Cousin Dorawa being baptised in the sea. This memory of Cousin Dorawa was refreshed in 1985 when Christa, my sister and spiritual advisor, also went through the waters of baptism. I admired her deep faith and love for Jesus which she always, readily and openly, shared. She was confirmed in 1978, at St Pauls Cathedral and water baptised in 1985 in the Pentecostal Church. At the time of her baptism I felt as though she was on a higher spiritual ground than the rest of us and wanted to be there with her. Other members of my family were also being water baptised. My aunt, Mammatee's sister, was first, then Mammatee. They were both staunch Anglicans but were water baptised in the Pentecostal Church. Mammatee explained in her letter to me the reason for her water baptism; she hoped that I would understand that it was a step she was called to take. I understood and told her so in my reply. I further explained that she had to do what was right for her. In the same reply letter I shared my own desires on the subject of water baptism.

PASTOR TOM

One day, as I walked down the road from my house on the way to the shops, I spotted a figure much like Pastor Tom coming in my direction. As we got closer, I realised that it was him.

"Pastor Tom you are back! What are you doing here? Nice to see you! I want you to baptise me!" I shouted in one breath.

"Hello sister Williams, it's good to be back. I came all the way from Jamaica to baptise you. The Lord has sent me. I was given the vision and you will not be alone. There will be four of you. Don't worry I'll take care of everything. I will call you. I am rushing to see a church sister."

"OK thank you so much."

We shook hands and went our separate ways. Two weeks later Pastor Tom called.

"Hello sister Williams I have booked a nice little church not far from you for your baptism. It will be on 1st October, invite your family and friends."

"Oh, that's so nice of you, bless you pastor," I replied.

MY WATER BAPTISM

I set about breaking my good news, first to Fitz, then to my family and closest friends, inviting them all. On 1st October 1993 I turned up at the hall with my large family including sister Dorada who was holidaying with me. Two friends from the few that I had invited also came. Pastor Tom also invited a couple of his church sisters. The service began but when my baptism was about to take place, we discovered that the water in the pool was cold. We continued the service, which was nice but omitted my baptism and postponed it for the following day. 2nd October everyone and more turned up. The pastor for the church we were using was also present. With more people in attendance the service was much livelier than the previous day, and the water in the pool was nice and warm.

My baptismal experience was like being out of this world. It is the only way I can explain it. I felt as if I was being buried and then lifted into a new life with Christ. I just knew that I was free from all my sins by God's grace and mercy. I am still free and forgiven through daily repentance.

When I came up out of the water Pastor Tom made an alter call, "Here is water! Who will be baptised?"

One of my nephews, Leon, answered the call, next was our family friend, Vincent. My sister Karen went outside and discussed with others the possibility of her entering the water, but she did not go forward, primarily because she did not have a change of clothes. Pastor Tom was adamant that there were to be four candidates for baptism because he said his visions are never wrong. Karen admitted that the night after my baptism she became restless, thinking she ought to have been baptised then, which meant that Pastor Tom's vision of four people being baptised was correct. As soon as Karen heard where the next baptism was taking place, she packed her clothes in readiness and put herself forward.

MY BIBLE STUDY GROUP

After my baptism I continued to attend the little Pentecostal Church. This was quite convenient because it was directly after the service at St John's Church and walking distance. I also started a prayer and Bible study group in my home; It began with two of us and gradually increased in numbers of up to twelve members from different denominations and non-church goers. It was one of my best ideas. The group was fun, we learned from each other and grew spiritually. My spiritual growth was observed at work and Faye began asking me about Jesus.

WORK AND CHURCH

Faye and I had been working closely in the office, so it was easy for us to communicate while on our computers. Her questions about Jesus were endless and I was happy to be of help. I carried my Bible to work, intending to do my devotion during my lunch break. I had to start work at 6 a.m. Monday to Friday, so that left no room for early morning study. Faye took her lunch break with me and shared my Bible readings.

One day Faye said, “Sheva, I am ready to be with Jesus.”

“What? You ready to die?” I joked.

“Whatever it takes to be with be with Jesus.”

“Ok, I think you mean you want to have him completely in your life?”

“Yes, that’s it.”

“Then, come to church with me.”

Faye agreed and later became a member of St John’s Church. We continued to read in the canteen during our lunch break. Sometimes, we were joined by two young men, both from different Pentecostal Churches. A Muslim lad was also keen to learn about Christianity. They accompanied us to the Tuesday lunch time service at St John’s Church when it was convenient for them, as the church was only a few minutes’ walk away from our workplace. We also paid a visit each to church assembly that the two young men attended, which we very much enjoyed.

When I told Faye about Pastor Tom’s church that I also attended, she asked excitedly, “Can I come with you?”

“Yes sure, that would be great.”

From that day we spent much time together, studying, learning and having fun.

CHAPTER 29

FITZ RETIREMENT 1993

Fitz's health began to play on my mind, it had started about the time of my baptism. It appeared that because of his irregular hours of eating, due to his shift work, he developed stomach ulcers and he had to be treated under the hospital. One night he was in a lot of pain, his medication just did not help. He lay on the bed groaning with his eyes closed. He was not aware that I placed my hand on his stomach and prayed until, I guess, we both fell asleep. When I awoke in the morning, I had expected him to be in the bed, but he was gone. *How did he manage to get up and go to work after such a rough night?* When he got in that evening, my question was, "Fitz, you really got up and went to work after all that pain you were in last night?"

"Pain, what pain? when I woke, I was fine, so there was nothing to stop me from going into work."

"That's good. Did you know that I put my hand on your stomach and prayed for you?"

"I knew you put your hand on my stomach, but I had no idea that you were praying, and I probably fell asleep."

Fitz never suffered such harsh pain again. Nevertheless, at the end of that year he took early retirement, and his health was no longer a problem.

VIRGIN GORDA 1994

In 1994 I became genuinely concerned about my youngest brother Harran, who was now having minor health issues. I had not seen him in 33 years, that was before I emigrated to the UK.

I wrote to him asking if I could visit, his reply was that he thought no one remembered him. "When are you going to come? I can't wait," he wrote back. When I shared the news with my family they were delighted. I rang Harran and told him the date I had in mind, it was fine by him and his fiancée. He briefed me on the best airlines and route to Virgin Gorda where he still resides. I followed his instructions. My flight stopped in Antigua for fuel and to collect passengers, but we were not allowed to disembark. From there we flew to San Juan airport, in Puerto Rico then on a helicopter. Whoa! This was scary! Thank God we landed safely in Virgin Gorda. Harran and his family were waiting for me.

It was a treat meeting them, as we drove from the airport, he kept stopping to introduce me to the people we were passing along the road. It's such a small island they all know each other. Everywhere on the island was clean and beautiful.

When we visited his special friends, one teased him saying, "Harran you really have a sister!" This was because he often spoke of his siblings. I was the first to visit. Harran just laughed and commented, "One day you will see them all." One afternoon they took me out for a drive and when I got out of the car, they blind folded me and led to where they wanted to surprise me. When my eyes were uncovered, I could not believe the beauty that lay before me. A large pond in a cave by the sea, supplied by water from the constant waves, all I heard was the echoing of voices and the sound of the sea. The place is called the Bath, I was captivated by its magnificence and the wonderful works of God.

I so loved Virgin Gorda, when I returned home to London and told Fitz about the natural beauty and attraction of this little island, I noticed that he was caught in the spell, "Would you like us to retire there?"

"That would be great." I replied.

I wrote to Harran and asked him to keep an eye out for a house for us. He found one but when we thought things were progressing it fell through. It was not meant to be, we lost money through the failed transaction, however, it did not get us down because we believed that God's will was done.

FITZ AT HOME

Fitz was enjoying his retirement. He kept himself busy at home, cooking, decorating, gardening, reading, chatting with neighbours and collecting Lee from school. He just did all the things he loved but never had time to do before. He also joined my Bible study and prayer group and was able to attend church services regularly. When I told him that World Vision for Christ, my second church, was having a trip going to Israel and that I was thinking of going, he encouraged me. Faye was also interested in joining the trip, so we booked a shared room.

ISRAEL 1995

The church had two to three trips a year. We went in January because we were advised that it was the coolest time of the year, the best time to go. When we arrived in Israel, everything was organised for us. The coach and its driver that picked us up from the airport remained with us throughout our stay so that he became part of our travelling team. We visited most of the places where Jesus walked, and all the other famous attractions: The Mount of Olives, the Dead Sea, Bethesda, Cana, Bethlehem, the Nativity, and the river Jordan. It was like walking through the Bible because it came alive to us. Most of all was the tranquillity of the place and the feeling of holiness. The two weeks went too quickly, many people say it is a once in a lifetime trip, but it is a trip I would certainly love to do again.

THE BIRTH OF HANSON MARCH 1995

Two months after my return, gorgeous Hanson was born to Glenda, now my sixth grandchild. A brother for Stacy and little cousin for Lee. Thank God I was present at his birth. I offered him up to the Lord as I did with the two before him. Hanson was not christened but was blessed in church by our vicar and we had a lovely little family party with special prayers at my home. He was the first of my immediate family where the tradition of infant baptism was broken.

FAYE'S BAPTISM 1995

Later that year, Faye entered the waters of baptism in the very pool that I was baptised in two years before. She was later confirmed at our parish church, St John's. I felt very blessed to be her spiritual advisor. Faye and I continued to attend both churches and went on a weekend crusade to Dim Church with our little Pentecostal assembly. One night, during a prayer meeting at Dim Church, I heard an angelic voice singing; it was coming from one of the sisters. It touched my soul and brought tears to my eyes. The next day I asked why no one mentioned the singing, as it was rather unusual for something so significant to go unmentioned. To my surprise no one else heard the voice but the sister knew she was singing quietly.

"So you heard?" she asked, smiling.

"Yes, it was angelic," I replied.

When I got back, and I shared the story about the singing voice I heard that no one else did. My friend Hatti said that voice was sent by God for me; it certainly increased my faith.

MENTORING

As days and months went by, I felt the spirit of God moving strongly in and through me, I had no fear of ministering His word; my friends were catching on and being drawn to Jesus. One by one they started attending church. One night I telephoned brother PJ, we had a good long chat about the way we live and what the Bible says about how we ought to live. I sensed that he wanted to go God's way. A few days later I called him again, to find out how he was doing. He answered saying, "I have been thinking about our discussion and was hoping you would call to chat some more."

"Really?"

"Yes, I am anxious to hear more. I thought you would never have asked how I am feeling."

" I tell you what, I am sitting in the garden reading a book for a course I am doing on Christian studies why don't you pop down?"

In less than 15 minutes PJ was at my gate.

"Good heavens that was quick! How did you manage that? And why are you only wearing one sock?"

"Well, when you told me to come, I was so eager to hear the word, I could not stop to get the other sock on. Anyway never mind that, let's talk," he urged.

PJ'S DECISION

Without hesitation I read some practical Bible passages and explained them to PJ as the Holy Spirit guided me. Before I was finished PJ declared that he wanted to be baptised and confirmed, so I invited him to my Anglican Church. He attended regularly. When I heard that there was to be a baptismal service at Christa's Pentecostal Church, I spoke with her pastor, Pastor Smith, about my brother wanting to be water baptised, he was pleased to hear the good news and said, "Sister Williams, you are doing a great job! Bring him along." At the service Pastor Smith gave me the opportunity to speak of my Christian faith to the congregation. I began by singing the song, 'A Wonderful Saviour Is Jesus My Lord, A Wonderful Saviour to me.' Then I explained how God was using me to reach others. After PJ was baptised, he became a member of my prayer group; this was another tremendous blessing for me.

STACY

Stacy, my granddaughter, was now seven and she spent a lot of time with her granddad and me, I think one of her reasons was that she loved to hear stories of Jesus.

Her love for the stories of Jesus reminded me of myself at that age. When her mum was not able to go to church she would ask her mum, "Please can you take me to nanny's? I want to go to church." She stayed over some Saturday nights so that she wouldn't be late. One Sunday morning while we were on the way to church, we caught up with, one of our church sisters who lived a few yards from me. As we walked Stacy said, "Nanny, I had a dream about the little church."

"Is that so? What did you dream?"

"Lots of people were there, but it was not the same. There was no service and some people were arguing, and everyone was asked to leave. I don't want to go there today, Nanny."

"OK, darling, you can return home after the service at St John's Church with aunty."

When I met with Faye and PJ at the end of our service at St John's Church, I told them about Stacy's dream and that she did not want to go to the little Pentecostal Church. They were not deterred and the three of us went as usual. We were amazed that everything happened just as in Stacy's dream, the minister of the church was accused publicly of having an affair with one of the members. Both parties declared their innocence, and the minister's wife stood by him. I guess that this was a lesson to remind us that there is persecution in the church. That was the last day we went back to that church building. The minister and some of the members attended another church and we joined them. Whenever we went, Stacy went with us, she also joined me in our parish church choir.

WEDDING IN CANADA JULY 1995

Exciting family news was in the air. It was announced that my niece, Victor's daughter, living in Montreal, Canada, was engaged with a date set for the wedding, and the entire family around the world was invited. Many of us accepted the invitation. I decided to take Stacy and Fitz agreed to join us. I set about making Stacy's outfits and shopped for mine. We flew to Toronto and spent some of our time in Mississauga with sister Dorada's daughters, but mostly with Esther and her family. Fitz was excited to meet Esther and her husband as they really enjoyed each other's company when they spent some time with us in 1977, and Stacy loved it at Esther because she had three children, one was Stacy's age.

On 10th July Esther drove us to Montreal for the wedding, we could not believe the number of bugs on the highway, the car was covered, we had difficulty seeing the road.

The bride looked fantastic as she walked arm in arm with her handsome husband, every guest smiled. It was a lovely day and a beautiful wedding. During our stay in Mississauga, our family group of about twelve visited Niagara Falls, Lake Ontario and CN Tower. Then the three of us flew on to New York and stayed a week in Queens with Fitz's brother Toni and his family. While we were there, Fitz's niece and two of his nephews, went with us on the circle line boat cruise, down the Hudson Bay to the Statue of Liberty. One day during that week cousin Franado came from the Bronx to visit us, and we went with him back to the Bronx to visit cousin Dorawa. We had a great trip, but it was tiring. I looked forward to being back at home to prepare for my graduation by the bishop at Chelmsford Cathedral.

CERTIFICATE COURSE IN CHRISTIAN STUDIES

A few days after my return my vicar drove me to the Cathedral for the service. I was pleasantly surprised to see the many friends at the service supporting myself and others, this was very uplifting and encouraging. During the service, the bishop presented us with our certificate for completing the 3-year course in Christian studies. Our certificate was not an end to studies but a gateway to further learning for Mission, Evangelism, Teaching and Preaching to build up the body of the Christ. Cynthia, my colleague went directly into further training to become a Licensed Lay Reader. I went two years later.

During those two years I began reading the Bible from the beginning, hoping to quickly get to the end. This was my first attempt to read the Bible from Genesis to Revelation. I had much difficulty getting through the book of Numbers; there were too many names that meant nothing to me, so I skipped most of it and got to Revelations in three months. The strength and encouragement that I received from the New Testament enabled me to begin again but this time, I started with prayer and succeeded, even though I still struggled with the pronunciation of names in the Book of Numbers. However my desire for learning and obeying the word steadily increased. I wrote a study course on the Book of Ruth and presented it in a seminar to the women at my Pentecostal Church. My home group was doing amazingly well. Also, my work colleagues saw me as a true follower of Christ, although Brenda criticised me for knowing too much Bible.

One day while I was preparing to send work through to head office on my computer, a voice from within said*, go to the ladies! But I don't want to go to the ladies! Go to the ladies now!* the voice repeated. *OK.* I pressed the sent button on the keyboard and went to the ladies, as I pushed the door, I heard someone crying, my ears and eyes followed the sound. There she was, a young lady sitting on a bench in the cloak room, head in her hands in agony. Yet still, I went past and into the loo, although I did not need to go. While in there I prayed, "Lord what shall I do?" *Go to her!* the voice replied. I obeyed.

I asked her gently, "What's wrong?"

Still holding her head, she answered, "My head! My head!"

"Do you believe in Jesus?"

"Um, yeah," was her faint reply.

"Would you like me to pray with you?" I asked.

"Um, um, um,"

"Does that mean yes?" I asked to be sure.

She repeated.

"Yes, um."

"Do you mind if I touch your head?"

She nodded again and said, "Touch! touch!"

Very lightly I touched her head and prayed in the name of Jesus for her healing. Within seconds she began to relax with sighs of relief, saying, "Thank you! thank you!"

"Thank Jesus." I said to her.

I had no idea a first aider went to her before I saw her and went to get another to help. When they came, she said to them, I am better now. One turned to me and asked, "What did you do?"

"I prayed for her."

They became cross and told me that if she collapses, I will be held responsible because they were going to take her to the hospital, but now it's up to me. They suggested that I should see her to her home in a taxi. However, she said she had no money, so I went back to the office and explained to the manager all that had happened. I was given money from the petty cash for her taxi fare. I saw her safely in the taxi, she was happy to go home alone. Besides, I needed to catch up on my work. In the days that followed I enquired about her, but no one seemed to know. It turned out that she was a Saturday staff providing cover on the day she took ill. One of the office managers doubted that the girl's healing was from Jesus and went on to say that it was the warmth of my hand on her head that caused her to relax and relieved her pain. I knew she was wrong but said no more.

A few weeks later I was in conversation with a student, Jeff, who worked on the shop floor and sometimes in the office. He told me that he recently got involved with a few guys he met on the street talking about Jesus and that the leader, Sam, visits him at home, but he wished he would stop, because he kept asking for money which he did not have. On the day Jeff and I spoke, he was expecting Sam to come to the store to collect money. Jeff looked so worried. I said to him that does not sound like the work of a genuine Christian, and asked, "Would you like me to have a word with him?"

"Yes please! If you don't mind!"

"I don't mind, just put a call out for me when he comes."

As I was always under pressure to get my work done, in my heart I prayed: *Lord, please let the conversation with Sam be short*. When Sam arrived, unbeknown to him, Jeff called for me. I went to where they were. "Hello," I greeted Sam.

"Hello" he replied, looking shocked at my presence.

"It's OK." I said, "Jeff told me you are a Christian. It's nice of you to be encouraging him to get to know Jesus."

"Thank you!" Sam replied. With that Jeff left.

"I believe you are here to collect money from Jeff, does he owe you?" I asked Sam. Sam was stalled for words, so I spoke again, "Surely you are not charging Jeff for helping him to know about Jesus?" Sam still did not speak but began to look away. "I am a Church elder and what you are doing is not right, you should not come on Jeff's job to confront him about money or anything else."

Sam finally spoke.

"But I am not working!"

"Then find a job!" I said. Sam quickly left.

When I got back to the office and explained to Jeff he was pleased. "Well done, Sheva!" I heard from some of the staff. That was the last time Jeff heard from Sam.

CALLED TO PRAY

One afternoon I had an urgent call to go to Mr Cowdry's office, my heart missed a beat. *Oh my God! What is it now? What have I done?* I went immediately and knocked on the door.

"You want to speak to me?" I asked nervously.

"Yes, have a seat."

How strange? I've never been offered a seat by him before, but I accepted with a thank you! Although I still kept wondering what was going on. Mr Cowdry hesitated to speak. Wearing a worried look he said, "I have asked you here because I am in a bad spot right now, can you pray for me?"

"I'll be happy to do that." I replied.

Without questioning him about his problem I went directly into prayer. I held the palm of my hand over his head without touching and prayed sincerely for God to deliver him from whatever was troubling him, and to help and guide him forward. After my prayer he wore a smile and thanked me. I told him it was no problem as praying for others was my Christian duty. I watched as he relaxed in his seat, and I returned to my work.

What took place in that office was between him, me and God. From then, Mr Cowdry paid less attention to complaints he received from Brenda about me.

MY BROACH PIN LOST AND FOUND

It was hard to believe the strange things that continued happening to me. It all began when I suffered from that nervous breakdown back in 1973. I feel positive that those angels who visited me when I was in hospital and pinned that broach on me saying it would make me better really worked. Was there some magical connection? All I can say is that from the time I was given the pin my recovery was rapid. I was also able to console others in many ways and still managed to overcome the problems I was going through.

I only wore the broach pin on special occasions. One day I decided to wear my church coat, which the broach pin was on, to work. When Nettie saw it, she remarked, "Oh, your broach sparkles! It dazzles my eyes, it's so beautiful! It will look better on me."

I told her that it was a very special gift, and I was never taking it off. Months later I realised that my broach had disappeared. I looked everywhere but it was nowhere to be seen. I was positive that it was not stolen, I was almost in tears.

One early morning, two years later, I was the first person to walk through the shopping mall, just as it was being opened by the security guard. The ground was cleanly swept, and as I approached the slope, I was dazzled by a light from the ground about ten feet ahead of me.

When I got to the spot, it was my broach pin! I picked it up with great amazement and marvelled at how such a thing could be! There was no one around for me to share this phenomenon with, I just praised God. Later I told my story to Fitz and our children, they too were astonished.

MY OPERATION

Two days later I received a letter from the hospital concerning an operation I was to have that kept being deferred. I did not hold many hopes for this new appointment, but still I went to see the consultant, Doctor Dickson. As soon as he saw me, he looked concerned, "You have been waiting for a very long time, but you won't have to wait any longer. I will do this operation myself." I smiled and thanked him in relief.

He took me through the necessary procedure and explained that the after pain would be excruciating. When he saw how scared I became he offered to pray with me, which of course I gladly accepted. I could hardly believe my luck that I would be operated on by a genuine Christian. Not wanting to cause further delay, he got me booked in for the following day. I went home nervous but smiling at this wonderful man of God.

On the day of my operation Doctor Dickson prayed with me again and offered me tablets to calm me. But he said, “Let your faith guide you as to whether you should take or leave them.” I took a couple and wished my faith was stronger to not take any. While on the operating table, Doctor Dickson held my hand and said, “Think of somewhere nice that you would like to be right now.” I thought of the clear and shallow blue waters of the Caribbean Sea in Grenada and of my sister Manda. With that thought I knew no more, until I realised that I was singing a hymn. My eyes opened and there they were, my surgeon and his nurse smiling at me. Doctor Dickson said, “I love that hymn.” The nurse echoed that she did too.

The after pain was awful, so bad that I did not want visitors, especially not my vicar. Bless him, he came out of goodwill, but I refused to let him see me. The blanket was my shield, so all that was visible was a huge, covered lump on the bed. He heard only a faint, “um, yeah,” to the questions he asked. Even when Fitz visited, I was unable to converse with him. I stayed for two days in the hospital. Although my operation was minor, my pain was severe. My nephew Dingi collected me and drove me home. Instantly I went to bed. The next day while still in bed, I was visited by three ladies dressed like nurses. White uniforms and white caps, like they wore in past years. They smiled and waved at me from the door, I returned the smile, and they were gone. I knew that they had to be angels, who else could have suddenly appeared and disappeared? Besides, I felt healed and wonderful.

The day the angels visited happened to be the Tuesday before Christmas, which was also the day for St John’s Church’s Tuesday lunchtime carol service. After they left, a strong urge came over me to get up and go. I had only one hour to get ready and to be there. Somehow, I made it just in time. As I entered the door my vicar was surprised to see me.

Nonetheless, he handed me the open Bible, pointed to the chapter, and said, "You read." I took the Bible and smiled. I had no fear that the pain would prevent me from reading. Whilst reading I felt the power of God upon me, the words came from my mouth like music.

After the service, my colleague said, "I have not heard you read like that before. It was very moving." I explained my supernatural experience to her, although I hoped she did not think I was mad as some people do when you talk about angels, but she believed, understood, and thanked God. About six months later my beautiful broach pin went missing again, I just could not understand why. I told the whole story to one of my vicars about how the broach came into my possession, was lost, found and disappeared again. He said it came when I needed it and now it has gone to someone else whose need is greater; I was glad he did not think I was crazy, and his explanation left me with a comfortable feeling and happiness for the one who received it.

The pin had left me, but God kept me safe. One evening while alone at home I decided to have a long soak instead of a shower. I lit my scented candles, turned off all the lights and locked the bathroom door. I was never in the habit of locking the door.

After being in my lovely bubbles for about ten minutes I heard movements. I wanted to call out thinking it might have been Fitz or one of our children, but my inner voice said, *just relax you will know who's there in time.* I obeyed the voice, closed my eyes, and after another ten minutes all went quiet. When I got out of the bath, I opened the door and called for Fitz but there was no reply. I was immediately hit by a strange bad odour and instantly I knew that I was burgled. My bedroom was ransacked, and my jewels were missing. Did the thief realise that I was in the bath and left before completing what was intended? I would never know but I am forever grateful to God that He inspired me to lock the door. Just to think, I could have been found in a blood bath.

Luckily, money from a partner hand, for which I was in charge that belonged to my colleagues at work, was still where I kept it. The burglar could not have seen it. My jewels were insured. I made a claim and was able to replace them. The next day when I broke the news to my manager at work, I was granted the day off. Not wanting to go home, I went to church and told those who were there. I received a great big comforting hug from Cecilia, it uplifted my spirit.

CHAPTER 30

ACCIDENT AT MILSBORN SUPERMARKET

One day in December 1996, towards the end of my ninth year working at Milsborn, I was very much looking forward to our Christmas celebration, having a fun night. The annual event was organised by a couple of staff members when the unexpected happened, as I opened the office door to exit, I instantly tripped over some large, heavy boxes that were placed to the left of the door. My God, I went flying forwards, then backwards, before falling. My neck and shoulder banged on the sharp edge of the top box; I could not move. With pain and dizziness someone helped me up to sitting position and another staff member drove me to the hospital. After examination and x-ray, I was ordered rest. The x-ray result showed a bruised neck, upper back and shoulder. I stayed off work for a while but returned as soon as I felt able to manage; some days I coped well, while other days were stressful. The constant strain of looking down on the keyboard aggravated the injury, so that further sick leave was unavoidable. Mr Cowdry was very sympathetic when I was on duty, as he allowed me to go for a walk when the cold office temperature worsened the pain.

One day a nurse from the firm came to see me for a chat without prior notice. We used the secretary's office and were given one hour of privacy. The nurse knew from my records that I was a Christian, it seemed like everything known about me was recorded.

"Hello Sheva, I am Stella, a nurse from the company. I am here to talk about your health. How are you feeling?"

"Up and down. Some days I manage well, other days I struggle through the discomforts."

"I understand you are a Christian."

"Yes, I am."

She said, "So am I."

We talked a little about our faith, then she told me about an issue she was facing at that time. We prayed together for each other. Afterwards she calmly said, "Sheva I am going to put you off work." I burst into tears because, I loved my job, and I did not want to be at home permanently. Stella tried to comfort me. "Don't worry you will be on full pay. Perhaps sometimes you can invite one or two of your church sisters to tea. You can also do all the things that God opens up to you. Your wages will gradually go down but after one year you will be given retirement benefit." That was all good to hear, but I knew I would miss my friends and the social life we shared, I could not stop crying. "You can go home right now," said Stella.

I did not want to, so I returned to finish the job I had in hand, but I could not concentrate. Sadly, I said goodbye to all and left in tears. Everyone asked, "What's wrong?" Not wanting to explain I waved and walked out the door.

At that time, my sister Manda from Grenada was holidaying with me. When I got home and told her the full story, she threw her arms around me and sang sweetly in my ear - 'Jesus is my Papa I will not beg for bread.' It was the first time I heard that song and thought she composed it specially for me. She even recorded it for me, and I still cherish it.

One month later my phone rang, the voice on the other end asked, "Have you had an accident in the last three years."

I answered. "Why? And who are you?"

"We fight claims. No win, no fee! You can't lose, so have you had an accident in the last three years?"

"Yes, I have had."

"Well, if you give me your name and address, I'll send you the claims form."

"OK!"

When the forms came, I completed and returned to sender. The investigators replied in a letter saying I had a good case. The long process of investigation began. To my surprise the consultant that was chosen to check the injury I sustained was Doctor Mann. We knew each other well from my job at the hospital, the injury I had sustained there, my treatment with him and from his advice to me on making a claim. When we met, he asked, "Why did you not take the case to the solicitor you had before?"

"I never really thought about it, I had no intentions of suing the firm, but I answered a phone call, asking, "If you have had an accident in the last three months make a claim with us, no win, no fee."" Doctor Mann made no reply. I suddenly recalled someone had told me that my previous solicitor and Doctor Mann were related. I also remembered that he was a good solicitor, but it was too late for me to turn back.

I did not think highly of my present solicitor, I had to put most of the case work together myself. Debbie his personal assistant complemented me, "You ought to work as a PA. You'll be excellent." Just before the end of that financial year, Mr Cowdry and Netty, the union representative, paid me a home visit. They both congratulated me on my lovely home. Mr Cowdry asked, "How will you manage to stay in the style of living you have become accustomed to?" I must admit I was concerned, but I made no reply. I have always trusted in God to see me through.

"Is there any part of the store that you think you might manage without pain?" enquired Mr Cowdry.

"I don't know."

"You can always come back," he said.

That was good to know but I also knew that if I had to go sick again, I would lose the offer that was already decided by the nurse. “Thanks, but I will leave it as it is.” I replied.

“We will fight you in court. We are a big company you will not win.” He then explained my pension and benefits.

A letter came from the solicitor stating we had a good case and that the report on my injury from the consultant looked promising. Four weeks later I received another letter saying the consultant had changed his statement, the case was no longer in my favour, and do I want to continue? I telephoned the solicitor’s office and spoke with the PA. I said, “I've got this far I might as well continue.”

“You will need two witnesses,” she explained.

“I will try,” was my reply.

I went into the store to speak with Joan, the one who helped me to sit up after my fall, and Faye, who on hearing my scream rushed to see what was wrong. Luckily, they were both there when I went. I spoke first with Joan.

“Hi Joan, good to see you. How are you?”

“Fine and you?”

“I could be better. I am here because I need your help. Do you remember what happened the day I tripped and fell?

“Yes, I saw when you fell and helped you up.”

“Can you be a witness for me in court?”

“Oh no! I do not want to get involved.”

“That’s ok, thanks.”

I went to Faye next and asked. “How you doing?”

“I should be asking you,” she said.

I smiled and got to the point not wanting to keep her from her work. "Can you remember what happened the day I tripped and fell."

"Yes of course I remember."

"Will you be a witness for me in court?"

"Yes sure."

"Thank you so much."

I called the P.A. to let her know that I only had one witness. I explained that Joan who assisted me when I fell did not want to get involved and the colleague that drove me to the hospital no longer worked for the firm and I could not locate him. She decided that we'll just make the one witness do. I prayed that all this effort of seeking justice would not be in vain.

On the day in court the consultant was the first to give statement and left. I was called next to give mine. I spoke as it happened, the judge asked me two questions.

"How far were the boxes from the door?"

"They were immediately behind the door.

"How many boxes were there?"

"Two" I replied.

"You may return to your seat," said the judge.

Faye was called next. In her statement she said that there were three boxes. I had no idea there were three boxes. Faye and I were not allowed to discuss the incident. The judge called me up again and said, "Mrs Williams you are the most honest person I have ever met, it's a credit to you." He went on to explain about my honesty, but I was too overwhelmed to grasp all he said. He awarded me a reasonable sum for my damages which the solicitor thought was not enough and asked me if I would like to contest. "No thank you! I have been through enough, thank God it's over." I thanked him and his PA for their efforts and bid them goodbye with God's blessings. End of an awful chapter!

MEMOIRS OF A SMALL ISLAND GIRL

CHAPTER 31

JOY BELLS

Joy bells rang as Patsy announced her wedding for the summer of 1997 and entrusted me with the catering and the making of Stacey's dress. Stacy was her only bridesmaid. I was honoured that Patsy trusted me to make Stacy's dress, and I looked forward to presenting my best. We did everything together, beginning with shopping for her outfit, then the material for Stacy's dress which was designed by Patsy. I also made aprons to match Stacy's dress for my friends Hatti, Faye, and two others who kindly offered to serve on tables. Hatti was in charge of the table service on the day. We were fortunate to get a newly built hall that did not need much to make it look lovely. I planted flowers in troughs to match the colour scheme and displayed them on the windows. I prepared and cooked all dishes in advance. I am happy to say that on the day the wedding went just as planned, the couple looked amazing as did the bridesmaid and all the guests. The hall looked beautiful in burgundy and gold and the food was delicious followed by great music. Fitz and I were proud parents.

1997 ST VINCENT & GRENADA

New month, fresh thoughts. *Well girl, time for a break in the sun, perhaps it would bring some healing to the bones. SVG. and Grenada, why not? Well don't just think, get on with it! OK! OK!* I made calls to Prince, Winnie and my sister- in- law, Claire, who was now in St Vincent, then to Manda, in Grenada. I told them about my plans to holiday with them over a period of fifteen days. They were all happy to accommodate me and made provisions for me to get from the airports to their homes.

I went first to Grenada. On my second day, Manda's Friend drove us around the Island. We stopped for a paddle along the sea front of Grand Anse Beach. Next, we went to view the Grand Etang Lake, and from there he took us back to his home where his dear wife had a lovely meal prepared for us. By the end of the day I was so tired I had a nice nap before we were driven back to Manda's home. In St Vincent I spent time at all three homes, but I was based at Claire's because she lived alone and had wanted me to stay with her. Both her and Prince drove me around the island, nothing was too much for them to do for me. While at Claire's, most mornings we went to the sea for a couple hours swim and enjoyed the company of those we met and others who came after. On the other early mornings we went for walks up the road from Claire's house to Calvary's Mountain. That road also goes up to Mount St Andrews. Although the road is good and jeeps go to the top of the mountain to service Cable and Wireless Communications, we did not venture the steep and winding climb. We got to a flat clear area that was covered in soft green grass, there I knelt and gave thanks to God for his great creation, before descending. Later, at the cool of the day, I walked through the village greeting family and friends.

I had a lovely surprise on hearing that Manda's, daughter sent her a flight ticket to holiday in St Vincent. She spent some of the time with Winnie. Christa and her husband were also on the island. One day Prince discreetly took us all up to Mount St Andrews, the climb that I dreaded. According to Prince we were not going to the top, but he took the lead and kept saying, "It's just around the bend." We followed with much difficulty until we came to a freshwater spring that flowed through the rock. We drank and were energised. We got to the top and saw the building of Cable and Wireless Communication. The descend was just as difficult as the ascend. Manda suggested we walk in a zig zag pattern, and it worked. I was grateful to Prince for giving us the experience however I promised myself to never do that journey again.

One day Claire and I went to Lowmans windward to visit my husband's sister. Claire was a good driver. She had never driven that way before, but she took extra care along some narrow roads with unexpected bends and sharp drops. On some other days we travelled to different parts of the island just for sightseeing.

It was a joy to explore the island and to meet with everyone, especially seeing my grandchildren again and visiting families, friends, and churches where I knew some members well. It was also good that I had time to enjoy the calm waters of the blue Caribbean Sea, to bask on the warm sands and also to feast on the lovely cuisine of both islands. I had a splendid holiday and looked forward to catching up with Claire on her next stay in London.

1997 HAPPENINGS

On my return, Fitz was offered a job as verger in our church. He accepted and enjoyed the position, but this resulted in him spending much of his time at church, much more than me. He always joined the church outings I organised to the seaside once or twice a year, depending on the weather. Family and friends also joined us, we had great times socialising.

Both Fitz and I loved celebrations. Each year we celebrated our birthdays together as they were only one day apart. We sometimes received cinema and theatre tickets as gifts from our children. Fitz always remembered Valentine's Day and presented me with a card. New Year's Eve was party night for extended family and friends, but that ended when our church started a midnight service.

In 1998, Philemon, my dear brother in Christ desired to be water baptised. I spoke to Pastor Smith about it and he was happy to carry out the baptism. Pastor acknowledged me before his congregation in the same way as he did when he baptised PJ. I went forward and announced Philemon for his baptism. Philemon was already a member of my prayer group, who admired the gift he saw in me as I prayed and helped others. One day he came to me and asked if I would kindly go with him to the home of a friend who was very ill and awaiting an operation. I agreed.

When we got there the lady was in bed, we prayed with her and read a psalm. I blessed a cup of water and gave it to her to drink as suggested by Philemon, she sat up and drank it. After about ten minutes she went to her kitchen and brought us food. When she went to the hospital for her pre-operation test, she was told that she no longer needed the operation. *I thought what a wonderful God we serve.*

Philemon encouraged me to become a trained Christian counsellor. He began by introducing me to read the booklet 'Every day with Jesus' by Selwyn Hughes and paid the subscription for my first year. This I have continued. He also wrote to the Waverly Christian Centre and recommended me for training in counselling. I did three weeks of in-depth study on counselling theory, strategy and practise, an accredited course, and received a certificate of recognition in Christian Counselling for the Association of Christian Counsellors. Philemon also introduced me to Fresh Fields Trainers in counselling, in 2001, where I did an eighteen-hours course for facilitators and counsellors and again I received a certificate.

READER TRAINING

In 1998 after many interviews, I was accepted for training to become a Lay Reader in the diocese of Chelmsford. My training lasted three years. It was tough, but God brought me through because it was His will for me. Others on my team also agreed that it was not an easy course. I believe the love we shared in the time we spent together helped to enrich us and kept us positive.

There were times when I studied all night and never grew weary. When morning came, I only knew when I saw the natural light, yet I carried on. I bless the Lord that my husband did not object. At times all he said was, "Sheva you've been up all night!" I would smile and reply, "I know, I just want to get it right." I passed my pastoral project with a distinction. General comments on all subjects were excellent, and character references from tutors showed me to be honourable and worthy of my calling. I received my licence in 2000 to teach, preach, take funerals and to support the bereaved, but I had to continue training for another year.

I received full support from my church, my entire family and my friends. My sister Christa was my spiritual advisor. I preached my first sermon at our sister church, St James' Church, which I was also assigned to. My siblings and their spouses attended. My granddaughter Stacie and my sister Selda's granddaughter helped me with actions. My sermon went quite well, and I was given top marks by the vicar and my tutor.

My second sermon was at my placement parish. The vicar said that my talk was overwhelming, as in powerful. I thought about it and did my best to be moderate with other sermons.

My final sermon during my training was at my tutor's church where he was vicar. My sister Karen kindly offered to drive me there and my brother PJ came to support me. We had difficulty in locating the church, so I rang my tutor to say that I had problems with directions, but that I was on the way. Regrettably, we got there late. Thankfully, my tutor, worked around the sermon and left it until I arrived trusting that I would get there. I have to say that I did very well, and everyone congratulated me. One lady said that it was well worth the wait!

A year on from receiving my licence, I was invited to preach in two services at Selda's church in Rainham, Essex. I was pleased with how well they went. I was complemented and presented with a generous gift.

I enjoy teaching and preaching, which I continue to do at my main church and at others when invited.

VILNA AND SOLOMON'S WEDDING

1999, the year that I began Reader training, my youngest daughter Vilna and her partner Solomon announced their wedding plans. Gosh it was so exciting! I began to wonder how I would be able to fully assist her and still carry on with my studies. It was as if she read my thoughts when she said, "Mummy all I want you to do is make my cake and Stacey's dress. She will be my bridesmaid and Hanson my pageboy. Dad can make his waistcoat to match Stacy's dress, then you can sit back and enjoy my wedding day!" I smiled because I knew I could make these well in advance. I also knew that Anita, a family friend, would ice and decorate the cake.

The day of July 25th, 1999 dawned with a bright sky. The wedding was at our usual parish church. Everyone looked amazing in gold and dark green. Fitz and I were once again proud parents, as were Solomon's, when our children made their vows. The reception was kept at the beautiful Tower hotel in Aldgate, where we decorated the hall to our liking with everything matching. Fitz's speech was cracking, the food was delicious, and the music kept us on our toes. It was a splendid day and a superb wedding. Fantastic couple!

HOLIDAY FROM VILNA

Great surprises from my children kept springing up. "Good morning mum!" chirped Vilna in a surprise visit.

"Morning Vilna, it's good to see you! How was your honeymoon trip?".

"It was excellent, mum. We had a great time!"

"That's so nice to hear."

Vilna then said, "When you get a chance, open this envelope. It's for yours and dad's birthday, but don't leave it till then."

"In that case I'll open it now. "Whoa! A holiday in Spain? Thank you! Thank you! But how can you afford it?"

"Never you mind mum," Vilna replied. "If you want it, just tell me the dates that will be best for you and dad."

When I revealed this exciting news to Fitz, we both smiled happily. We then decided on the dates and Fitz booked his time off from work. We flew from London Heathrow to Santa Maria where we boarded the minibus to our hotel. During our stay we visited San Miguel, the parish church, and Gibraltar. We also went to the Montserrat mountain and the monastery, where we saw the Shrine of the Black Madonna.

HOLIDAY CLUB MEMBERSHIP

We were returning from our walk on the beach when we were stopped by a couple of time share sales representatives. After listening to their offers for about fifteen minutes we went with them to their business quarters. There, we decided to become members and invested in a studio apartment for one week each year in Portugal. At the same time we joined another company called RCI through which we could exchange our week for other destinations as well as cruises.

Our assigned apartment was in Albufeira. Our first trip was in November 1999, we both loved it. It was like home from home. We went on trips organised by the holiday company. On the way to Lisbon, we stopped in Seville for a break after driving past the statue of Jesus, and we had a chance to look around. We met a young Australian lady who was touring Europe. She asked, "Can I stick with you guys?"

"Yes sure." Fitz and I replied.

"You can be my adopted parents," she said.

We both smiled and from then she called us mum and dad and spent the remainder of her holiday in our company.

When we reached Lisbon, it was surprisingly cold, but we still enjoyed the walking tour. At the end of our holiday we gave the Australian lady our home address as she was flying to London. She visited us but, as years went by, we lost touch.

On our second trip we went through the RCI and stayed in a lovely Villa in Quinta do Lago, in an exclusive golf course and residential resort, in the company of Karen and Larry. It was about a thirty-minute walk from main attractions and buses were few and far between. Because we were not golf players, we took time to enjoy the scenery. We first walked to the beach; the naturistic trail to the sea was fantastic, as were the sand and sea. The following day we walked to the town, explored, and had a meal before taking the bus back. Other days we strolled around the grounds and watched the golf players, while we feasted from the picnic basket we prepared.

It was a nice quiet break, but not a place that I would return to without a car. Fitz and I then upgraded to a one bed apartment to allow us to take another couple with us on other holidays.

JUNE 2000 NEW YORK ANDY'S GRADUATION

Great news from New York! Andy was about to graduate with a bachelor's degree in science. I could not miss that. Because of circumstances, I had already lost out on so much in his life. He was over the moon when I told him, "I'll be there, God willing."

I arrived two weeks before the graduation date so that I was able to meet with many relatives and visit places of interests with them. Andy picked me up from the airport. I stayed at his home for the duration of my holiday. He drove me around as much as he could. My sister Dorada flew from Canada just to be with me. Her son, Terence, also lived in New York, so she stayed with him. Terence was great as always; he drove me around when Andy couldn't. We went to the home of a nephew who I had not seen in years and together we went to Canarsie Pier where we had a lovely walk and ended our time with a meal. It was all very exciting and a very special time for me.

Terence also drove me to Andy's graduation at New York City Technical College as Andy needed to be there early. When I spotted him in his seat, he looked splendid. He already had many achievements in various subjects, but he was still intent on studying further to get a master's degree.

The next week, Andy drove me to the airport. Parting was never easy. I found it was best to just say, "See you soon."

Some months later Andy called to say that the university where he was teaching had awarded him a master's degree. I was so proud of him.

PORTUGAL HOLIDAY NOVEMBER 2000

We were thrilled to be accompanied by Christa and my dear friend, Shelley, on our first stay in the apartment in Algarve. During our stay we made our way, independently, by bus and taxi to Gipsy markets and walked along the beaches wherever we went. We also went to Lisbon and drove past the statue of Jesus, which Fitz and I did the year before, so we were able to point out to our companions where we were as we drove along. Shelley's birthday was on the 24th and on the day, she treated us to a delicious dinner in a posh restaurant. We had a super break and I looked forward to the next.

CHAPTER 32

HEALING CAFÉ

During the month of August, still in 2000, I was greatly inspired by a team of Christians called Through Faith Missions. The team did extraordinary missionary work for one week with our church and in the wider community. I admired their work, and the blessings God was pouring out on everyone around them, so I decided, with the permission and full support from my vicar, to start a Tuesday morning healing session, which we called 'Healing Café. This replaced the Tuesday coffee morning meetings. We began with two prayer ministers from 11 a.m. to noon and another two from noon to 2 p.m. Our aim was and still is to befriend whoever comes to us. We offer tea, coffee, biscuits, a listening ear, a reading from the book of Psalms and prayer, also personal mentoring and prayer if requested.

Over the years things have changed for the better. We still begin at 11 a.m. but with at least three prayer ministers. Other assigned prayer ministers arrive at different times. We have included a lunch for which a small donation is welcomed. The lunch is prepared by some of us prayer ministers and at times a couple of church members help. Numbers attending range from about seven to twenty people. Once a year we go on an outing, usually to the seaside, and we have dined out for a couple of Christmases but for past three years we stayed at the church and prepared delicious three course meals, enjoyed by all. We also celebrate birthdays. Over the years attendees have expressed the fulfilment they have gained through the Healing Café. Sadly, because of the Covid-19 pandemic we were not been able to meet for most of 2020 and 2021.

HEALING SERVICE

Oh what a morning, that day when I woke at six by an inner voice instructing me to hold a healing service. I could not switch the voice off, the harder I tried the more powerful it came to me. In the end, I grabbed a pen and paper and began writing as the voice commanded, and within twenty minutes I had a complete layout with everything that was needed for the service. I was given the names of all who were to take part and what each one role was to be, also the way in which I ought to advertise for the service. As soon as the church was opened, I rang my vicar to tell him of my vision. His response was, "Hmm! Yes! Sounds good, bring it in let's have a look."

I got to church as quickly as I could. Reverend Paisley looked at the layout and said, "Good, but too long! About sixty minutes too long!" He cut four songs and omitted some verses from another two and promised to apologise if he was wrong about the cuts. I was grateful that he allowed it to go ahead even in the order that was given. We agreed that the service would be called, 'Prayer, Praise and Healing,' to be held on Sunday 15th October 2000 at 6:30 p.m. With the help of a church colleague, I set about designing and printing handouts and posters. In the handouts I clearly stated that we are not miracle workers, but Jesus is working miracles, so come with an open ear ready to hear and receive from him.

I distributed invites widely to all neighbouring churches and throughout the community. I also posted to some people in other parts of London that I knew would be interested. I hung posters in every place that the Holy Spirit directed me. The turnout on the night of the service was magnificent, and it went exactly as was given in my vision.

So many people came forward for prayer and anointing that none of the songs and verses from the original layout should have been omitted; the ones we retained had to be repeated to fill the gap. That very night Reverend Paisley's wife said to me, "God is saying to you, "Well done my good and faithful servant!"" The next day Paisley handed me a letter that read:

> Congratulations on the service last night everyone I have spoken to said, "What a lovely service!" Well

done for vision, content and organisation. Even the schedule worked out.

I had faith that it would go as planned because I only followed the instructions I was given, so the Glory I gave to God. It was His doing.

MARCH 2001 HOLIDAY IN TENERIFE

Good families are special treasures. Once again Karen and Larry gladly joined Fitz and I on another of our RCI exchange breaks to Tenerife. It was so nice that we were able to visit other parts of Europe through this extended plan. We visited churches, markets and other interesting places. The highlight of our trip was a boat tour to see dolphins. There were many, they even went under the boat that we feared it would capsize, it was a treat watching them in their fun splash. One night we went for a walk on the beach, we came to a restaurant where there was live music. The band was from the Congo, they played so well that we could not resist stopping. We danced and bought drinks. The musicians showed us such appreciation that the following night, which was our last, we went back there to dine and dance the night away. On our way out the musicians were grateful for our donations, and we thanked them for their wonderful entertainment.

2001 FITZ'S 70TH BIRTHDAY HOUSE PARTY

I guess by now you have realised that I just love to be on the go. As soon as I got back, I began to organise Fitz's seventieth birthday party with our children. We decided on having it at home, Fitz heard us whispering and demanded to know our secret.

"Why are you lots always whispering? I want to know!" he demanded. Eventually we told him. He made sure I invited some of his friends from church, also his brother, sister and cousin who lived in North London. Two days before the party, he went shopping and came back with a goat, chopped and ready to be cleaned. He cleaned, seasoned and cooked it to perfection. He loved cooking. On the day, everyone was happy for Fitz, especially Thomas, who was much younger but quite ill, still he made the extra effort to be present. When Thomas arrived, we were running out of seats, he held on to Fitz's jacket and said, "Come on man, get up and let me sit. You are strong!" Fitz quickly gave up his seat. We had a great evening of prayer, praise, fun and delicious home cooked food.

2001 THOMAS'S DEATH

Two months later on Boxing Day the phone rang and the voice at the other end said, "Thomas passed during the night."

Thank God we had that time together on Fitz's birthday, because that was the last time we saw him alive. That was a sad end to 2001 for all the family. We were told that although he was sick, he went shopping for the Christmas. Fitz and I spent that Boxing Day at his home with his family, comforting each other and waiting for his body to be taken to the mortuary. He had a lovely funeral attended by relatives from as far as America and Canada.

CHAPTER 33

2001 PRAYER MINISTRY STARTED

My vicar suggested that I would be good at coordinating and training a team to become responsible prayer ministers during Sunday morning and evening services. I was delighted at the idea and prepared material for the training. I began with four sessions but later I condensed it to three for the benefit of people who worked one Sunday a month. I also wrote a refresher course which I mentored twice a year then reduced it to one. Over the years I have trained many people. Some have moved away for various reasons and others came. Many have now joined the saints in glory. I was later asked by a vicar, a very dear friend, to train some members of her church. I agreed and felt highly honoured. I further wrote a one-day training seminar from the same material at the request of two other vicars and taught it at their parishes. Those who attended were very grateful to me.

During two different sessions at my church, there were two young women on the course, the Holy Spirit pointed me to them concerning pregnancy. I honestly did not know how to begin, so to each I said, "I believe that God wants me to pray for you for the fruit of your womb, is this something you are thinking of?"

They both looked amazed and said, "Yes please!"

I prayed as led by the Spirit of God. One year later they both gave birth to healthy babies. They thanked me for the prayers and explained that they were praying and hoping to become pregnant for a long time. "Give God the glory," I said, "I only did what He asked me to do." When their children became toddlers, both mothers, on separate occasions, asked me to pray for them to have another. I did and by God's grace, they produced.

This prompting by the Holy Spirit to pray for another young lady happened again. One day I attended an induction service, a couple were standing close to where I was sitting when out of the blue that still small voice from within me said, *go over and pray with that couple for them to have a child. I can't just do that, when I don't even know them and look at so many people around. I would look and feel like a fool.* I dismissed the voice, but it kept coming back until eventually I had to go.

"Hello! Excuse me, I'm sorry to bother you. We do not know each other but I have just received a message from the Lord to pray for you to give birth."

They were both shocked and looked blank for about sixty seconds, then the man spoke. He explained that he was a priest and that he and his wife beside him were friends of the incumbent who was inducted. He went on to say that his wife kept losing their babies, and doctors had no explanation. She had never gone past three months of her pregnancies. They suspected that she was pregnant again, and so they were very concerned.

"Would you like me to pray?"

"Yes please!" they both answered.

I had to be very discreet, however, I did it, and I felt happy and free. The couple took my email address to keep me informed. Eight months later an email came with a picture of mother and baby daughter doing well in hospital, with a note saying, "Many thanks for your prayers." Two years later I received another email with a picture showing the progress of their little girl. Early 2020 when I thought they had forgotten me I received a family picture. I thought, *how amazing!*

CHAPTER 34

RUBY WEDDING 2002

"Fitz, how would you like us to get married again?"

"Married again? How do you do that?" was his reply.

"Well, we do what we did when we got married and a bit more but no signing of Registrar. After all, we only had a tiny wedding!"

"If that's what you want," Fitz said, "fine by me. Organise it!"

I informed our children of our decision. They were excited for us and were ready to help. Next, I spoke with my relations and close friends; they were also willing to assist. I then consulted our vicar; he turned and looked at me with a big smile, "Umm! Sounds good," he said. We fixed the date and booked the church hall for the party.

I knew exactly what I wanted and set about working on my plans. My niece, Pearl, designed the invites and I sent them out early. My nephew, Dingi, was happy to be in charge of the music and, another of my nephews, was also pleased to be master of ceremonies. Patsy's husband made a fantastic video slide of different events that Fitz and I shared over the years. I made the cakes well in advance which Anita iced and beautifully decorated as always. I also made Stacy's outfit, an off-white trouser suit that looked great on her. She had become the family's bridesmaid girl. Next, Vilna and her husband, Solomon, took me to Calais to buy the wines. It was more like a day out because we had a lovely French meal. I then booked a week away on a sun cruise using our timeshare exchange. We intended to make the most of our agreement with the club, although Fitz did not like travelling on boats, he plucked up the courage to say, "Yes, let's go for it!"

When my wedding anniversary plans were under control, Fitz and I went on a four-day coach trip to Scotland. We stayed at two different hotels on our outward journey and observed a wedding in Gretna

Green where the bride and groom invited us to join their event. On our return we had a four hour stay in Bath, so we went window shopping. Whilst walking, I spotted a ruby dress in a shop window, we went in, I tried it on, it was my perfect fit. I was so happy we did not realise the time until we got a phone call from the coach company saying that they had to go without us, but not to worry the feeder coach will pick us up. Thankfully, it did. A few days after we got home, I filled in whatever else was needed to be done for the party, such as buying Fitz's shirt and tie to match my dress. I did not need anything else because my hat, shoes and my gold accessories from Glenda's wedding served well. The evening before the wedding anniversary, we decorated the church. Family and friends assisted with the catering.

When Fitz and I stepped out of our house on that beautiful day, unknown to us Vilna stood at the gate and took pictures. Dudley drove us to church in his nice new silver car. Vilna continued to take pictures in all the right places at the right times. I felt ten feet tall as Fitz and I walked slowly up the beautifully decorated aisle. All I saw were smiling faces, most of our guests wore complementary colours. Our vicar did us proud as did my nephew's wife, who during the church service sang a very uplifting solo. Everything went as planned and we all enjoyed the party.

A week later we were off on our seven nights' cruise and stay holiday across the Mediterranean and the Atlantic. We flew to Tenerife where we boarded the ship, Carousel. After one night at sea we realised we had made a big mistake by booking a cabin below deck. Whoop bang! whoop bang! was what we got all night from sea waves.

The next morning bright and early we headed to reception and asked to be changed to a cabin above deck. Luckily, there was one available and it was given to us with compliments from the captain when we explained that we were celebrating our ruby wedding anniversary.

After dinner that night the captain took pictures with us. Overall, we had a lovely time on our cruise. We visited Morocco, Lanzarote, Agadir, La Palma and Gran Canaria. The island we loved best was Lanzarote because there was much to see, the fires in the volcano beneath us was most thrilling, and we loved the sea. A few years later we returned there for one week. Our last two nights were spent at a hotel in Tenerife. While there, Vilna called to say that Kaleb, our dear friend, who had been ill for some time, died peacefully. Such sad news as we expected him to make a full recovery. For the remainder of our holiday we could only think of Hatti and her family. As soon as we got back, we went to support them. Hatti gave Kaleb a lovely funeral.

After Kaleb's funeral, Dudley presented us with a video which he had made of our wedding anniversary. Vilna also brought us a beautiful album made by herself of the pictures she took. The family and I still enjoy watching these.

COUSIN DORAWA'S DEATH DECEMBER 2002

I know that I am repetitive by saying I consider it a blessing to have relations in many parts of the world, but it is heart-breaking when one of them becomes ill and you cannot be there for him or her, and worst still, is receiving news, gone to glory. My dearest cousin Dorawa began her career as a teacher, moved into the nursing profession as mentioned in one of the earlier chapters. Sadly, an operation for an eye problem left her totally blind. She was given early retirement from her role as nursing supervisor when she was just fifty. Not once did she allow her blindness to change her inwardly. I once asked her in a letter, "How are you managing with no sight?"

"The Lord has given me inner vision so that I am able to do what's necessary," she replied.

I was strengthened by her response and in the knowledge that she still wrote her own letters. Earlier, I briefly mentioned that on my trip to New York in June 2000, cousin Franado drove me to cousin Dorawa's home. On that visit she had prepared a meal in advance for us, it was just as if she could see us when we spoke. As a matter of fact, she said she could. We knew she that meant in her mind's eye. Her blindness did not ruin her happiness, she made the best of what life offered. When we were leaving, she walked us to the door and waved good-bye. Although we still corresponded, she was no longer able to write her own letters, so she dictated to her niece, who wrote and posted them to me. Meanwhile Franado kept me informed by phone. He was in tears when he explained that she had taken for the worst and was in hospital. December 1st, 2002, cousin Dorawa passed on to glory. How sad that I was not able to be with her in her final days, not even for her funeral. The flowers I sent by Interflora was the best I could have done for all the years of love and care she gave to me.

When I think about life, it is full of the unexpected; it comes with joys, sorrows and times of calm; I have learnt to keep an open mind. From January 2003, I was in for a spell of joy which lasted a few years, even though it was invaded by a little sorrow. I had become better at dealing with sadness and sorrow, and I have been helped through the kindness of wonderful people in my life.

SUPERVISING

January 8th, 2003, my friend Faye, who was now administrator at church, asked if I would consider paid work as supervisor for one evening a week. I happily accepted and enjoyed meeting the different groups. My favourite group was the writers' group, I listened to some of their stories when I was free, and they invited me to their end of term parties. I was only able to attend one, but it was enough to get better acquainted.

A few years later, one evening after work about 9:45, the street light was not working. I crossed the road from the church into the darkness, tripped and fell on an unsecured pole used by the market traders. I banged my knee and could not get up. Two people passed on the other side, saw me lying, and went by. A third one came, helped me up and walked me to a policewoman standing a few yards away. "She ought to help you." He said and saw my gratitude just by my reaction. He made me think of the story in the Bible of 'The Good Samaritan'. The policewoman asked me how far did I have to go. When I told her she said, "That's not far, just take your time." Normally the journey was seven minutes but that evening it took me thirty-five minutes. When I got to the door, Fitz stood with a worried look.

"Thank God you are here! I was just about to send out a search party for you."

This happened on a Thursday. The following Tuesday I explained what had happened to me to my friends at the healing café. One said that I must report it. I had no idea how to go about it, so she took me to a building where there was a local government office for reporting accidents. The officer took my statement without questioning. The very next day the pole was put back into place and the street light was fixed. The following week I received a letter of apology from the council with a claim form for compensation. I completed the form and was compensated for the injury I suffered.

2003 HOLIDAY TO FRANCE, GUADELOUPE AND DOMINICA

Although Kaleb had passed, Fitz and I kept up the friendship with his siblings through Hatti, his widow. One of Kaleb's brothers kindly invited Hatti, Fitz and myself to join him on a round trip, first to France then to Guadeloupe and on to Dominica, back to France then London. He had homes in both France and Guadeloupe. We were happy to be invited and we did not hesitate to say, "Yes thank you." I think his intention was to lift Hatti's spirit after Kaleb's funeral.

We enjoyed the scenery in Paris. When we got to Guadeloupe, Hatti and I had much fun in the calm sea water and exploring the market. From Guadeloupe we sailed to Dominica for the weekend. Our guest house was just three roads up from the seaport in Roseau, walking distance, but strangely no one seemed to know where it was. We took a taxi and the driver drove all around before finding it. We were later told that the driver just wanted to make more money. Reluctant to use a taxi again, we did our sightseeing in Roseau on foot and took a short bus ride out of town and back. The owner of the guesthouse, Mamma, as she was called, wanted to treat us like children, so we left early and had breakfast in another guesthouse nearby. To our surprise Mamma came looking for us while we were in the middle of our meal. We had a good laugh, but Mamma, hand on hip and shaking her head, was not pleased. All in all, we had a pleasant trip thanks to Kaleb's brother who joined him in heaven a few years later.

CHAPTER 35

THE BIRTH OF NELLIE

February 2003, such joy it was looking forward to Vilna and Solomon's long awaited first baby. She was born on Valentine's weekend, our Valentine's baby, Nellie. Thank God, once again I was at the hospital, and waited outside the labour ward during her birth. When I was allowed in, I hardy believed my eyes. Nellie's midwife turned out to be the very lady whose home I was taken to by my friend, Philemon. The lady who was in pain and awaiting an operation and after we had prayed with her, she felt better and no longer needed the operation. I was surprised that she remembered me but sad to see how little care and attention she paid to Vilna. Her attitude caused Vilna to decide against giving birth again in that hospital.

I presented Nellie to the Lord our God and thanked him for Vilna's safe delivery, just as I did with my other grandchildren. Vilna had had a rough time. Nellie was tiny but bigger than her mum was at birth. Like her mum, she was slow at sucking her milk and needed to be fed often. Her parents were constantly worried about her, but she did well and was a happy baby. Nellie was blessed during an open-air Sunday morning church service, keeping to the tradition that I started of no infant baptism. It was a pleasure to see all my siblings and most of their children in attendance also all of Solomon's family. It was a wonderful service followed by a nice celebration at Vilna and Solomon's home. I cared for Nellie while her mum worked, which was my joy. Solomon's parents provided fantastic help; sometimes his mum collected Nellie from nursery and brought her to me. Often, we sat and chatted over a cup of tea.

GLENDA'S WEDDING 2003

It was so nice to look upon Glenda's beautiful smiling face that day when she turned up with her partner. After our initial greetings, Glenda excitedly informed us, "Mum and dad, we are going to get married!" We were happy for them and consulted our vicar, who was as always pleased to assist, and together we set the date of 23rd August 2003 for the wedding.

Glenda made wise choices in keeping costs down. With the consent of Vilna and Solomon she hired a fabulous marquee, and two toilets for their spacious garden, and held the reception there. I did not follow the custom of making the bridesmaid's dress for Stacie, as Glenda chose to have it readymade. I made the cakes, which were iced and decorated by Anita, who also organised flowers. Anita and I decorated the church and the marquee. Glenda's other friends took care of the catering. I was thrilled to accommodate Fitz's brother Elvin and his lovely wife, Florin, from Queens New York and Glenda felt honoured that they came for her wedding. Once again Fitz had an amazing speech tucked up his sleeve, he was becoming an expert. White and beige with a touch of blue were the colours of the day, everything was beautiful from beginning to end.

SURPRISE LEAVING PARTY

September 2003, my eyes could not believe the surprise invite I received, from Jeana. *How could Jeana and Lennard do this to me? Leaving London! Returning to live permanently in St Vincent! How on earth did they keep that secret? Oh well, I'll just have to get accustomed to them not being around anymore.* My family and I went to the party. Our friends were happy to be going so we were pleased for them. We knew that they would pay regular visits to London to see their children and grandchildren, and we would see them then. We certainly did. We also met with them when we were on holiday in St Vincent. Sadly, Lennard is now in heavenly rest.

CRUISE HOLIDAY NAVIGATOR OF THE SEAS

Fitz and I were determined to make the most of our time share. May 2004, we went on a two-week holiday; one week cruise and one week on land. We invited brother PJ, his wife Hilda and Patsy. They gladly accepted. It was so nice that Patsy joined. We flew to Miami and boarded the ship, Navigator of the Seas. It was the most fabulous ship I had ever seen. From Miami we sailed to the Eastern Caribbean islands. We saw and did a lot on our days at sea. The ship was like a palace with streets, theatres and many stores selling all sorts. I bought jewels, a gold chain and matching bracelet cut to my required length. Then there were swimming pools and Jacuzzis which we made the most of. At times we just enjoyed the view as we sailed past lush islands and other large cruise ships. Food and drink were delicious and available throughout the day. Night entertainment was fantastic; we danced to live music, watched great shows and films; there was never a dull moment.

Our first stop was Nassau, the capital of The Bahamas. We hired a seven-seater taxi to take us around, the driver was amazing he took us to all the best places of interest including Atlantis. He wanted us to meet his family, but time was precious. At every port of call we hired a taxi. Our next stop was Cozumel, Mexico. We strolled along the beach and had a quick swim in the sea. Then we sailed to Jamaica, where Patsy and I left the others waiting in the taxi - their choice. We went to Dunn's River and climbed up the slippery fall. We also had a few minutes of fun in the sea, time was all too short. This was definitely another place for me to visit again, which I did.

Next, we went to The Cayman Islands, it was the wettest day of our travel. We all bought plastic macs that were sold along the streets. Patsy decided to go shopping alone instead of sightseeing. The taxi we hired had a lady driver, as we got chatting, we were all surprised to learn that her family in London were PJ's friends and neighbour. Such a small world! Whoa! She sang a couple of Bob Marley's songs to us which we recorded. Then she exclaimed, "Today you are going to Hell!"

"Hell?" We all replied simultaneously, "What are you talking about?"

"Everyone goes to Hell! You cannot come here and not visit Hell."

We then caught on that Hell was a place. Due to the heavy rain fall and much of the island being below sea level we were knee high in water. It was difficult for us to look around in Hell, and we simply could not wait to get back in the van. When we caught up with Patsy, she was pleased that she made the right choice to go shopping in the in-door market and was well chuffed with her purchase.

When we got back to Miami for our week stay, we had a three-bed house at Pompano Beach. We only had to cross the road and we were by the sea, it was fantastic. And to our joy Fort Lauderdale was just a bus ride away. We went, enjoyed the food at a popular restaurant then we explored the market and Hilda and I bought beautiful hats and dresses. On our second day we rang my sister Thelma who lived in Palm Bay. She was thrilled to hear from us and arranged for Terence our nephew, who had also moved to live there, to pick us up.

Next day Terence collected us as planned. Patsy and I stayed the night at Thelma's, she looked after us and took us around, while PJ and Hilda stayed at sister Dorada. Terence returned next day to take us back to Pompano Beach. Our company was much appreciated by both sisters, as they both lived alone, and we were very happy to see them. Thelma gave us the phone number for a cousin who lived in West Palm Beach. I could hardly believe that she recognised my voice when I called. We had not spoken to each other in over twenty years. I guess Thelma told her to expect my call.

"Sheva, it's nice to hear your voice, please come and visit me. I will meet you at the station." Not knowing our way around we had to find the station near us before deciding. We found out that the train station was not far from where we were staying, and that there was a train from there to West Palm Beach. So I called my cousin again to let her know we would be there, in the next couple of days. She was as excited to see us as we were to see her. She picked us up from the station and drove us to her home, where she had a meal ready for us. Her home was beautiful, but she lived alone, and she said that she did not get many visitors but thankfully her daughter did not live far away. We had a refreshing time with her, then she drove us ever so slowly back to the station. We got back to our house safely.

On the day of our return flight to London, we hired a taxi for the day and left incredibly early. We spent some of our time along the beach in Miami gazing at the scenery, we also went on an airboat tour along Sawgrass Recreation Park watching the alligators. When we got back in our taxi, PJ and Fitz had an eyeful of enjoyment watching the bikini motorbike race. The men drove the bikes with their women clad only in bikinis at the back, a sight PJ and Fitz never forgot. That was two weeks well spent - a trip of a lifetime. Thanks to Patsy for her positive leadership. When we arrived home, I was amazed to behold my garden in full bloom, flowers everywhere, Vilna did well in keeping it watered, she also made my day by stocking our fridge, breakfast was sorted. Fitz and I felt so blessed.

BIRTHDAY CRUISE

It's great having a large family. I am hardly ever alone, and it makes finding travelling companions easy. October 2004, Selda and PJ accepted my invitation to accompany Fitz and myself on another cruise and stay trip, to celebrate our birthdays. We flew from Stanstead to Valetta, Malta and sailed on the ship called Seawing, along the Mediterranean for one week mainly around Italy. We docked in Venice, Sicily, Rome, Dubrovnik and Dalmatia in Croatia. We went sightseeing by taxi in each port as we did on other cruises. The day before my birthday, unbeknown to me, Selda had informed one of the servers on our table of my birthday. On the day, some members of the crew serenaded me and presented me with a cake. It was a lovely surprise and I smiled into the night.

We spent our second week in Malta, and soon discovered the friendliness of the Maltese people. They were the most loving of all the other countries we visited. They happily assisted us with directions, even when we did not ask but seemed puzzled. Another thing I loved about Malta - it was so easy to get around, especially as the bus station was not far from where we stayed in Paola. We went to Marsaxlokk harbour and walked along the rugged rocks to a Jewel factory and bought silver jewellery, then popped into the old church, Santa Katerina, after that we strolled through the street market. A couple of times we went to the beautiful Mellieha bay and had great fun in the sea and on the sand in the sun. Malta was on my list for another visit.

SELDA'S 65TH BIRTHDAY

Well, well, well! I did not realise I would be going, so soon, on another big-time fly and cruise holiday but when Selda announced that she wanted a Caribbean cruise for her 65th birthday I said, "Sister, count me in!"

In November 2005, twelve of us - family and friends - flew to Miami. From there we boarded a bus to Fort Lauderdale to begin our two-week cruise to Eastern and Central Caribbean. We were at sea for five days before reaching land, but we had much to see and do and most of all, to enjoy. We had great fun, great food, and excursions. Best of all, on my sister's birthday, my nephew Darren joined our cabins, by removing the partitions, so we could share balconies. Together we celebrated his mum's birthday - drinking, singing, and dancing in private.

Our first port of call was the island of Tortola where we had eight free hours. In that time we took a boat to Virgin Gorga to visit our brother, Harran, his wife and their two sons. They met us at the seaport and drove us first to their beautiful home, built by Harran's own hands. We had lunch, took many photos and made videos, then he drove us around the island and stopped at The Baths, the place that I loved so well on my previous visit.

When we got back to Tortola, we took a taxi up a very steep hill to meet with Harran's wife's sister. After quick greetings we briefly looked around in her gift shop, purchased a few items and hurried to get back to the ship.

Next port of call was St Martin. We had just enough time to get a taxi for a short drive and to take photos. To me, this was another beautiful island with many hills. In my haste, while getting out of the van to video the scene from a hilltop, I tripped along a busy road and fell on my camera. It got damaged but thankfully it protected me from falling flat on my chest.

Next, we went to St Kitts. Christmas carols and calypso were being played in the market. Our long drive took us to a beautiful hotel which we explored but because a storm was forecast, we shortened our tour of the island and returned to the ship.

We reached St Lucia the following day. Although I had been there before, I never had the opportunity for sightseeing. We went to the market, then we visited an arts and crafts centre where we saw some intricate wooden sculptures being made. I resisted the temptation to purchase.

From St Lucia we went to Barbados, one of the islands I have had the privilege of visiting a few times before. After driving around, we stopped at the home of Selda's in-laws. They were expecting us and laid on an amazing spread.

As we sailed from Barbados, St Vincent, the land of my birth came into view. I was thrilled with excitement, especially as we had a splendid welcome that surpassed all the other islands. Immediately after we docked, I rang my friends, Jeana and her husband, to let them know that I was on the island and would be stopping at their gate to greet them. As we drove towards their house, we spotted them standing at their gate as planned. We chatted for five minutes, and then set off. I had also rang Gaylene, my granddaughter, and arranged for her to meet me at the Botanical Garden. When we got to the gate, Gaylene was there and joined us to travel onto the Leeward end of the island to meet other relatives and friends. Gosh it was so good to have her near me! We continued our drive to Lowmans Hill.

Our first stop in Lowmans was at the home of Selda's son and his family. Then we went to Claire's home where most of the family gathered to be with us. After refreshments and chat, we drove to Layou to more relatives and friends, then to Barroulie to meet Ian, my second grandson, and his mum Flora. This was my first-time seeing Ian who was now 20 years old. I was so happy and even happier to introduce him to his half-sister, Gaylene. He wore a beautiful smile and was instantly loved by all. Finally, we went back to Lowmans to Prince and his family where we were also entertained. I don't quite know how we managed to consume all the food set before us. My niece, who could not meet with us, had sent me gifts, but unfortunately, I was only allowed to take one small bag back to the ship.

When we left St Vincent, I was so filled with joy that I was ready for home. However, the next day, the sight of Venezuela brought refreshing thoughts. I remembered from a child that Pappahen had said that we have relatives living in Venezuela. So when we went ashore, I somehow felt connected to the inhabitants. I wondered if the lady driver, who drove us to the salt mines, was a distant relative. Only God knew.

Our journey took us past the famous Bellefonte hotel, and also the tiny homes where African slaves lived, who were brought to the island to work the salt mines. We were also fortunate to see beautiful flamingos. When we got to the mines, we collected small portions of different quality salt.

Before boarding the ship, we went for a quick dip in the sea, which was very lovely and refreshing. Our next stop was Curacao - there the heavens opened. This happened to be the result of the warning from the storm that was circulating when we were in St Kitts. The showers were mighty. We thought of staying on board, but curiosity got the better of us. Covered in rain macs we waded through what seemed like rivers to the nearest set of shops. Our eyes caught the jewels in a window, and we went in. Myself and another of our companions purchased a watch each and off we went back to the ship, feeling well pleased that we bought something.

Our final stop was Aruba, but it was also raining there. Nevertheless, we went out. Can you guess where to? Hahaha...another jewellery store! There, I bought a bracelet that matched the watch I purchased the day before in Curacao. That was amazing.

We set sail to Fort Lauderdale with fantastic memories and many treasures. We were thrilled to be entertained first by a Vincentian steel band and thoroughly enjoyed dancing to their great music. They were the best band we had on the trip. The long delay at Miami was a bit disappointing, but we had fun with Selda's grandchildren in their running games. Eventually, we had a pleasant flight back to London, thanks to God for another great two weeks away.

SUMMER 2006

In the Summer of 2006, Harran and his family came to visit. They were joined by Winnie and her daughter, Elvie, it was so nice to have them all. They shared some of their time with our other siblings. When Winnie was leaving, I had a small barbeque farewell party, which I started and ended early because Stacy was being baptised later that day.

My friends Hatti, Faye and Shelley attended along with my immediate family. I was surprised to see how Elvie took over the cooking, she was no more than twelve. Cooking was her chosen career, so she had fun doing it and it was done to perfection.

After the party some of us made our way to support Stacy. A few years previous our dear Stacy had found herself a new church, and like me, although she was christened as a baby, she wanted to go through the waters of baptism. She openly testified of how the spirit of Jesus was moving in her life. Her testimony was very touching. We were all proud of her and still are. The baptismal service was quite moving and uplifting. Many other young people were baptised and also gave amazing testimonies.

The following day Winnie and Elvie left for St Vincent. They were great company to me, I wished they didn't have to go but I believed that one day they would return, and I would visit them too.

JANUARY 2007 SISTER DORADA'S DEATH

I knew that sister Dorada was unwell. Many times she spoke of her pains, which I detected in her voice. She relied on her wheelchair to get around the house. Sister Dorada was generally a happy person. It was sad to hear of her decline and not being able to assist, being so far away, divided by a vast ocean. Thank God her siblings and relatives who lived close to her did their best to help. It was a shock when Esther, her daughter, rang from Florida to say that they had just taken her to the hospital and in no time, she was gone. My siblings and I immediately made plans to be there for her funeral. Manda and Christa were not able to be there. PJ, Karen, Selda, and I flew over from London. Winnie and Prince flew from St Vincent. Harran and his wife went from Virgin Gorda. We met with Thelma and our other family living in Canada and America. We were privileged to have eight siblings together, five sisters and three brothers.

All sisters stayed at Thelma's. Brothers and their wives stayed with friends. I am sure we were of great comfort to sister Dorada's five children, and the togetherness made the grief much easier for each of us to bear.

At the funeral, the five of us sisters sang the hymn, '*The Old, Rugged Cross*'. Prince read the first lesson, I read the second and fought back tears as I read. Victor was supported by his son as he gave a moving tribute. Tribute was also paid by Annie, a granddaughter, followed by a niece. Sister Dorada's five children stood together as one spoke of her love and dedication. Sister Dorada was embalmed, which she had arranged and had informed us of long before her passing.

As the coffin was lifted to the top floor of the mausoleum, I sang the song, '*Steel Away to Jesus, Steel Away Home*'. Everyone joined in. That was followed by '*Amazing Grace*'. I must say, watching the coffin go up was not as painful for me as the many I have watched go down into the ground. That was a new experience for me.

After the reception we all went back to sister Dorada's house. Prince and others cooked. We ate, drank, listened to music and later, one of sister Dorada's grandsons entertained us well as he sang, '*Jesus Loves Me*' and '*Amazing Grace*'.

While we were in Florida a granddaughter was born to Victor, her parents decided on 'Dorada' for her middle name. My sister was gone but her name lives on in the family. A lovely and thoughtful idea.

CHAPTER 36

DREAMS, VISIONS, PROPHECY

About one month after returning from Florida, I dreamt that there was a fire at Heathrow airport. When I told Fitz he said, "Tell someone it might help!"

"Who can I tell?" I asked. "People will laugh at me."

Later that day I was shocked to hear the news, a fire at Heathrow airport.

I recall another dream I had back in 1984 of a threat on Margaret Thatcher's life which actually happened. It took place in Brighton, but she escaped unharmed. As far back as I can remember I have had dreams and visions that came to pass. There were also times when some things that I had spoken, happened. For this reason, Fitz often pinched my lips when he assumed that my words were prophecy - he called me a witch. I am still learning to be careful about what I voice.

TRACY'S WEDDING

Tracy wore a straight face when she said, "Mum and dad, Mark and I are ready to get married". She was so casual that I wondered if she really meant it. I reflected on the day when Mark proposed to her in our garden at a barbeque party. It all happened so quickly, he went down on one knee in the presence of myself, Fitz and our children and asked, "Tracy will you do me the honour of becoming my wife?" Tracy gave a big smile but no reply, until we all said, "Go on, answer then!" I am sure she must have said, yes! Everyone was in fits of laughter and all the time I thought, *whoa! That was brave of Mark, so very much like my husband.*

"Are you both sure?" I asked them.

"Yes, we are serious," they replied.

"I hope you and dad won't be offended...we do not want a church wedding." Tracy added and went on, "We shall be having everything under one roof on 20th May 2007 at Devonport House in Greenwich."

Fitz and I were a little surprised, but it was their life, and they had every right to choose. Tracy continued, "Mum, we want to keep the tradition, and have you make our cake, and if you don't mind, please can you ask Anita if she would decorate it? I am also hoping that you come with me to choose my dress. And lastly, can we have some white lilies from your garden for our side table...and I would love you to help decorate the hall." Tracy had everything nicely worked out. I was more than happy to fulfil her requests. She chose her colours to match the lilies and wore off-white. She looked amazing. It was just like a church wedding. Her guests wore colours of their choice. I wore navy and gold. Mark and his children made excellent speeches. Fitz had now become an expert in giving speeches; this was his fourth time giving speeches for our daughters' weddings. The wedding went well from beginning to end. Everyone danced and sang along with the live band. Having everything under one roof was much easier. Tracy was a good organiser.

LOUISE'S WEDDING

More great news! An invitation to the wedding of my sister Thelma's daughter, Louise, and her fiancé in Florida came about the same time that Tracy announced hers. Because it was the week after I did not think I would have been able to go, but my daughters encouraged me. "Mum you have to go!" they insisted, and I took their advice, especially as I did not have much to do for Tracy's wedding.

I booked my flight to travel with Karen and her children. We stayed together at sister Dorada's house. Our other siblings and their children stayed with Thelma but most days before and after the wedding we got together and had great times. One day I went out with my nephew, Delboy, his wife, and their baby, to the Kennedy Space Centre. A fantastic day that was!

Louise and her husband's wedding on 27th May 2007 was a wedding with a difference, the first I had seen of its kind. The bridal party danced in pairs on entry into the hall, each to a different tune. It looked quite romantic. I believe that for them, it was a dream with a fairy-tale ending. They now have a daughter and a son, bless them all.

KELLY'S BIRTH

"Mummy," said Nellie, "I do not want a brother! I want a sister!"

"Nellie, what will happen if mummy has a boy?" I asked her.

"Well she can't bring him home!"

Nellie was so adamant it was worrying. On 21st August 2007, Vilna gave birth to another gorgeous baby girl. Thank the Lord! Nellie was overjoyed, and so were all of us. This was the first time that I was not present at the birth of a grandchild born in England because I was needed to take care of Nellie. As soon as I was able to visit, I went and presented Kelly to the Lord with thanks and praise, and for Vilna's safe delivery. I did not look after Kelly as much as I did her sister.

Kelly was blessed in church when she was about three months old. The service of thanksgiving was attended by close family and friends followed by a small party back at Vilna and Solomon's home. Kelly and Nelly have always been inseparable, they are now beautiful teenagers. Nelly was water baptised in 2018. Kelly was also baptised in 2020 but due to the pandemic she could not be immersed.

CHAPTER 37

THE AWFUL PAIN

What is this pain in my heel all about? My God, it's too much! I cannot bear it. I know I am good at bearing pain but this one is unbearable. Lord God in heaven, please take it away. You will have to go to the doctor! whispered my inner voice. I took heed and went. It was in the year 2008 when this happened. The doctor referred me to a specialist at my local hospital. The specialist asked me a few questions, then he diagnosed my pain as Achilles heel. He advised me that it needed to be operated on.

"How would you feel about having an operation?" he asked.

"I don't care if the foot is chopped off, I cannot bear the pain anymore," I exclaimed.

"No, you don't want that. You just want to feel better. I am the surgeon, and I will do my best for you." His voice was calm and reassuring. I felt at ease and trusted him.

On the day of my operation, my surgeon knelt beside me and said a little prayer. I was supposed to be an overnight patient, but he said, "You will not be staying, I do not want you picking up infection. When you recover, you are going home. If there will be no one to collect you I will put you in a cab, even if I have to pay for it myself."

God had placed me into the hands of another Christian surgeon, just as He did before. I know I did not deserve such grace but as I received it the peace of God was upon me. After my operation I came through singing the song, '*There Is a Redeemer, Jesus God's Own Son*'. My surgeon said that he knew the song I was singing and smiled.

Patsy and Jacob came to collect me. My first few days at home was a real struggle as I was on two crutches. Fitz was employed at church as a Verger and had to go to work.

I think everyone, including myself, thought I would be fine but when push came to shove, managing was difficult.

However, God showed me a plan. I had a basket with a handle, I hooked it onto one crutch with all that I needed to see me through until Fitz got home and hopped back to my seat.

I was rather pleased and laughed to myself, I could not wait to share my achievement with Fitz. Our church warden, God rest her soul, was kind. She visited regularly and as soon I was hopping better, she walked with me to and from church for the mid-week service. When I was able to hop out alone, one neighbour saw me and asked, "What's wrong?" I told her about my operation. She remarked, "You will never walk properly again." In my heart I was annoyed at her words, but I rebuked them in the name of Jesus.

My timeshare holiday in Portugal that year would have been a very significant one. Fitz and I were to be accompanied by our children and grandchildren for Tracy's 40th birthday. They had to go without us, as I was not fit enough to travel. Thank God each one reported that they had a fantastic time.

HOLIDAY TO MADERIA ON CRUTCHES

When I was much improved from my operation, Selda joined Fitz and me on a trip to Funchal, Madeira. Selda did her best to take good care of me. We stayed in a beautiful clubhouse on a hill and were given free transport to the town which was close to the beach. It was quite fun hopping around on crutches, but Selda was rather scared for me. We bought bus passes for the week and enjoyed riding around the towns. Sometimes we bought hot dinners at the local supermarket just before catching the free ride back to the hotel and enjoyed the meal in our lovely spacious apartment. Selda happily prepared all our other meals.

One day we went on a coach trip to another seaside resort. As we lay on the beach a kind man came to me and said, "I have been watching you on your crutches, if you cover your leg in the hot sand where the sea water is coming up, you will no longer need those crutches." I did as he advised but by then, I could only spend a short time in the sand because our coach was already waiting to take us back. However, the hot sand remedy did help. I found myself walking with just one crutch and at times I carried it.

My healing continued and the ankle was no longer painful but rather stiff. My surgeon was pleased with my progress and booked me in for physiotherapy. Physiotherapy and long walks helped but a couple years later, in 2010, I was advised by another surgeon to have a second operation to get rid of the stiffness. I enquired about the surgeon who did my operation and was informed that he was unwell and had returned to the country of his birth. I agreed to having the second operation, but on the day, even though I was dressed ready for theatre, I had doubts about the surgeon. When he spoke to me, he did not sound too well. I was told that he had just returned to work from burying his mother. The voice inside kept saying, *get up, get dressed and go home.* After hearing it for a few times, I made up my mind.

When the surgeon came and asked, "Are you ready?"

I answered, "No, I am not going through with it."

He seemed relieved and said, "That's Ok, I have a busy morning." He offered to see me again in a few months at his clinic.

Fitz, who was seated beside me, said, "I was so worried. I am glad you called it off – something did not feel right."

On our way home, I said to Fitz, "I need a holiday to forget about this worry." He turned his head to look at me, tenderly and gently he replied, "If that's what you want, go for it."

I stopped at the home of my dear friend, Shelley, and Fitz popped into church. Shelley always had an open ear ready to hear my troubles and a warm heart to comfort. Standing in the doorway I began to explain what happened. Shelley interrupted saying, "Come in my child, sit down, I'll make you breakfast while you tell me all about it. I know you're hungry, you've been on a twenty-four hour fast." Shelley quickly went into the kitchen while I continued talking, and in no time, she came out with a full English breakfast.

Wow, it was tasty, and I certainly felt better. Shelley hugged me close and prayed for me. I thanked her and said, "I am going now to ring my family in New York to see if they can accommodate me. If yes, I shall book a holiday."

NEW YORK - ANDY'S 50th

Andy was overjoyed to hear that I would be coming as he wanted me to be there for his 50th birthday, but because of my operation I had to decline. The cancelled operation made it possible for me to be there for his birthday. Patsy said, "Mum you have been to New York a number of times, but you have not seen that much, and you have never had a night out, so I am coming with you for four days to take you around." I was over the moon! Patsy booked us a sleep only accommodation on Broadway in Manhattan. Shops and restaurants were everywhere, local transport and night life were just walking distance. Our first visit was to Brooklyn to see Andy and his family, we had a great reunion. He drove us to Manhattan Bridge, parked up and together we went for an enjoyable walk before taking Patsy and me back to our hotel.

Next day we went to the beautiful Staten Island and Patsy was in her element visiting museums. I also liked it but it became hard on my troublesome ankle and aching feet, even though I had my walking stick. On another day, we walked through some famous streets, popped in and out of stores, then took the train to Long Island and had a good look around. We also went to the Bronx to the Yankee Stadium. We were just in time for the start of a baseball match and of course Patsy could not resist, I did other things but we both had fun.

On our last day at the hotel we went on separate horse drawn carts through Central Park. It was great. We ended the day at a club on

Broadway with dinner, followed by a live show called 'Fella' and finished with some dancing. What a day! It was fantastic. Thanks to Patsy's thoughtfulness and generosity towards our brilliant four days stay.

We left the hotel in separate taxis. I headed to Queens for a week with my in-laws, Elvin and Florin. As I entered the cab, Patsy stood beside her cab and shouted to the driver, "Take care of her, she's my mum!" I was in fits of laughter for neither of us knew the driver. I watched as she got into her taxi to take her to the airport.

Elvin and Florin warmly welcomed me and treated me kindly, each day my health improved. From there I spent two nights with Franado and his lovely wife. Franado took me to meet his son and family in Connecticut. His wife shares my birthday. We had a lot in common and much to chat about over the lovely lunch she prepared for us. When we returned home, I briefly met Franado's youngest daughter and her daughter. The following day I went with Franado and his wife to Manhattan, to visit the eldest daughter in her condominium. They took me for a meal and later I watched with Franado a video of the funeral of one of his younger brothers. It was a joy to meet my cousins, it was my first time seeing his grandchildren and I had not seen his daughters since they were little girls.

From there I moved to be with Andy and his wife Gloria in Brooklyn. Gloria was only home at the weekends, I looked forward to her home coming. We did lots of shopping together and Andy took us out to dinner. I made Andy's birthday cake the day before his birthday when I was home alone, but the scorching heat melted the icing, so I had to redo it on the day. It looked and tasted great.

Andy enjoyed his birthday, and it was also his wedding anniversary. Some of my in-laws came from Queens and some cousins, whom I had never met, were present. We all had a good time.

During my stay, Andy took me to visit some family and friends who lived on the other side of Brooklyn. One Saturday he took me to a Seventh Day Adventist Church. He really wanted me to meet his friend who was the pastor, but he did not stay for the service. The pastor had his eyes on me as he preached which made me feel a little uncomfortable, but he soon welcomed me as did the members which I appreciated.

After the service, the pastor came directly to me and said that I looked just like someone he knew, who had passed a long time ago. He told me her name. "She was my mother." I said. He was shocked and called his congregation together and told them that he was my mum's neighbour back in St Vincent. They greeted me warmly and gave me a big lunch and a takeaway bag. I made my own way home safely by bus. Andy was happy to hear that his friend recognised my face as that of my mother's and had treated me well. A couple years after my return to London, Andy rang me saying that the pastor died. It was sad because he was young and had so much to live for.

One day, while home alone at Andy's, I went for a long walk to Kings Plaza. On the way, I popped into a restaurant for a snack. As I walked in a lady called me to sit with her. She seemed to be a nice person, so I accepted. She advised me on the best lunch for a good price. I had a pleasant time in her company. When we parted, she pointed me in the right direction to the Plaza.

When I got there, I sat in a massage chair. I was surprised to hear someone saying, "Hello aunty Sheva." I looked to my left in the direction of the voice and beheld one of my nieces, with her son walking towards me. It was incredible! We chatted for a short while and then they went.

Another surprise! Up came an old friend, who kindly drove me home after I window shopped. We arranged to meet again another day. When we met, we went for a meal, then he drove me to see Prince's daughter Andrea.

Andrea introduced us to her fiancé and announced her wedding for the summer. She said, "Aunty, I need you to come back and do my wedding blessing." I was delighted and agreed. I knew my family would have wanted me to assist Andrea.

Before returning home all stiffness in my ankle was gone. God had been good to me; I believe it was his will for me to reject the operation. My tongue is not good enough to praise Him, yet I know He accepts my feeble praises. I felt no sadness when leaving the family in New York as I had faith that I would soon return. Andy was also happy to know that I would not be away from him for long.

When I arrived home, everyone was pleased to see how well I had recuperated from the trauma with my ankle. They were also happy to hear that Andrea was getting married and agreed that I should go back for her wedding.

CHAPTER 38

2010 ESTATE REGENERATION PLANS

I eagerly entered the church to meet with my colleagues and to resume my duty in the Healing Café. I was shocked to hear the disturbing news from Cecilia, my Vicars wife, about the future of the Carpenters estate, my home for over forty years. Our beautiful homes that we moved into when they were first built were to be demolished by the local council and regenerated to accommodate more people. With Cecilia's expert help and advice, I drew up petitions for restoration in opposition to regeneration and hung posters in protest around the estate. I then knocked on the doors of the residents for their views and signature if they agreed to my petition. Almost everyone signed the petition, including family and church members. Some council tenants refrained from signing as the deal they were offered was too good for them to turn down. Some tenants were not happy with what they were given and regretted that they moved. Many homeowners protested that to their dying day they wouldn't relocate. Some did indeed protest to their dying day.

Fitz was a member of the Tenants Management Organisation for the estate. I joined the Steering group to voice my opinions and to be a voice for others. For many years I attended council meetings, which mostly consisted of talking and listening to the local Mayor who always refused to listen to our views. In the last meeting, held at the Stratford Town Hall, the Mayor walked out on us in anger saying that he had too good a deal on the estate to back out. I took the case along with a few of the residents to speak with the London Mayor. Unfortunately he told us, "I sympathise with you, but you have to go back and listen to your local Mayor," which led us back to Stratford.

With the help of my church, family and friends, I organised a service on the estate. We prayed regularly in church, did prayer walks and sang carols during the Christmas season on the estate. In 2018 the local Mayor with whom we were battling was deselected. There was much rejoicing among many including me. Our new Mayor seemed to want the best for us; I am watching, praying and hoping that she does not change.

CHAPTER 39

ANDREA'S WEDDING

Back to 2010, once again Andy met me at John F. Kennedy airport, and he was expecting me to stay with him. Andrea came to Andy's home and was adamant, "Aunty, you are here for me so you will be staying with me." Of course she was right, I was there because of her wedding.

Her two little girls were my delight, they reminded me of my granddaughters. I loved the creative things they made me and their prayers each night were quite touching. They abandoned their beds and slept with me. We went to parks, interesting riverside walks, and shopping. When Andrea's parents arrived for her wedding, we all visited their families. After our initial greeting and pleasant conversations we tucked into a delicious big meal. The day before the wedding we went to view the venue, *wow!* was our impression. Andrea and her bridesmaids looked beautiful on the day. Everything was well organised. I performed the wedding blessing to the best of my ability. Everyone enjoyed the day. They were, and still are, a lovely gentle couple.

TENERIFE WITH SHELLEY

In the same year of 2010 myself and Fitz spent our birthdays in Tenerife on our timeshare exchange, in the company of our friend Shelley and her daughter. We stayed in Adeje and travelled around on the local buses using day passes to Santa Cruz, Los Cristianos, and San Miguel. It was nice being able to show our friends some of the places we had visited before. We were pleasantly surprised to meet again with one of the staff at the Christian centre in Los Cristianos.

I discovered that a member of the staff there was the daughter of a couple from the *Through Faith Missions Team*. They often stayed with Fitz and me during the years of their mission in Stratford. I did not get to meet their daughter in Tenerife as she was usually away on holiday. Some years later her dear dad, my friend, passed. We got to know each other at his funeral, and I had hoped to meet with her on my next trip to Tenerife. I had no idea that this trip to Tenerife would be the last of my exchange holidays.

PORTUGAL WITH LEE

March 2011, Fitz and I returned to Portugal along with my grandson, Lee, and his girlfriend. We were on a two-week break, the first week we all stayed together in our allocated apartment. The second was a bonus week. Fitz and I were given a luxury apartment in a hotel nearby; it was rather grand in comparison to ours. Each morning there was a water aerobics class in the basement, and I made sure not to miss any. We tried hard to stay clear of the management team as they were always aiming to get us to upgrade our apartment, and we had no intention of spending any more on an upgrade. This time we were in when they knocked on our door. We explained that our grandson was with us and that he might be interested, so they made an appointment for us all to meet. After listening to their proposal, we declined their offer. As a matter of fact my grandson explained to them, that there were better holiday deals on the market than what we had with them. That was the last year we paid our maintenance and exchange fees to the timeshare and holiday exchange companies, even though the timeshare kept sending us threatening letters, which we ignored. Fitz was content to give up the timeshare as he became tired and no longer enjoyed trips away.

2011 DALAMAN TURKEY

I have mentioned before, but I am saying it again. It is wonderful to have a large, loving and caring family.

In the year 2011, my darling niece, Alice, invited me to Dalaman, Turkey. We stayed in Marmaris, a nice friendly holiday resort, not too far from the sea. The food was amazing. There was a grand buffet three times a day, with snacks in between and free drinks, brought to us at the large pool side. Evening entertainment was also grand. A couple of times we went for late walks and a meal along the sea front. My highlight was our trip to Ephesus where we visited The Library, the Church of the Virgin Mary and other ancient ruins. I was thrilled to be walking where the Apostle Paul walked. Thanks to Alice for not thinking me too old to be her travelling companion.

I now looked forward to holidays at least once a year. Between these, I always had something to celebrate. If not with immediate family, it was with my wider family or church family.

ST VINCENT WITH PATSY

In 2012, I began to feel a longing for St Vincent. Perhaps it was because my brother, Victor, kept asking me to come down and spend some time with him in his lovely home. Patsy was long overdue to see the island and to meet with relatives. She was meant to accompany me on one of my earlier trips but changed her mind with the passing of her driving test and the excitement of her brand new first car. I was so pleased for her. She readily joined me on this trip in the month of March. Victor picked us up from the airport and we stayed with him for the duration of our time. I spent five weeks, Patsy spent two.

My niece, Esther, flew from Canada to be with us. She stayed with her bother, Prince, and his family but met with us daily at Victor's. Together we visited many relatives and went to places I had never heard of. Prince did most of the driving as he knew the island well. We went to Owia and stopped for a light lunch before descending the steps to Salt Pond. Another day, Prince's son, Dan, accompanied us to Mount La Soufriere to see the Crater Lake, an active stratovolcano. We approached La Soufriere from George Town on the Windward; it took us three hours to get to the top of the mountain and two to return. The path was rough, steep, rugged and dangerous. Dan took my hand whenever I struggled.

On the way up, we met with a Rastafarian guy going to tend his plantation. He kindly cut me a walking stick and took his time walking with us. When we almost got to the top, he quickly went his way that we suddenly realised he was no longer with us. We finally reached the top. I crawled on my hands and knees as the air was dense and scary. I took one look down into the crater and had no desire to hang around. The downhill was even more dangerous than the going up. When we got back to George Town, Dan took us for a meal in a restaurant that he had booked in advance as a surprise. After we had eaten, we went to Black Rock Tunnel where the slaves took sugar to the ships which sailed to Britain. I was too worn out to fully enjoy.

Another day we went to the Vermont nature trail on the Leeward, then later to the Botanic Gardens in Montrose and to Fort Charlotte, where we had a spectacular view of a good part of the island. It is also known as View Fort. Before Patsy left, Gaylene and Ian spent some time with us at Victor's; it was a joy to have them with us. We also met with one of Patsy's half-brothers and had a nice walk with him. On the day that Patsy left, everyone, including Christa and her family who were also on holiday, went to the airport to see her off. It was there that we met with one of Patsy's half-sisters.

During my remaining weeks I continued to visit relatives. I also went with a friend on a one-day island hopping boat cruise. Another great, unforgettable holiday.

2012 PRINCE VISITED

I am repeating myself by saying that by having a large family circle, there are very few dull times in my life. When Prince called saying, "Hi Sheva, I would like to visit."

I answered, "Yes sure, come on up! We would love to have you stay with us."

Prince has never called me Aunt, simply because we grew up together and we are not too far apart in age.

In one of my earlier chapters, I mentioned that when Reverend Daley and his family went on sabbatical to the Caribbean, they stayed a week in St Vincent with Prince and his family. I thought it would be nice for

Prince to meet with the Daley's, so I rang and informed them that Prince was about to visit the UK.

"That's fantastic! You must come up! We shall be expecting you, just let us know when, and I will meet you at the station," said Daley eagerly.

"Thank you, I will." I responded.

Prince made his own way from the airport to my house. It was good that we were able to be together again after such a short time. 2012 was the year of the Olympics in London, a great year for Prince to visit, as there was a lot for him to see and it was so close to my home.

When I explained to Prince that I had plans for us to visit Daley and his wife, Fiona, in Bradford-Upon-Avon he was pleased. We bought our return tickets and informed Daley of the date and time we would be with them. Prince also rang my nieces who were working and studying in Bristol, and we arranged to meet with them there that same week. Unfortunately, we missed our train to Bradford-Upon-Avon and had to purchase fresh tickets, only to note that the ticket inspector did not even concern himself about the time of travel, we thought, what a waste of money!

When we got to Bradford-Upon-Avon, Daley was already at the station to receive us. It was such an exciting moment. I was expecting to see Fiona at the wheel as always, to see Daley driving was a nice surprise.

"How long have you been driving?"

I can't remember if he answered that question, but I know he said, "Well, living in these parts you need to drive."

Daley was an excellent driver, and it was good that he picked us up because it worked well for Fiona; it gave her the extra time to prepare for us. She had a meal waiting just ready to be brought to the nicely laid table. I have always enjoyed Fiona's cooking but this one topped them all. It was absolutely delicious.

After lunch we went for a walk along the river and watched the boats. We also visited the church that they attend. When we told them that we were off to Bristol in a couple days, they looked at me in surprise. "You ought to have stayed with us and go from here! It would have been much better for you as it is not far away," Daley exclaimed, and Fiona agreed.

"That's so kind of you, it would have been nice, but we did not think about it." I replied. " And we cannot change plans because we are going in the company of a dear church friend, who once lived there and promised to show us around."

I went on to explain that my friend had some business in Bristol to take care of. Luckily for us she sorted out our tickets and helped us to get the best deal. Daley and Fiona understood. Daley drove us back to the station; we had a great day.

COACH TO BRISTOL

The following week Prince and I made our way by coach from Victoria to Bristol with my church friend, who knew the area well, and took us to where we had arranged to meet with my nieces. It was good to see them, they had both stayed with me at different times whilst visiting from St Vincent. The eldest stayed in 2003 and the other came with her friend in 2005. We had an interesting walk along the bridge across the River Avon, also through the parks and nature attractions, before having a late lunch in a smart restaurant. My niece insisted on paying. After eating we said good-bye and went in opposite directions. We got to the station just in time to catch our coach back to London. I slept most of the way. My friend kindly covered me with my coat for comfort. When we got off at Victoria station, I realised my phone was missing - it must have fallen out of my coat pocket. I rushed back and searched the coach, but it was nowhere to be seen. I had no options but to purchase another.

Prince is such a likable chap, he got on well with all my friends. When I told my friend, Sandra, that he was in the country, she offered to take him to the rehearsal for the opening ceremony of the 2012 Olympics. Her and her daughter, were very much involved in helping out. I could not go as I was on duty at church. Prince reported that the ceremony was very enjoyable. The following week Sandra brought us free tickets to the show called, 'The Harder They Come.' We had some good laughs. Prince and Sandra got on well, he spoke very highly of her. When he left, everyone missed him. My home did not feel quite the same without him.

During the time of the Olympics our church organised many different activities held in the yard, lots of people turned up daily. Each day the yard buzzed with fun and everyone who joined us had a wonderful time. Sadly, one evening at closing time Fitz accidently injured his back while putting instruments away. He ought to have waited for help, but knowing him, I guess he just wanted to get it done. From that day he was never the same and found it difficult to get to work. Sometimes he went but was often late. Fitz was not one for giving up, he always believed that his pain would go away and bravely said, "Tomorrow I will be better." Eventually in 2013 his job had to be given to another. Fitz spent more time in bed trying to recuperate. He had many hospital appointments, which he endeavoured to keep, and he was determined to continue cooking and doing the things he enjoyed. When Prince rang to say that he was returning with his wife Becky, for a couple weeks, we were both happy to have them. Actually I was overjoyed, it was nice having visitors.

Prince now knew his way around London, so he took Becky out daily, sightseeing and visiting relatives. I saw little of them. It was good that Prince was able to meet with Sandra and her daughter again and introduce them to Becky.

How quickly the time went, all too soon Prince and Becky were gone. Nevertheless, I had plans to visit them a few months hence.

MEMOIRS OF A SMALL ISLAND GIRL

MAY 2013 BARBADOS AND ST VINCENT

Glenda was determined to celebrate her fiftieth birthday in Barbados in the company of immediate family and a couple of her children's close friends. Fitz was the only family member who could not be persuaded to join us, no matter how hard we tried to convince him that he would be fine with all of us around. He insisted, "You lot go ahead without me." He was an independent man, but while we were away, family and friends still kept an eye out for him, and I rang him daily.

This was the first time that I was on holiday with all my daughters, their husbands and my grandchildren. I shared an apartment with Glenda and Stacy as we were the only three single ladies in the family. Patsy, her partner and her son also had apartments in the same hotel as well as some others in our party. Vilna and her family stayed in a fabulous resort about three miles away. Tracy and her husband also stayed in another lovely resort a distance away.

We visited each other and enjoyed the different pools and beaches. Some days I took a slow walk to the beach and spent time chatting with the people I met and joined them for a swim. When the sea was calm, I walked for miles to where there was land. From there I saw my hotel, but I had to get back quickly before the turning of the tide. When we were in the pool at our hotel, Lee took pleasure in lifting me high and carrying me towards the deep end to hear me scream.

The group regularly met for food, fun, outings and night life. One day we took a taxi to Mount Hillaby the highest point on the island. The view was spectacular. The Friday nights we went to Oistins, for the famous fish fry market, ate and danced in the open air to fantastic music. Another day we visited Sam Lords Castle, an amazing place. Thank God I was fit for church on the Sunday mornings, and that it was just a short walk from my hotel. I was warmly welcomed into the church and the service was uplifting, much the same as my church at home. On leaving, to my surprise, I was given a gift which was very unusual.

On the second Sunday after finishing at the Anglican Church, I went with Stacy and her friends to another church, a branch of the one she attends in London. They treated us as if they had always known us, I thought *how wonderful!* We celebrated Glenda's birthday in our apartment. It was cramped but we enjoyed every moment, and Glenda was happy. At the end of the two weeks stay everyone but me returned to London.

STAYING WITH PRINCE IN ST VINCENT

I flew to St Vincent for a further two weeks with Prince and his family as we had planned. They looked after me well. On their wedding anniversary I was invited to join the family for a celebration meal at the newly built Buccament Bay holiday resort. It was nice to see how well the place was built.

On one of the days we had a splendid barbeque beach party. Many of their friends turned up. Another day we took the ferry to Bequia, where a friend of theirs drove us around the pretty little island. We stopped for a meal at the restaurant of another friend and while waiting for the ferry, we passed at another friend who kept turtles. Some were huge - they were all gorgeous.

Another day we drove to see the work in progress at the Arnos Vale airport sight, which is now in operation. I had a brilliant day and another wonderful holiday.

PJ'S DEATH

I returned to London feeling exuberant. When I arrived at my home it was unusual to see my daughters and their other halves waiting for me. I happily began greeting each one not realising that something was wrong until one said, "Mum, sit down."

"Sit down? I don't want to sit down!" I protested. "It's good to see you all. Is Dad ok?"

"Dad's fine! It's your brother."

"Brother? Which brother?"

"How many have you got?" someone asked.

"Three," I replied.

"Let's get to the point," said another.

The next few words I heard was "Mum, Uncle PJ is dead."

"No! No! it can't be, I left him good."

"Sorry mum, but he's gone. He did not suffer - he was getting ready to go for his exercise. He passed while putting on his trousers."

I bawled like a cow. Someone handed me a sweet drink. After drinking it, I calmed down and said, "I want to see him." Patsy took me to his house. Of course he was not there, but it felt better to be there with his wife and children. As soon as we were given consent to visit him at the funeral home we went. He looked peaceful; I knew that he was safe in the arms of Jesus.

5th July 2013 was the date of the funeral. It was large and well organised by his children. His eldest daughter, her children and grandchildren flew in from Canada in good time. All my siblings from near and far attended. Only Harran was unable to make it. Death is sad but having a large family to support is comforting. I fought back the tears as I read the eulogy. Dingy, his son, and his grandchildren wept when presenting their tributes. The final tribute was the song 'Help' sung by his daughter-in-law. When they lowered his body in the ground, I truly wished it were me and not him. I miss PJ so much, he always made me feel special. The lovely things he said to me and to others about me were sometimes embarrassing. My memories of him are beautiful. Sweet sleep my darling brother until we meet again.

SORROWS KEPT AWAY

I thanked God for the events that were forthcoming. As I thought of the joys, the sorrows were kept away. I had already booked a trip to Egypt for my 70th birthday, a one-week cruise down the Nile and one week stay in the company of my daughter, Glenda, her children Stacy and Hanson, and also my niece Pearl and her daughter, Alice. And more excitement was in store for the following month of November - the wedding of another niece, Pearl's sister, Sherlene, in St Lucia.

2013 MY 70TH BIRTHDAY TRIP TO EGYPT

Visiting Egypt was my dream from the year I went to Israel, but weeks before my travel one of my friends warned, "Be prepared, you will get sick." She informed me that she got sick and that everyone gets sick, and that it might help if I eat hot food only. I worried for a while, but it did not deter me. We landed at Sharm El Sheikh airport and from the moment we entered the ship we started being careful. Everything was beautiful, the buffet was inviting. We stuck to hot foods for a while and we were ok, until temptation from the dessert section got the better of us. We gave in and enjoyed but one by one we began to feel ill. Pearl had it really bad, yet we tried not to let the sickness confine us to the ship.

Throughout our seven days we braved the excursions on land by coach and visited the magnificent Valley of the Kings. Some of us went to the Pyramids in greater Cairo to the great wonders of the ancient world. There, we rode on camels along the desert. We also went through the Aswan Dam on a small boat, waved to natives who were doing their washing and stopped at a little village where we purchased tiny handmade souvenirs. Finally, we visited Cairo by night. Each night on the ship there was joyful entertainment. On the night of my birthday my family sang to me and showered me with love, and others on the ship joined, which was great. The last night was the best. Everyone wore something Egyptian and danced the night away. We were not aware that we were being judged as we danced, and to my surprise, I won first prize! Although, I was called to do another dance before receiving my bottle of champagne.

At the end of our cruise Glenda, Stacy and Hanson returned to London while Pearl, Alice and I went to Hurghada by the Red Sea for a week stay. The resort was fabulous, it had everything we needed, and the food was good. Alice and I recovered from our sickly feelings, but Pearl was still a bit rough. When she was up to it, we explored the compound. I bought some nice beach wear. While they were still shopping, I went to the sauna and finished with a dip in the cold pool. I was the only one there; that was the biggest mistake. As I entered the pool, I went dizzy and could not see. I struggled to the side rail. Luckily, a young man happened to be walking by. I waved and shouted, "Help! Help!"

"What's wrong?" he asked.

"I am dizzy. Please take my hand."

He did and helped me up the step from the pool. By then the worst of my dizziness had passed. He went for his manager, who came with a chair for me to sit then he massaged my head, I soon felt better. I thanked them both and went to find Pearl and Alice. I did not have to look far because they were on the way to meet me. When I explained to them what happened to me, I don't think they quite understood how scared I was. Well, that was first and last time I went into a cold pool after a sauna.

One day we took a taxi into the old town and shopped around. My nieces could not resist buying the beautiful jewels. Another day we went on a coach trip and visited a famous mosque, a Catholic Church and some other places of interest.

My best experience was in the Red Sea. We walked for miles to the other side of the sea in shallow water. For this reason I went wind surfing without fear and loved it.

It was a great holiday, but because of the sickness that we had to deal with, I have not been back.

SHERLENE'S WEDDING

A couple weeks at home and I was off again to the lovely sunny St Lucia for Sherlene's wedding. Everywhere I walked at Heathrow airport I heard the sound of voices that I recognised. We were all heading in the same direction for the flight to Hewanorra international airport. When I got on the plane it was already like one big family party, even though I did not know some members in the group, we were full of smiles and gentle laughter.

Sherlene was a great organiser. She booked everything well in advance so that almost everyone on the beautiful resort in Rodney Bay were her wedding guests. Prince and Claire, Sherlene's mum, came over from St Vincent. Thelma arrived from Canada, and also Sherlene's aunt from the United States. Patsy, Tracy and their husbands were the only ones from my immediate family that were able to attend the wedding. Tracy and her husband stayed at another resort on the beach, but they came to us daily. I shared an apartment with Pearl, Alice and Vena, Pearl's foster daughter.

Everything was wonderful. The food, the swimming pool, the evening entertainment, and the company. The calm blue Caribbean Sea was within walking distance, so sometimes I went to the beach alone. The police station was nearby. One sergeant advised me to wave as I go by so they could look out for me, which I did.

I was honoured to be asked by Sherlene months in advance to do the wedding blessing and to give a speech at the reception. I prepared well. The wedding ceremony was held on the beach in a marquee on Pigeon Island. Sherlene had organised minibuses to take us around on the day. The marriage was done by a Registrar. We were all in fits of laughter when Sherlene and her groom jumped over the well decorated broomstick. This reminded me of stories I heard from my parents when I was a child; couples jumped over a broomstick to show that they had crossed the threshold from single status into marriage. My prayer and blessing for the couple followed next, it flowed well. I was satisfied and was praised by the couple and others.

From the beach we went to the reception hall. It looked spectacular, very well decorated. Many great speeches were given. I am often reminded by a great niece that she can never forget my amazing speech based on roses. The dance music was so good that not many people sat down. We even had the limbo. I had a go and surprised myself that I made it quite low.

A few days after the wedding we went on a boat trip to the other side of the island. That was a lot of fun. Good swimmers jumped overboard for a swim, not me. I made sure the boat stopped and went into the sea only after others tested the depth of the water.

One day myself, Pearl, Alice and Vena went to the market in Castries. I bought myself a beach dress and they bought jewels, then we went exploring. We popped into a church, knelt and prayed. From there, we visited some other historic buildings. On another day most of us went to the lovely Marigot beach, before going to the Sulphur springs where we had a mud bath. We then walked to the lake on the opposite side of the road to wash off the mud and there we experienced the spectacular waterfall.

The night before we left, we all went to a street dance at Gros Islet, where I encountered an unpleasant experience with a determined guy. It was good that a couple from our group came to my rescue. I was glad when the dance ended. The day we left the island, we had a kind taxi driver who chatted with us on the way to the airport. He insisted that we had to eat bread from the best bakers in the world, so he drove us the long way in order to get to the bakery. When we got there, he went in, bought bread for me, said it was a gift, and that my husband would enjoy it. When I got home Fitz was in good form, and he enjoyed the delicious bread while I shared my stories with him.

MORE PASSINGS

One evening in early November 2013 I went to visit Solomon's mum, who was ill in hospital. It was dark as I walked the along the path, unfortunately I tripped on a concrete block and fell. I was there for a few minutes before I was able to get up. When I did, I went to the reception and reported the incidence. I was advised to call an ambulance to take me to the outpatients at the general hospital, but I declined and went on to visit Solomon's mum. She also advised me to go to the hospital, but still I did not. I did not stay long with her, when I got home, I had a hot bath and went to bed. I ached for about six weeks, but I managed. The hospital compensated me for my injury that was caused by the negligence of the work men. I continued to visit Solomon's mum until she passed in January 2014. I attended her lovely funeral along with some of my siblings and my niece Pearl. Strange how things turned out, Solomon's mum was always concerned about her husband who was ill long before her, but he outlived her by one year.

18th November 2014, my dearest sister-in-law Hilda, PJ's wife, went to be with him in heaven. She had been ill for a while. Like Solomon's mum PJ was always concerned about her poor health, but God took him first. No one knows when his or her time on earth will end, it is good to live in the love of God. Hilda did well for one year after PJ passed. She was helped by her immediate family who lived close by but after four months her health deteriorated, and she was gone. Her loving daughter-in-law, myself, and the Vicar of the church that Hilda attended, organised the funeral service. I sorted and printed the hymns that were sung at the graveside. Her sons took care of all the other arrangements.

On the day of her funeral I gave the eulogy. Hilda's children and grandchildren paid tributes and those from Canada were all present. Her body was laid to rest not far from her church, she had a nice reception just the way she would have wanted it.

2014 PATSY AND ME WENT TO IRELAND

God always makes ways to help us fulfil our greatest desires. When I was a child, I was taught some Irish folk songs, which I loved, and sometimes my siblings and I sang them while playing in our garden on moonlit nights. I still sing and listen to the lyrics, especially 'Molly Malone'. For years I pondered with the idea of visiting Dublin, then one day came the thought, *why not go now? Perhaps Patsy might love to join you.* I was spot on. When I asked her, she willingly said, "Yes mum! I would love to go."

We went for a weekend and stayed in a lovely hotel, a fair walk from the town. We walked just once. There was so much to do; first we booked a two-day bus tour and rode around the town a couple of times. I was fascinated whenever we went past the singing statue of Molly Malone. I really wanted to sing along but no one else did, so my heart sang instead. I must have hummed aloud because someone explained to me the meaning of the song. We also went to the Guinness factory for a tour and enjoyed sampling the delicious stout. Patsy wanted to go to the museum, usually a must for her when on holiday, but it was too late - we would have missed the last bus back to the hotel. That night we went back into town on a Ghost Bus tour at Christ Church Cathedral. Some of it was a bit spooky but not enough to scare me. On the last day we went to Croke Park to the sporting arena. Patsy was at her best when we entered the museum. I was surprised at how much there was to see. We had an excellent albeit rainy weekend.

My trips abroad were fewer as Fitz began needing some help. He was given a carer for an hour and a half, one day a week, arranged by the local council and the NHS which we happily paid for. They assisted by fitting a hand rail along the stairs, grips and other aids in the bathroom and toilets, they also put stable legs on his chair so that he was able to sit and rise comfortably, and finally a keylock for carers to get in. But Fitz was not happy for them to just enter, it unnerved him. He preferred to let them in as he was still capable, but I was mostly at home to receive them.

2015 CAPE VERDE WITH TRACY AND MARK

Our children realised that it was essential for me to continue having holiday breaks.

One day when the phone rang, "Hi mum how you doing?" it was Tracy.

"I am fine, and you?"

"Well, I was just wondering if you would like to come to Cape Verde with me and Mark."

My eyes lifted, and my face broadened with the smile. Without hesitation I answered, "Yes please!"

Fitz was happy for me to go. While I was away, our other children and grandchildren paid him daily visits.

We went to Sal. This island and resort where we stayed was unlike others I have visited; the resort had everything we needed and more. We had a three-bedroom villa, with our own pool - although we did not use it. The staff on the resort were friendly, food was excellent, and we had a good choice of restaurants. The sea was just at the bottom of the resort. Some days I walked a couple of miles to where I found a little pool all to myself. I felt quite safe, so there I would lie for about an hour or so.

The first day, Mark came looking for me as they became worried. When he found me, and saw that I was fairly safe, he seemed to relax the next time I went, but they warned me not to stay too long. Mark and Tracy did not need to go on many trips as they regularly visited the island and already knew most places. I went on a trip around the town, then to the salt mines and finished up with an enjoyable float in the Salt Lake. I also went on a shark spotting trip.

There were many sharks, they even came ashore, which caused me to feel uneasy the next time I went alone to my favourite spot on the resort away from anyone. Although I was informed that they did not come to the resort area, I was still cautious.

Another day Tracy and I went by public transport into the town and had a good walk around. We were drawn to a pretty little girl walking along the street in her beautiful island costume. She carried on her head a lovely little basket, nicely arranged with craft items made by her mum. Her mum kindly allowed me to video her. I still watch this video and smile. I did not want these two weeks to end. I will always be grateful to my daughter and son-in-law for inviting me, and I promised myself to visit the island again. On my arrival back to London I stayed the night with Tracy and Mark. The next morning I took the train home but left my luggage with them. Tracy brought them to me a week later all nice and clean.

It was good to be back with Fitz, and to see that he had been well cared for. He had always been a strong man, never had any serious illness and never needed hospitalisation. He tried to hold on to his independence for as long as was possible. He was not supposed to go out alone but once, while I was having a bath, he took his walking frame and went to the doctor. It was a stormy day, and the wind got the better of him. Thank God someone saw what was happening and offered to help him home. I went out to find Fitz, and luckily, I walked the same road that they were returning on and so met with them.

Another time, I was dressed and about to go to the funeral of Fitz's sister-in-law, when out of the blue he said, "I am off to the hospital." I called a cab to take him there and told him to get the receptionist to call another to bring him back. My children and I returned as soon as we could. He was home and ok, bless the Lord.

CHAPTER 40

ALZHEIMER'S

In 2015, I renovated our house to make it easier for Fitz to get around. I upgraded one bedroom with an ensuite shower room and two years later, I bought a suitable bed to help meet Fitz's needs. Alzheimer's is an awful disease, which Fitz found hard to accept, and I knew very little about. It was difficult to understand how such an intelligent and strong man could be his perfect self and become someone else within minutes. Even though he was not as bad as some people I had seen with dementia, watching him slowly degenerate was sad and depressing. I will be forever grateful to Alzheimer's Society and the carers' group that I was advised to join. Listening to the concerns of others who cared for Alzheimer's sufferers educated me and helped me to accept what I could not change.

The leaders of the carers' group invited the group to join various mind activity classes. They took us on outings to museums, river boat trips, lunches and visits to the seaside. They also engaged us in jewellery making, films and writing stories. These helped to relieve the stress we were under. I tried to get Fitz to join me, but he objected. He was taken to different group sessions for stimulation, and when he came home, he would happily show me the dance moves he did. Nevertheless, he was always reluctant to go and stopped after about one year. He did not like to be with people who were frail and suffered from dementia, he felt sorry for them and wished he could help. So he ended up staying home every day. God bless our thoughtful friends from church who regularly phoned to see how we were, especially those who sometimes brought a home cooked meal and fruits to cheer our hearts. One Ghanaian sister, in particular, visited regularly bearing gifts. On nice days she walked him into our garden and sat with him, giving me the opportunity to get out without worry. And while she was there, she watered my plants. Such a wonderful person!

During this time, I received exciting news of the birth of my first great grandchild. He's named Tommy, born in New York to Keisha, the daughter of Andy, my first son. I had only seen Keisha twice; when she was ten, and again when she was twenty. I became anxious to visit them. After one year I was able to go. My loving family willingly covered Fitz's care.

2ND MAY 2016 NEW YORK TO SEE TOMMY

Andy collected me from Kennedy airport. Our meeting brought many smiles and lots of catching up. When Andy and I were not chatting, he was studying, working or sleeping. It was also great to be with Gaylene who now lived with her parents, having received her right to stay in New York, although she was not one for chatting. On my second day, Keisha came with Tommy. That was such an exciting moment, too much for words. When Gloria, Andy's wife, came home at weekends, we went everywhere together. Gaylene attended college, but when she was free, she went out with me. One afternoon we went to Kings Plaza to window shop and ended our day with a tasty meal.

Whenever I decided to go out alone, Andy became worried. He wrote down every detail of how I would get from 'A' to 'B', and he would keep ringing to make sure that I was on the right track. Once when I told him that I was not going to take the bus, because it had changed its route just for that day, he said, "Mummy stay there, don't move, I am coming." Within ten minutes he was on the spot. He then explained that where I was going to change transport is a dangerous area. He took me to a subway that he felt was safer. I was feeling more confident each day, and I travelled to Queens, where I spent a week with my in-laws, Elvin and Florin.

On the Sunday morning I joined them in their brilliant church service. Elvin drove me to meet other relatives that Fitz always spoke about. It was good to know them and when I got back, he was happy to hear all the good news about them. Florin insisted on treating me to dinner at Red Lobster. A few of us went and I certainly enjoyed it. She also took me shopping and refused to let me spend. Such a generous lady, God bless her.

During my week with them, cousin Franado came and drove me to meet his wife at their lovely new home in the Bronx. We had a good time together catching up while feasting on the tasty lunch prepared by his wife.

At the end of that beautiful day, I was driven back to Queens for my last night with Elvin and Florin. The following day Andy called me to meet him at a subway station. I had no trouble finding it. Andy's plan was to collect a friend and drive us to Coney Island for a buffet dinner. The food was good, but I found myself silent in the company of his friend.

Now back in Brooklyn I went to see my great-niece, Andrea and her sweet little family. I did not think the girls would remember me, so I asked, "Do you remember me?"

"How can we forget you?" The eldest one replied.

I was then welcomed with generous hugs and kisses. They made my day - sweet little angels.

When Andy was free, he took me to visit relatives. He only trusted me to go alone, if he believed the area was safe, and never without his written directions. One day I went to visit a dear friend, Bartholomew, the son of one of the ladies from my home Bible study group. I got to know him first when he was visiting his sick mother and when he came again for her funeral. He drove me into Manhattan, where he worked, and dropped me off at the square by Central Park. I had the day to look around interesting places, like Trump Tower and the University where Andy worked as a lecturer. I also stood and watched actors performing along some streets. When I had had enough of walking, I sat in the park and listened to live bands. At lunch time, Bartholomew came to find me and took me to lunch. After lunch I was on my own again window shopping until Bartholomew rang saying he was ready to leave. I waited where he dropped me off, and he took me to see his home and his church. They were just next door to each other. We had a drink before he drove me back to Andy's. I had an interesting day thanks to Bartholomew; it was kind of him.

A couple days before I was due to return to London, Andy began to show jealousy and discontent for not growing up with me and his siblings. He seemed to think that I did not love him. I tried to explain the reason why he did not grow up with me, but I could not get a word in edgeways. His abusive words had me in tears, that I immediately wanted to leave the home. Gloria tried, without success, to make him stop. I called Patsy in London to listen to Andy's bitter words and his tone of voice in the hope that he would stop, but it did not help. I said to him, "I will never come back, and I do not want to see you again, and when I die do not come to my funeral."

Later, I very much regretted my words. When Keisha came, she rebuked him. He looked at her, smiled and stopped - she was the only person he seemed to listen to - but he never left the subject alone for long. I called Bartholomew in the hope of spending my last night away from Andy. Bartholomew drove to the block where Andy lived, and I went out to meet him. We had a chat about the issue, and he helped me to compose myself that I felt better and decided to stick it out at Andy's.

The day that I was leaving was Keisha's birthday. I took her and Gaylene out for a birthday lunch. Andy was sound asleep when we left, but when we got back, he was awake and realised that we went without him. He was not pleased with Keisha, but he said nothing to me, as we no longer conversed. It was time for me to leave for the airport and wondered if I ought to call a taxi, but Andy showed willingness to take me. Nevertheless, I asked Gloria to come with us because Andy was still in a bad mood. He talked nonstop all the way to the airport about his grievances, without allowing me a chance to speak. I was very sad for both of us. Andy knew that I loved him, and I knew he loved me, but regrettably, unforgiveness ruined our chances of making amends at that time.

When I got home, I hurried upstairs to see Fitz. He looked fairly well, and as we embraced, my tension slowly eased. Although he was ill, he listened to my concerns and understood. Some months later I received a card from Andy; he apologised for his bad behaviour. I felt relieved until I read to the end where his last statement wiped away his apology, and, once again, I was in tears. It was even more upsetting when I read his remarks on his Facebook page. We no longer communicated but Gloria and I conversed regularly, and she did her best to keep Andy and me informed about each other. Andy and I always loved to hear that we were both well and he was always in my prayers.

CHURCH DUTY CONTINUED

I continued with my duty in church as Prayer Ministry Trainer and Coordinator. My supervising job ended, and I no longer preached during Sunday services, although I sometimes led the opening. I was responsible for the service once a month on Tuesdays, unless the vicar was away, then I would cover. Concentrating was hard, as one ear was always trained on Fitz's needs, so preparing sermons took longer, and it was my constant aim, with Gods help, to give my best.

Unfortunately, Fitz became prone to falling. Most times he got up with little help. A couple of times I called one of our lovely neighbours, who came almost instantly. I thank God for him, he has a heart of gold.

PEARL AND ME TO GHANA

In August 2017, Pearl invited me to her friend's wedding in Ghana. I gladly accepted and increased Fitz's care to three times a day daily. Social services explained that all carers were entitled to breaks and they would cover the cost of the carer. Although each time I went away, they sent me an enormous, frightening bill. The thing was, sometimes no carer came but they still sent a bill charging for service. Our girls, including our granddaughter Stacy and niece Alice, took turns to be with Fitz, so they knew when no carer came. I had to be constantly fighting Social Services over their wrong invoice each time I got back from a holiday break.

My trip from home to Ghana was most interesting. We had an unexpected overnight stay in Istanbul with no information on what to do. We just sat with all the other passengers and waited. After a few hours, we were given meal tickets and were later led to a bus that drove us miles away to the most amazing resort where the garden was fabulous. We sat in it until dinner. Our room was spectacular. Dinner and breakfast was a large and superb buffet - I could have spent my holiday there. The following morning, we were driven back to the airport. The scenery along the way was breath-taking. We landed safely in Accra and felt at home with the friendliness of the Ghanaians. The first two weeks we stayed at a guest house in St Mary, a short walk to the high road. From there we got the 'chocho', the name given to the local buses, and changed mostly at Central to whatever destination we had planned. We chose to go to the places we thought would be of greater interest to us - Cape Coast, Elmina Castle, Volta, Kumasi, Akosombo, Aubrey Gardens, Kwame Nkrumah Memorial Park and Mausoleum, and some others.

Chochos were always full, and roads were busy. At times, some people assisted us in our attempts to cross the very wide roads. As a matter of fact, some willingly offered to walk with us to where we wanted to go. Accra market is extremely large, so we kept getting lost. One day we went to a store, then the next day we went back, feeling sure we would find it. We never did, although many people tried to help.

The day that we went to Cape Coast, the driver of the chocho rang a taxi to pick us up from where he left us, to take us to Elmina Castle. He told us how much we should pay the taxi driver. He added that if the taxi driver told us to pay more, we should call him, so he gave us his number. When we got to the taxi, he asked for a lot more than the driver of the chocho quoted. We kept the taxi driver waiting while we called the driver of the chocho and relayed how much we were charged. He told me to pass my phone to the taxi driver so that he could speak to him. We did, and instantly the taxi driver reduced the fare. We thanked the chocho driver, and we had hoped to travel with him on the way back to Central but when we arrived at the point of pick up, he was not there. We had no choice but to travel back with another. Days later, he spotted us in Central and came running to find out how we were doing and if we enjoyed Elmina Castle. Pearl and I thought how amazing, where in the world would anyone care so much about a couple of strangers. We both explained how grateful we were to him and that the history and scenes in the Castle had us in tears, and how happy we were that we went there.

At Kumasi we had a lovely walk along the beach, it was packed with children and lined with many brilliant restaurants. A staff in one of the restaurants was so pleased to meet with us, a couple of Caribbeans, that he insisted that our meal was his treat, and he took pictures with us on the beach. Before leaving London, I was told that I would not find a sea within reach of where we would be staying, but hallelujah! we found the sea. Pearl had no intentions of missing anything and I was up for it.

We spent a few days in Akosombo in a hotel by the Volta River, organised by the receptionist at our guest house. As usual we travelled by the chocho. The hotel owner, known as 'Chief', picked us up from where we got off the chocho and took us back at the end of our stay. The hotel grounds were fantastic. We had our meals at the restaurant and bar overlooking the river. While we were there, I called a friend of one of my Ghanaian church sisters who had kindly arranged for him to take us around. He drove us to the beautiful home of my friend's late sister, who I was privileged to meet when she came to London. He also took us to the school where she was headmistress and to the library that she started, to help the children. Sadly, she passed while it was in progress. He then took us to the amazing dam to see the Hydro Electric. From there he took us to all the places of interest before driving us back to our hotel. He was a very lovely guy, wanting to do more for us after he had already done so much.

We returned to our hotel in Accra two days before the wedding, which was held over two days. The first day was traditional and took place at the magnificent family home. The second was at the bride's church in Tesano. Everything was fantastic, and they were a great couple. I was so happy that I accepted the invitation to be a part of such a wonderful family. We checked out of the guest house after the official church wedding and moved into the family home for the remainder of our stay, where we were lovingly taken care of by the family.

One evening a friend of the family, who Pearl knew very well, took us to a dinner and dance mainly to see the night life. We thoroughly enjoyed it. Another day, we went to visit Pearl's elderly Dominican friend and his very ill Ghanaian wife. She got out of bed just to greet us but after the greeting, she returned to bed. She welcomed me into her bedroom, and I prayed with her for a moment - she was most grateful. We were well entertained by their adopted son and carer. Ghanaians are wonderful people. The history of their suffering has not embittered them.

On my return to London and to my church, I became a member of the Ghanaian group there. If in the past, through ignorance, I had doubts that I was an African, even though I had read books and watched films, my visit to Elmina Castle changed every wrong belief I had. The writings on the wall about the history of slavery and the awful way in which they were shipped to the Caribbean, including St Vincent, my homeland, gave me a true sense of awareness about my origins, praise God!

Early 2019, Patsy became curious about my ancestry and did a DNA test. It shows that I am 65.7% African (45.5% Nigerian, 12.8% West African, 3.2% Sierra Leonean and 4.2% North African) . The balance shows 34.3% European (12.5% Iberia, 5.3% Italian, 13.9% East European and 2.6% Baltic). Now I know my heritage, thanks to technology!

CHAPTER 41

FITZ'S FALL

Not long after my return from Ghana, Fitz tripped and fell from the last three stairs in our home. I think I felt it more than he did. I checked him out and he seemed ok but there was a lump on the back of his head, so I called the ambulance. I was shaking and crying so much that he told me to pull myself together and be strong. The ambulance arrived within ten minutes. Because it was night, they advised me to stay at home and said they would keep me informed, which they did. The hospital also updated me. When morning came, I went to him, and he was quite comfortable. Our conversation revealed to me that his memory was better than before. I thought, *how strange it was? Did the blow to his head bring his mind back to normality*? But while in the hospital he caught a cold and after a few days he was transferred to our local hospital. I went to him daily and tended his primary care.

One evening as I was about to shower him, Stacy visited with her friend. He kindly offered to shower him for me, I thanked him but declined. The next day I caught a cold, I ought to have known because whenever Fitz had a cold, I too became ill. Too ill to visit, I spoke to the doctor and care worker on the phone about Fitz's progress, and our children visited daily and kept me informed. Fitz improved well. The social worker called to say he was ready to come home, but I was still unwell. Thankfully, Stacy and her friend brought him home. They settled him in bed and made him tea.

Watching my soul mate suffer and deteriorate in his golden years was painful and stressful, not many people understood. I found it difficult to share my deep feelings with some church members, even when I asked prayer ministers to pray with me. I came to realise that some Christians believe that those who live in the love of Christ should be strong enough to bear and forbear all things. I was careful in choosing who I discussed my troubles with, and often it was with those who had turned to Christ through my inspiration and teaching. They listened and prayed with encouraging words, without judging. The people in my Alzheimer's group were always the best helpers; we shared our problems and learned from each other. Our meetings always ended with smiles and hopes for the better. Still, my doctor referred me to Mind for counselling. The Mind Clinic was close to my church and, being a Christian counsellor, I was embarrassed to be seen by my church family entering the clinic for counselling.

JAMAICA OCTOBER 2017

Pearl invited me to her sister-in-law's wedding in Jamaica. This was fantastic! I always hoped that one day I would return to Jamaica for a holiday. We flew out on the day before Fitz's birthday. Our children did their best for him while he was in hospital. We flew first to Toronto, from there to Montego Bay. At the airport I exchanged what money I needed to spend on the island, having been told that they had the best rate and that I would not lose when I buy back - I was tricked. We took a taxi from the airport to our guest house in St Mary where myself, Pearl, her two daughters, sister Joanne, and some members of the bride's family stayed. Pearl and I shared an apartment.

Two days after arriving, we celebrated my birthday on the 23rd. A young man, whom we got chatting to, organised a boat cruise for my big day. He drove my nieces and me to the docks to get the boat. On our walk to the boat we came to a pool called 'Healing Pool', and we were told "It's a must", so in I went. It was great, but as time was against me, I quickly got out and headed for the boat. We sailed to Dunn's River and got out of the boat for a brisk walk and a quick dip in the sea.

On my return to the boat, I danced to the music that was specially played for me, chosen by my niece. My great niece, Alice helped me off the boat for a deep-sea float. I was really scared, but I was assisted by one of the crew until I got the hang of it, then I wanted to stay longer. At the end of our cruise, the organiser picked us up where he dropped us off. My nieces saw to it that I had a super fun day. When I got back to our apartment my children video called to wish me well, and Fitz sang happy birthday to me. It was a treat to see him, he sounded so well. He never objected to me having breaks, I guess he knew he would have more time with our children he loved it when they were around.

My nieces and I began making our way to different places. A couple of times we walked to a bay nearby, but we were rather disappointed to see that the beach was divided. One half was well kept for paying visitors; the other half was extremely run down, more like a rubbish dump, with many sunken areas where sand was dug out and taken away. That was where we decided to go, because we felt like we fitted in with the less well-off natives.

We were also just a few bus stops from Ocho Rios, so most days we went there to shop, or for the hairdresser, beach, bank or just to look around. Joanna, Pearl's older sister and I went to the beach there and paid an extortionate amount to get in, but it was fantastic as I was able to float alone in the sea without fear.

A few times we travelled from Ocho Rios by bus and taxi to different places. One day we went by taxi to Spanish Town in St Catherine and enjoyed the town centre. Another day we went by bus to New Kingston, we had to change at Half Way Tree, a very busy place. We walked through many streets in New Kingston and were pleased to see that some were named after other Caribbean islands. We then made our way to the famous Devon House where I unexpectedly bumped into a friend, one of the managers from my carers group. We were so excited to see each other we screamed and jumped for joy, drawing everyone's attention. We knew that we were both off to Jamaica but had no intention of meeting up. We ate our tasty ice cream with much joy and laughter.

When we left Devon House, we had no idea which way to turn to get back to Half Way Tree. Upon asking for directions, one very fit and kind elderly lady, who seemed to be about ten years older than me, took my hand and said that she would take us there. She walked so fast that I struggled to keep pace; Pearl and Joanne had no problems. The lady went a good distance out of her way to help us, then pointed us to our bus stop, but refused to accept a little monetary gift. She just told us to be careful as we were not in a safe district. Thank God we had no problems and got home safely.

The wedding was on the Saturday after my birthday. We were all asked to wear white. All the guests arrived at the church in good time but there were some setbacks, because the bride was running late. To speed things up, the bride wore her second outfit to church, a zipped dress, instead of her corseted dress. I thought she looked very nice and seeing everyone in white presented a look of purity. The ceremony was brief to make up the time lost. The reception hall, not too far from the church and on the same compound as our guest house, was well decorated. The bride changed into her first bridal outfit, and she looked fantastic. We had a great evening with no problems getting home, just a stroll around a corner.

The next day the wedding guests were invited to dinner at the home of the bride's daughter. On that day I became well acquainted with all who were present. We had a great night. I thanked God for placing me in the company of lovely people. The family organised a trip to Negril. Many of us went and a few of us walked down some steps to the sea; a couple of brave people dived in from the top. Not long after we got there it rained hard; however we enjoyed the scenery on the way and our meal at the nearest restaurant.

A few days later, I visited the birthplace and mausoleum of the famous Rastafarian reggae star, Bob Marley, in Nine Mile, along with Joanne and Pearl. We went by taxi. It was difficult deciding which taxi to travel with as every driver kept saying, "Don't go with that one! Come with me, I am the best and the cheapest." We were not sure that we chose the best. When we got there, we realised that our driver was not truthful, he had led us to believe that our entry was included in his price. When we asked him why he deceived us, he answered, "I brought you here, you don't have to go anywhere else!" We realised that everyone who offered to take us was just desperate for the job. We had to pay to go up to the birthplace and mausoleum and extra for a guided tour. I did not have enough money on me, luckily Joanne had enough to pay for me. It would have been awful driving all the way there to then miss out on the best.

After our organised tour we were taken to a kitchen, where in the yard all kinds of bush was being boiled on a large coal fire. The brew was sold to treat different ailments. We were given few drops to sample. Although I was a bit nervous, I tasted it. Joanne and I bought a small sleep potion between us. Perhaps sharing it was not a good idea; we drank it before going to bed, but it had no effect on either of us.

The following Sunday morning, Pearl and I went in search of the nearest parish church. We had a good little walk before we found it and we were just in time for the start of the service. The welcome was not as warm as I had hoped. On our way back they all drove past us in their lovely cars. It would have been nice if we were offered a lift to the high road.

The next day Joanne and I took a bus to Port Maria and visited St Mary's Anglican Church, the Civic Centre and all the interesting places. We were unaware that we were watched by a plain clothed police detective. When we got chatting, she said she observed that we were strangers so when she saw that we were entering an unsafe zone, she came to tell us to turn back. We became scared and took the bus back as it was also getting dark.

We were all set for our return to London. All went well until we got to the airport. I bought some alcohol and the store clerk sealed it in what she called the duty-free bag, I thanked her and went on my way. Next, I went to the foreign currency exchange desk where I had exchanged my English pounds on entry. At the time of exchange I was told I would not lose when I changed back. I could not believe the low rate I was given when I changed the Jamaican money back to pounds. When I complained I was given a bit more which was no way near correct and I was very displeased with their dishonesty. Worst of all, when my nieces exchanged their money in Ocho Rios, they got a much better rate than I did at the airport. When we got to Toronto, I could not take the alcohol through because the staff on the desk said that it was packed in the wrong bag. He told me that the person who packed it in Jamaica benefited from my rights of duty free. He kindly instructed me to return to the check-in desk and put my alcohol in my checked-in luggage. When I arrived home, Fitz and I were both happy to see each other and he looked well. I thanked God and my family who cared for him in my absence.

FITZ'S SECOND FALL

A couple weeks after my return from Jamaica, Fitz met with a terrible incident. His leg gave out while going up the stairs in the small hours of the morning. He was just two steps from the top when he called to me. I tried to hold him, but it was impossible. He slew on his stomach to the bottom. As with the first fall, I was in tears. He was fully conscious and said that he was ok and just needed a hand to get up. I could not pick him up, so I called the ambulance. Thank God they came quickly, checked him out and confirmed that he was ok, but to be on the safe side they took him to the hospital.

When I went to see him next day, he was in a caged bed and wearing a brace. An X-ray showed that his neck was fractured. His mental health was good, and after a couple of weeks he was out of the brace and well improved. He was transferred to another hospital for rehabilitation. Sadly the care there was not as good as I had hoped, and he slowly became weaker and sad. I began to think of ways to make our home more comfortable for his return. I thought of moving his bed into our front room on the ground floor and installing a shower. However, I was advised by the majority of the group, consisting of carers and family members speaking on both our behalf, that returning home was not a good decision because of Fitz's determination to try to help himself; he would be in constant danger of falling.

We brought Fitz home for Christmas. It was so nice to have him, and with fifteen of us around he was well cared for. He wished that he did not have to go back, and we were all sad to see him go. After a couple months in rehab, we managed to locate a very nice care home for him where he felt at peace and happy. Sometimes he believed he was at home because of the regular visits from loving family and friends. One day, he asked me if I had rented out our other house, he even mentioned the address. Fitz was very ill but at times we conversed fairly well. A couple weeks before he became low, I asked him if he still loved me; he paused for a moment then said, "I will always love you." Most times when I was leaving, he asked, "Where are you going in the dark?" so I began to quietly slip away when I thought he was sleeping, only to hear, "I know you are creeping out". And when I entered silently, he would say, "Sheva, I know you are there." I had to laugh.

Although life had become very trying, God always provided opportunities that lifted my spirit. Nellie and Kelly's end of term school concerts always warmed my heart as did their amazing yearly theatre shows. That year, after watching a very enjoyable performance by Kelly and other pupils at her school concert, I went directly to visit Fitz. While on the way I walked pass a house and saw a chap in the front garden working hard at carpentry. I was impressed and called out, "Hi! What are you making?"

"Come in and have a look," he invited.

I was in a rush to meet Patsy, who was on her way to pick me up so that we could go together to the hospital, but I had a quick peep. His work was truly fantastic. He handed me his card and said that his name was Alan and that he does property maintenance. I took the card and quickly dashed to catch up with Patsy. My carers' group had advised me to do whatever work was needed to be done on my home. One month later, I dialled the number on the card to get a quote from Alan for the restoration of my bathroom that was long overdue. After getting a quote, which I was pleased with, he took me shopping to choose what I wanted. While shopping, I became so hungry that I thought I could faint, so we went to a restaurant. Next door, a friend of his had a shoe shop. We passed in to say hello and the friend said he would come with us for the meal. He brought his stepson along. He also decided to pay for the bill. My bathroom was completed in six weeks, as Alan had promised. It is beautiful and it gives me much comfort. From then, I gave Alan jobs to renovate some other rooms in my home. I left him building me a new kitchen while I made a trip to St Vincent and the Grenadines.

CHAPTER 42

TRIP TO ST VINCENT

I arrived in St Vincent in March 2018. My brother, Victor, collected me from the airport, and we had a great reunion. Throughout my stay he treated me kindly, as always. We made daily early morning trips to the beach for a swim, along with Claire. Later in the day, we would occasionally go shopping in town. A few times in town I passed to see Flora, the mother of my grandson, Ian, at her place of work. A couple of times we visited Christa and her husband who were also on holiday from London, and together we went to the nearest beach, and once or twice they came to Victor's home, where we had much fun and laughter. Victor's favourite pastime was fishing, he went with his friends. Whenever he went fishing, I visited Prince and his family or Claire or Winnie. One afternoon while I was at Prince's home, I went with his daughter, Lydia, to collect her lovely girls from their schools. Lydia took the opportunity of driving me to have a better look at the new airport. Although I landed there, I did not see it properly. On our return we stopped off at a resort for a quick look at the surroundings and treated ourselves to some delicious ice-cream. Another day, Victor and I went see our eldest relative, who had just celebrated her ninety-nineth birthday. She was full of joy, a treasure to us all.

When I was not about with Victor, Elvie, my niece, was my travelling companion. One day we decided to take a trip to Owia, which I had visited before on my earlier trips to St Vincent. Getting there was fine because we took a bus to Kingstown and then one to Owia. But getting home was a nightmare. We were told that there would be a bus to take us back, apparently, we were misguided. After we had waited for some time, we started walking the very lonely road. Vehicles drove past, some were full, others ignored us. Elvie could not stop laughing when I knelt at the side of the road and prayed for God's help. Shortly after praying we came to a house, I called out, "Is anyone home?"

When a man and his wife came out, we explained our problem to them, and that we feared that we were stranded. They encouraged us and gave us hope saying that there is usually a late van coming from Kingstown to go back and that it will not be full. We must stop it, get in and go back to Owia with them, so as to be sure of our seats back to Kingstown. While in conversation, a young man came walking in our direction. The lady knew him, and she told him to see us safely along the road to Point Village, which was in the direction of his hometown. It was a long walk uphill but chatting made and the journey easier.

When we got to the young man's hometown and came to where he branched off the main road to get to his home, we bid each other goodbye. I began to wonder, *what now?* We were told that we would be sure to get a bus when we got to Georgetown, so we carried on walking. A man came running up to us from behind, shouting and beckoning "Come, come!" We turned and went towards him. "Wait here!" he said. We waited as he went into a house, then came out with a bunch of keys and went into a van, drove up beside us and said, "Get in, I am driving you to Georgetown." I wondered, *how did he know about us and our dilemma?* When we got talking, he explained that he was the village pastor and that the young man who was on the road with us told him that we were stranded on the road. I thanked God for his great love and tender care in answering my prayer.

As we approached Georgetown, I offered the pastor some money, but he refused to accept it, so I said, "It is not for you, it's for the church." He smiled and took it with thanks. When we got to the bus stop there were many buses on the stand collecting passengers for Kingstown. We boarded the first one and slept for most of the journey. By the time we got to upper Kingstown, the bus was almost full of passengers for the return trip. We were asked to leave before reaching the final bus stand, so as to make room for people waiting to board for Georgetown. We did as requested and had to walk a little way to get to the stand for the Leeward buses. When we finally got on the bus to our home in Lowmans Hill, it was very dark, but we were so happy that we were in fits of laughter. Victor, Prince and Winnie were worried about us and were relieved when they saw us. On hearing our story they warned us never to make such trip again and explained that we were lucky because lonely roads are dangerous.

MAYREAU

Ian invited me to spend a few days with him in Mayreau, one of the Grenadine islands where he stayed and worked as a charge nurse. He returned to the mainland on his days off. He was happy for Elvie to join us. Prince arranged the trip for us, and we decided to stay for five days. On the mainland, Ian lived in Barroulie, so we met with him in Kingstown. It was great to see him, we were both jubilant. He then took us to his regular snack bar before boarding the boat, and treated us to roti, one of the islands favourite cuisines. It was so delicious. We then made our way onto the ferry that belonged to one of my cousins. We sat on deck to view the scenery. The sun shone like diamonds on the blue seawater, the fish jumped high above the surface, birds came down and caught some. My hat blew with the wind, I watched, laughed and said "bye" as it sailed the sea. The vessel sailed past many little islands and stopped at some to pick up and drop off cargo. The scene was absolutely breath-taking. When we stepped out onto Mayreau, I just knew that I was in for a wonderful time.

My grandson was very loved and well respected by everyone on the island and on meeting with Elvie and me, they extended the love.

The clinic managed by Ian was a short walk from his home, and sometimes Elvie and I passed to see him on our way to the beach and on our walking tours around the beautiful tiny island. As we walked, we enjoyed the panoramic view and took many videos and photos. Our best view was from the Catholic Church.

On Ian's day off, his friend drove us to Whistle Bay, said to be one of the most stunning bays in the Grenadines. We walked for miles along the beach and had great fun swimming and floating in the still sea water. On leaving the bay, another of Ian's friends handed me three small bottles of cocktails from her bar - they were her own recipe. I sipped them slowly at nights with much delight. We enjoyed our last dinner at Owen's chill spot, which Ian insisted was a must. I was glad that we went; the company was good, and the food delicious. I had a wonderful time on the Island. Saying goodbye, especially to my grandson, was painful. He saw us safely on the ferry and we watched as the little truck drove him off up the hill to his home. When we got back to the mainland, Victor was waiting to drive us back to Lowmans. To my surprise a young man handed my hat to me, it was in perfect condition. "How did you rescue it? And how did you know that it was mine?" I asked. He simply smiled and refused to accept my monetary gift.

TRIP TO THE FALLS WITH IAN'S FAMILY

A few days after our return from Mayreau, Flora organised an outing for me to Wallilabou waterfall, better known as, 'Dam'. Again, Elvie accompanied me. This outing gave me the opportunity to meet and enjoy the company of Flora's other children, grandchildren, and a couple of her friends. They are a lovely family. Her eldest daughter and I became quite attached. Flora did all or most of the cooking. Among the different dishes she made one of my favourites, roast breadfruit and saltfish. After eating, I tested the water in the Dam - gosh, it was cold! However, I braved it. It was just the right width and depth for me to feel safe. I joined others to climb the fall and found myself a comfortable rock to sit on and allowed the water to beat on my body. It felt heavenly. I thanked God for the wonderful works of His hands. One of Flora's friends gave us a ride back to Lowmans on his way home. Another glorious day.

I was disappointed with the call I received from Alan that evening, explaining that the kitchen would not be ready for my home coming due to delay in electrical work. He also said that my old kitchen sink had disappeared from my garden. I had hoped to use the sink in the garden, but I was not too bothered, I was more concerned about having no kitchen. I tried not to think about it and hoped for the best.

Victor drove me back to the airport on the day of my departure. I was rather sad because I had no short-term plan of returning. On my checking in through customs, I was given a hard time, one that I had never experienced before. A young man, who could have been my grandson, searched my case because the scan showed that I was carrying illegal stuff. My smalls fell on the floor. When I reached down to pick them, he shouted! "Don't touch!" When he did not find what he was looking for he just said, "You can pack it back now." I thought *how very rude, no apology!?* I was ashamed of the behaviour of this my young countryman and hoped that he would be more polite to others.

HOME FROM SVG FITZ WAS OK

My flight home was fine. When I arrived and went to Fitz, it was a treat to see his smile and how well he looked. He listened as I told him all the news of home. He asked if I had seen his sister who had gone down for a long holiday. He also said that she paid him a quick visit before she went. I explained to him that I did not see any of his relatives and did not know where his sister lived but while waiting at the airport on my way back, I happened to see the father of her twins. He told me where her house is and that she was still there. I was happy that Fitz was so alert, he also asked about my sister Christa and wanted to know when she would be coming back. He said that he longed to see her.

During this time we were all looking forward to the birth of Hanson's baby. His partner had just two months to her delivery date. When they visited Fitz, he touched her tummy and smiled as he felt the baby move. We prayed that he would still be there to hold his great grandchild.

While I was comfortable with Fitz's condition, I was not pleased to see that my kitchen was far from being ready. However, the care home had become my second home and I had little time for cooking. Still, I was satisfied that as soon as the delay with the electric was sorted, Alan would push himself hard to keep the work going to completion.

Fitz was having a lot of problems with his dentures, his new ones got lost at the rehab. He advised me to do whatever was necessary to take care of my teeth as I was also experiencing difficulties. When I told Pearl about my gum troubles, she told me about her private dentist, so I decided to go there. She accompanied me on my first visit. My treatment lasted approximately one year, and I have no regrets. Once when I was going, Fitz said to me, "Pick me up and take me with you". During those tough times I received good support from our friend, the reverend at the nearby church. After finishing one of the Sunday morning services, she accompanied me to the care home. Fitz was delighted to hear her voice, especially when she sang one of his favourite hymns to him.

FITZ ADMITTED TO HOSPITAL

Two months later, one evening in the month of June, I received a call from the care home saying that Fitz had been admitted to hospital. Although I knew he was ill, I was still shaken because he seemed to be doing well. I immediately informed our children and our vicar, and one by one we made our way to see him. The doctor's first report sounded promising, so we all hoped for the best. I was not there to hear the second report; it seemed to be the norm that whenever he was ill, I also became ill. The awful news that Fitz no longer wanted to co-operate with the doctors was given to Vilna. She happened to be the only one present when the doctor did his round. Fitz was moved from the open ward to a private room which made it possible for all of us to visit. When we broke the news to the children of his siblings, those who were able, quickly joined us. Fitz was pleased to have them present. We began singing songs to him from YouTube. When Reverend Paisley arrived, he offered prayers and words of comfort. I believe he was impressed with our little worship service, and joined in, it then felt official. He ministered to and prayed with Fitz who was able to show gratitude with a smile as he was not in pain. We all left after he fell asleep.

FITZ'S FINAL DAYS AND FAREWELL

Fitz was not kept in the hospital for long. Within two days the care home called to say that he was being sent back to them to die and that he was being given morphine to ease his pain. On receiving the call, I screamed, and called Glenda. I knew that I had to get to the care home quickly. "Calm down mum, Hanson and I are on our way, we will take you." I became nervous and impatient. Alan said that he would have driven me there, but he was just completing the tiling on my kitchen and the grout could not be left. I was hesitant to call a cab because on previous occasions the wait was too long, and once, they did not even show up. However, Hanson came quickly, and he took the long route to the care home to avoid busy traffic.

When we got there, Fitz seemed peaceful. He said he was not in any pain and that he did not need the morphine. Our other children, grandchildren and sons-in-law came as quickly as they could. From then on, we never left Fitz's side. I called Paisley. He came and administered Holy Communion to Fitz and me. Alice, who had just arrived from her long stay in Africa, came directly to see him. I also called everyone who I knew had not seen Fitz lately and believed would love to. Claire and Sherlene came that night and stayed late to keep my company. Although Fitz had become blind, he recognised the voices of people he knew. He had not seen Claire for a long time but as soon as she spoke, he said her name and they held a good conversation. Claire and others assumed that Fitz would last a week, but the next night on 11th of June, after our children left, I settled in a chair bed beside him. He slipped away at four in the morning whilst holding my hand on his chest. When I informed the night staff they could not believe because one said that she had just popped in and saw us resting peacefully. I called our children, and they all came quickly. We supported each other in every way. I was surprised at the wisdom and strength of Hanson. He held our hands and said, "Let us all pray" and commented "We are one, we must stick together now".

On the nineth night of Fitz's passing we held thanksgiving service at my home, with a few relatives and friends from church. They all kindly contributed food and drink.

FITZ'S FUNERAL

The funeral was prearranged by Fitz and myself two years previous. My children and grandchildren were of great help and support in every respect. Together, we organised the service order and designed the booklets, which were printed as a gift by of one of Hanson's friends. We just needed a venue for the reception, and to sort out flowers and music. Hanson drove me around until we found the best venue that had the perfect menu, and Darren connected me to his florist friend. She did all the flowers. Darren also put me in touch with the leader of a Caribbean steel band who played for us.

Fitz's brother Elvin, and sister, came from New York for the funeral. It was so good to have them. Their company was invaluable.

On the 28$^{th\ of}$ June, I had Fitz's body brought home for the night. An hour before the funeral service on the 29th, the florist brought the flowers. Flowers came also from Victor and from Fitz's sister-in-law in Canada. We also received flowers from our kind neighbours and from the community centre, where Fitz was once a member and did a basic computer course.

While the flowers were being delivered, the steel band arrived, and so did the funeral directors with the horse-drawn carriage and cars. It was a beautiful hot day; 28 degrees Celsius. The horses' plumes were the colours of our Vincentian flag as we requested. All who were travelling in the funeral cars came early. Daughters, granddaughters and myself were all dressed in white; the immediate family and Fitz's siblings each wore a purple flower. I did not think Fitz would have wanted us to dress in gloomy colours. The band played Fitz's favourite songs at our front gate and some neighbours came and paid their respects while he was taken from the house to the carriage. When we got to church, our Vicar's wife played the entrance music. The service was conducted and addressed by our Vicar, and was attended by all our church ministers, choir members, many parishioners, as well as ministers and people from nearby parishes.

Family and friends supported us; we were also blessed to have the company of some neighbours. Some paid tribute. Our son gave the eulogy, followed by a song from one of Fitz's nieces. Another niece and Vilna each read poems. Tributes were paid by Elvin and our grandchildren, as well as our dear friend, the Reverend who sang to Fitz. Stacy read the lesson which was followed by the hymn, 'The Lord's my Shepherd', sung by our church choir. We had a total of five hymns. Final prayers were said by another dear friend, a Reverend from a church in the borough. It was a beautiful service. After the viewing of Fitz's body, I paid my acknowledgement with a vote of thanks. On exit, the steal band played 'Sailing', a song Fitz loved to hum to, while my wonderful Ghanaian friends distributed water and small parcels of food that they made, mainly for diabetics.

On our arrival at the cemetery, the band continued to play. My five grandchildren and I each held a lovely white dove, which we released at the start of the graveside service. They took flight towards the sky, as we all sang 'On the Wings of a Snow-White Dove', representing Fitz's spirit ascending to heaven. During the internment we sang seven songs, all backed by the steel band. When all was said and flowers laid, we made our way to the reception venue. The band got there before us and played as we entered, then Dingi took over the musical entertainment, which was great. The hall looked spectacular; the food was delicious, Stacy's sister made lots of beautiful cakes. We were all pleased with the way the day went, and Fitz would have been delighted with his great farewell to glory.

Elvin and his sister moved from my home to spend their last two days with their sister, who by then had returned from St Vincent. I missed their company, but I had to start learning to grow stronger on my own. I continued to visit the care home that Fitz was in and chatted with the staff and the patients. Being there brought me much comfort. It was my intention to join the staff one day a week, but some of the information that was required, I simply could not recall. However on my recommendation, my late friend's husband was later taken into the same care home, and a few weeks hence, one of my brothers-in-law was also admitted there. I was therefore able to continue visiting the care home and maintain connections with the staff and other patients.

CHAPTER 43

LIFE GOES ON

Hanson and his partner organised an amazing baby shower, it served well to lift my spirit. The following week one of Prince's granddaughters was passing through London from Canada and spent a couple nights with me. She was so quiet that I hardly knew she was there, but it really made a difference knowing that I was not alone.

In August 2018, my niece Lydia arrived from St Vincent with her gorgeous four-year-old daughter along with a teenage friend. The following week they were joined by her lovely eldest daughter and two of her friends, they were all very nice girls. We had made this arrangement for their stay the previous year, however because of Fitz's passing, the time no longer felt right.

I was not up to entertaining, I tried to deter Lydia, but all her plans were already in place and it was not easy for her to change. She explained that she would manage the cooking, so I agreed. I felt sad not being up to helping them, usually I enjoyed taking care of my guests.

The day before they left, a dispute arose which led to an unhappy ending, adding more grief to my sorrow. Nevertheless I was not prepared to let the outcome ruin our love. I hugged them as they left and made it clear to Lydia that my love for her had not changed. Unfortunately she did not see it that way at the time, and communications between us got lost. Thank God that we were able to make amends and our love has continued.

Soon after Lydia and the girls left, Hanson's baby was born, a beautiful little girl Hailey, to a sweet mother. She has brought and still brings such joy into our lives. Sad that Fitz did not live another month to touch or to hold her. Hailey was blessed by our Vicar during a Sunday morning service as he normally does with every new-born, and one year later she was received into the family of God in one of our Sunday morning alfresco services. The following Saturday we had a wonderful party organised by her parents who are gifted in the art of throwing exciting parties.

MY CRUISE 2018

I decided to go on a lone cruise for my 76th birthday. I needed to get the feel of being alone abroad in strange places. I booked a one-week all-inclusive fly and cruise trip on a Spanish ship. Patsy drove me to Stansted airport for my flight to Barcelona. When I landed in Barcelona my taxi was waiting to take me to the ship. On entering the ship I noted that no one spoke English. I remained hopeful that an English-speaking person would show up but after three hours all I heard was Spanish. I began to wonder, *why did I book a cruise to Spain*? My first meal was lunch, I sat and ate alone but at dinner there was a great change. I was escorted to a table with three other British single women and on the opposite table were eight Britons, male and female. We instantly got chatting and I became friends with Sylvia. Sylvia had a slight disability and we felt that we needed each other, so wherever we disembarked we travelled around together. She relayed to me, that when she told her daughter on the phone that she met with someone nice, her daughter said, "Mum stick with her."

Sylvia was very slow, so our explorations were limited, which was not a bad thing because I am apt to going too far and losing track. Sylvia was an excellent navigator, with her beside me I was saved from getting lost.

Everyone on the cruise went on a guided tour to Pompei, but Sylvia sat in a café by a market square and waited for us to return. Another day we both hired a taxi to view Florence. Again, Sylvia sat by the falls we came to during our walk and waited for me while I did my exploring. I went on a brisk walk, travelled too far and lost my bearing. Yes, I panicked and when I got back to where I left Sylvia she was not there, but the taxi driver rang me to say she was safe with him. He had to direct me back to where they were. The next day Sylvia was too tired to leave the ship and said, "Today, I am letting you go out alone. Perhaps you ought to stay close to one of the others and be careful!" I did not stay close to anyone as the others went their separate ways. However, I was sure to mark my tracks well and stayed where I was insight of the bus stop. The following day Sylvia was still not up to being out and about so when we docked at Napoli, I went out alone. The walk from the ship to the town was straightforward and I bought souvenirs along the way. Technology is a great thing because every so often while walking, I conversed with my loved ones back in London. The week went by so quickly. All too soon, one by one, we said goodbye and went our separate ways on disembarking the ship as our flights home were at different times. I took my taxi back to the airport. On my arrival at Stansted, Patsy was already there to drive me home. My week was great, and not exactly lonely. The following day, I rang Sylvia. She encountered problems at the airport in Barcelona, but she said thank God she was helped by a kind man. Since then we have spoken twice and discussed the possibility of travelling together some time – lovely lady.

Home alone, knowing Fitz was no longer with me and no more trips to the care home to see him was a very daunting realisation. Worst of all was when darkness fell. I found myself playing all Fitz's old records of love songs and sang along. Sometimes allowing a tear or two. I had his tomb stone erected six months after he passed, and six months after that I held a Service of Prayer Praise & Thanksgiving to his memory at St Johns Church, led by Reverend Paisley. Following a dream I had seeing Fitz in his lovely blue shirt, I decided for us all to wear blue, his favourite colour. Two of our other Reverend friends took part in leading prayers, while a couple of our children and grandchildren read passages from the Bible. Patsy and Cynthia, my church warden friend, read their own written poems and tributes were paid by Stacy and Christa. One of our dear friends sang a song. We sang three other joyful hymns and one song. Cecilia, the Vicar's wife, played the organ. The service was well attended. I thanked everyone for their generous help and support throughout the year. We ended with light refreshments in the church hall.

JULY 2019 CAPE VERDE

My niece, Sherlene, called me to say that she was organising a trip to Cape Verde and asked if I would like to join the party. "That would be lovely," I said, "Just say when." Within days she sent me all the information, which I agreed to. Two weeks after Fitz's memorial service I was on a plane, in a group of eighteen, back to that beautiful archipelago on the golden sands of Sal and staying at the very resort I stayed before with Mark and Tracy. Pearl and I shared an apartment, which to my surprise, overlooked the villa I occupied in 2015. There were many changes to the resort, what used to be the main dining hall was turned into a recreation centre and was much more welcoming and interesting. I also discovered that there were more restaurants with wider choices of meals. Being a large group, it was difficult for all to meet in the same restaurant for breakfast and lunch, but most evenings we made the effort to be together for dinner, especially when there was a birthday to celebrate. Oh yes, we had loads of fun and laughter. The bar and restaurant staff were super, doing their best to keep us smiling and we became very attached to a special young man named Martin. Most of us went to the after-dinner shows, which were outdoors and a good distance from the reception. Some people walked but myself and some others went on the free buggy ride. Gosh, the evenings were cold, too cold for the month of July. So although the shows were good, I never stayed to the end. When it came to excursions and shows, choices were left to individuals in the group. That way we were all free to enjoy whatever we wanted.

I spent a lot of time alone on the beach. One afternoon I was joined by Martin and his gorgeous toddler son. We had a lovely chat. His story was very sad but interesting to hear his triumph.

The following afternoon I retraced my tracks of the year I was there; my little pool had lost depth and was not as enticing as before so I was in and out quite quickly. Luckily, I came across a new bay not too far away, with ideal water for me to swim and float without fear and enjoyed the company of a lovely family. I also went on a jeep trip to the salt mines, and then to the lake. The salesman on the beach led me to believe that I was to be in the company of eight others but there was just three of us. Nonetheless it was great, they were newly-weds on honeymoon. We enjoyed being together and became friends. They left the resort before me, but we are still in touch.

I spent most of my last days at the recreation centre with Pearl and other members from our group whom I got to know fairly well. Sherlene's eldest daughter, my great niece, insisted on treating myself and her aunt to our final spa day. We had an amazing time together. The day that we boarded the bus to leave the resort, Martin came on to see us off. We all made a fuss of him, and we were looking forward to welcoming him to London one day as some of us became friends with him online. Well, things did not turn out for him the way he would have liked but we all did our best to help him at his point of need.

ANTIGUA MARCH 2019

Once again, Tracy called and said "Mum, Mark and I are going to Antigua for one week. Would you like to come with us?"

"Sure! Thank you but it would have to be two weeks for me."

"Well, if you don't mind being on your own, then book two weeks."

After my week alone cruise, I knew I would be fine, so I booked it. Just before we were about to go, our friend Anita, rang to say that she too would be in Antigua that same time. It was good to know that she would be spending some time with us there. I arrived at Gatwick airport, driven by my friend Alan, and met with Tracy and Mark. I slept a lot during our eight-hour flight. Between dozes, I was able to enjoy a few films. We landed to the welcoming blue sky, fresh air and hot sun. Our pre-booked taxi drove us to the resort in Saint John's and we enjoyed the scenery along the way. On entering the reception, we were greeted with nice refreshing drinks while waiting to be checked in and collect our room keys.

I was pleased with my double room and balcony that overlooked the beautiful garden towards the sea. Tracy and Mark had to go past my door to get to reception, so they knocked for me at mealtimes. Usually after breakfast most of our time was spent sunbathing on the beach. Mark had to slip out early in the mornings to get sunbeds for us, because we came to realise that that's what others were doing. Each day I joined the pool exercise class which I thoroughly enjoyed, and after the class I was in and out of the sea. Of all the many seas I have been in, this one became my number one favourite. Being a novice swimmer, the water was perfect for me. I floated and swam with confidence. Food and drinks were also excellent. The restaurant staff told us to order whatever Caribbean food we wanted to eat a day in advance, and they would provide it, as it was not usually included in the buffet.

Sunday morning I got dressed, ready for church, and enquired at reception about the nearest church. A taxi was called to take me there, it was fairly close. I received a warm welcome from the welcomers at the door. The form of service was the same as I remembered at the Cathedral in St Vincent. One lady invited me to her home for lunch but knowing that the others would have been concerned about me, I declined. After the service one of the members drove me back to my hotel and showed me where to wait for him the next week. I very much appreciated the kindness I was shown.

One afternoon we went on a boat trip and Mark went diving. I admired his bravery and skill, which was no surprise to his wife. We also drank in the beauty of the villages we sailed passed, and yes, we had drinks on the boat. Another day we took a bus into town and did some exploring. Before going back to our resort, we took a stroll around the one adjacent to ours. It was a yacht club. The boats were beautiful.

When Anita arrived, she only spent two nights at our resort as she was on a travelling break. We were happy to be in her company. All three left the island on the same day, so that I was on my own, but I had made friends with islanders on the beach, and they looked out for me. The traders that I had bought beach wear from always had a deck chair ready for me, and at times I sat with them. One day I went back to the town, and they kept my chair until I returned. In town, I followed my ears to a record shop and there I sat, listened and bought my chosen CD's, then explored some more of the town before getting a bus back to my hotel. The day came for me to say farewell to the island and its warm-hearted people. I left with smiles and gratitude for the love that was shown to me. I had a pleasant trip back to London. Alan collected me from the airport and on the way back, we stopped for a meal. Can I count my blessings? Never!

I guess my life sounds like one big holiday. Of course I enjoy holidays, they get me away from everyday routine. I often lose myself in doing too much. At one time wine making, beer brewing and baking were some of my hobbies. My pastime that is still with me today is gardening. In spring, summer and early autumn, my garden gets my full attention. Mowing the lawn, trimming the hedges, pruning the roses, weeding and clearing out the rubble has to be done. Occasionally I paint fences, doors and gates, repair damaged brick work and fill gaps between concrete slabs. My outdoor speciality is my flower and vegetable garden. Planting and cultivating them affords fun and harvesting is a lovely treat. Come November, housework and shopping takes priority in preparation for Christmas. I usually take things easy after Christmas and begin again in April, preparing for Easter. Christmas and Easter are glorious times in church but extremely busy with the extra services and practices. Nonetheless, I look forward to celebrating these events.

A couple of times on different years I have invited Pearl and Alice, and also friends who lived alone, to join us for Christmas dinner. My children and I try to be together on our birthdays; often we would enjoy a meal in a restaurant or celebrate at the home of the celebrant, and sometimes we go on holiday.

GREECE OCTOBER 2019

"Mum, Glenda and I are taking you on a four-night break to Greece for your birthday," said Patsy.

"Really? Whoa! How lovely, I am excited! I have never been to Greece. Where in Greece?"

"Corfu, and Jacob is coming too," Patsy reported.

"That's great!" I said.

All I had to do was to be ready for Glenda's arrival on the day of travel. When she came, we drove to meet with Patsy and Jacob. Glenda left her car at Patsy's house and Patsy drove us all to the airport. The flight was good, but the noise was awful. I did not think I would have been able to hear again, but after landing my ear soon cleared. Our resort was an uphill walk, but transport was provided. Glenda and I shared a lovely room with a pleasant view. Our fun began in the sea, under the sun, where doctor fish had a feast on my foot. At first, I was very scared of them, however, I soon got accustomed to their nibbling away at me. From the beach we went for a relaxing spa, followed by dinner and drinks. The next two days we took the bus to the town. The first day we rode around on the tram and alighted for a while to visit the Old Venetian Fortress.

The second day we went window shopping, but I was captivated by the work of the doctor fish in a health shop and made my way to have them finish the job that the ones in the sea had started on my feet. I must say it was scary because there were many of them, but they did a good job on my feet. While I was having my feet done, the others continued shopping. On the 23rd October, the night of my birthday, the girls had ordered me a cake, and free drinks were brought to the room. They all sang happy birthday to me. I had a lovely little birthday and a refreshing break. When I got home, more lovely surprises awaited me from my other children and grandchildren. I was welcomed with flowers, cards, dinner and theatre tickets.

CHRISTMAS 2019

Christmas preparations was my next focus. I enjoy decorating my house inside and out with fairy lights. I have always believed that it helps to lift people's spirits - it does mine - at the same time it reminds us that it's Jesus's birthday. As a Christian, I believe that He came from Heaven to Earth and brought new life and light into our dark world of sin. I always looked forward to the singing of Christmas carols with in my church choir in our city centre and in church. Sadly, I no longer join the choir as I was told that my voice sounded awful. I tried to accept the comment, but I began skipping choir and practices. Taking services also started to lose appeal because it meant I could no longer sing the lovely hymns and songs I had chosen to accompany the theme for the day's sermon. However, I persevered and still sang but tried hard to not let my voice be heard, as advised.

One day the organist said to me, "Sheva, I no longer hear your singing" and asked me why. He said that he needed to hear me in order to play. I explained that I was told not to sing because my voice sounded awful. He found it hard to believe and said that I was a good singer. I admit I struggle with the high notes in soprano, so when I was in the choir, I would find myself dropping to tenor when singing high notes. However, when leading a service on my own, I found this vocal change difficult. Nonetheless, I did my best at all times. When sitting in the congregation I found freedom being myself and it was with great relief.

Christmas 2019 was one of the best, both in church and at home. That year, Tracy came to me on the eve of Christmas instead of on Christmas day and together we went to the midnight church service. I had always dreaded going alone in the dark and had started taking the Dial-A-Ride, so it was great to have Tracy's company. Also, having Tracy in the home made such a difference; it reminded me of the old times when I was never alone. I felt so blessed to wake on Christmas morning with Tracy in the next room. My other children arrived, family after family; sixteen in total with their gifts and delicious dishes, some ready for the table and some for the oven, leaving me with nothing to worry about. I did only what I wanted to and when Hanson saw that I was doing too much, he lifted me out of the kitchen, took me to the front room and placed me in an armchair. I was left in fits of laughter. Our routine for Christmas day always seemed to go the same way, no matter how much we tried to make changes. Dinner followed by presentation of gifts, then games, TV and music with dancing, often rolling over into Boxing Day.

2019 - 2020

New Year's Eve was no longer a house party night for me. It had become another wonderful midnight church service, and had become customary for me to lead, which meant I had to be in church early. I booked my ride well in advance and thankfully they arrived on time. At the end I was given a lift home by my very kind friends and happily I cancelled my return ride.

Not all my children join me for the New Year, as some meet with their in-laws, so it's usually quiet compared to Christmas and Easter.

We were all excited about our plans and all the arrangements we had in place for 2020. Pearl had booked her wedding in Jamaica for the month of April. Every family member worldwide was invited and many accepted. My four daughters, three of my grandchildren, along with respective husbands and partners were set to go, as were my siblings and some of their families. Suddenly, talk of COVID-19 in China dominated the news. We had no thought that it was about to become a pandemic, we still expected to go to Jamaica.

Meanwhile, Faye wanted to do something special for her birthday in February. I decided to check out holiday breaks for her; it was not unusual for us to accompany one another on birthday breaks. By the time I found a reasonable all-inclusive week in Barcelona Spain, the news of the spread of COVID-19 presented cause for concern. But Faye was adamant that she would go alone if she had to. I could not let her do that, so I booked to go with her, as travelling was still fairly safe. We took the bus from Stratford East to Stanstead airport, and all went well until we arrived in Spain. Our pre-paid taxi kept us waiting for hours. We complained to the relevant company at the desk, but it made no difference. When we arrived at the little hotel, the staff at reception were welcoming. Our room was fine, food was good, recreation was poor, evening entertainment was enjoyable. On our second day we went for a nice walk along the beach, and the next day we walked again in a different direction and saw a train station. The following day we took the train to town and booked a two-day bus tour and that's how we spent the remainder of our time - riding on buses viewing places, window shopping etc.

The day we left the hotel, the pre-paid taxi did not come for us. We were told that we had to walk to another hotel and that the taxi would be there, but when we got there the hotel was not in operation and there was no taxi. We returned to our hotel and explained the outcome to the receptionist at the desk. She said that it had nothing to do with them. *How strange, when she was the one who told us that the taxi would be waiting for us at the nearby hotel?* It was all too much to take in and we ended up calling a private taxi for fear of missing our flight. The taxi was very expensive, twice the price we paid for the prepaid return taxi, but Faye decided to pay it. When I arrived home, I called the company I had booked with and complained that their taxi arrangement failed us. They offered me twenty pounds off my next flight and said that the taxi company refused to pay because, as far as they were concerned, the taxi came to collect us. Four weeks later we entered into a national lockdown, so that twenty pounds off our next flight became useless. We also had to abandon our trip to Jamaica for Pearl's wedding because of the lockdown. We remained hopeful but all hopes were lost. My suitcase is still packed.

CHAPTER 44

PHONE CALL TO ANDY

After years of stressing about the broken relationship between Andy and myself, I was encouraged by Patsy and Alan, my friend, to call him. So I called him on Valentine's Day. I was nervous as to how he might receive me, but I had no need to worry, it turned out that our feelings were mutual, and we both longed to be reunited. We talked for about three hours just clearing the air and putting right all misunderstandings. Neither of us wanted the conversation to end. We felt happy to have bridged the gap of silence and discontent, with the knowledge that peace and love had been restored. When Andy told his wife about our conversation, she rang me full of smiles as she explained her happiness. I also told my other children, and they too were happy for us, bless the Lord!

LOCK DOWN

At the start of the lockdown, I spent much time working in my garden. When I was not tending the garden I sat, slept and enjoyed the hot spring and summer sun. Over the years I have written many of short stories, most are scribbled but one has been displayed in a local library. I gathered these stories and found much pleasure in browsing through them. It was then that I decided to start writing this book, which had always been my dream. So I began in my garden with pencil and note pad.

The following month Andy's wife called me on video chat. While we were talking, I realised that Andy was standing beside her, she passed the phone to him. He said that he was not feeling too well, his asthma had flared up. I started giving him recipes of herbal remedies. After about ten minutes he said he needed the bathroom and that I should continue talking to Gloria. I gave her the ingredients, along with my method of making the remedy, which she took note of, and she promised to have the mixture ready for Andy as soon as possible. Andy stumbled and almost fell while leaving the bathroom, thankfully Gaylene quickly held him.

ANDY TO HOSPITAL

The next day Gloria called me to say that she went with Andy to see his doctor, who checked Andy and sent him home with medication. I thought Andy would have recovered at home, but the following day Gloria rang saying that he was still feeling rough, so he told her to call an ambulance to take him to the hospital. She also said that Andy asked to be taken to the hospital that was connected to the College where he worked, in the hope of receiving the best treatment. Gloria explained that she sat with Andy in the ambulance to the hospital, but she was not allowed into the hospital, and as they were about to part, he held her hand tightly and looked into her eyes as if he sensed something was about to happen. On hearing this news, I was panic stricken and informed my other children, my siblings, relatives, my vicar and all my praying friends, requesting prayer. When Gloria called again, she said that Andy called her to say that he was on an open ward and needed her to take him some clothes along with my remedy, but she said she was told that liquids were not allowed.

Patsy and some of Andy's friends reported that he also called them. Gloria relayed good news from the hospital that Andy did not have COVID-19; she was told to bring the medication that he received from the doctor. Gloria took the clothes and some lemons. Lemons were the closest she could get to my remedy, she said that she delivered them at the desk and left without being able to see or speak to Andy.

From then, I rang Andy's number a couple of times, as did others, but there was no response. I rang the hospital and spoke to a nurse explaining that I was Andy's mother living in London and that I was desperate to know about his condition.

"You know that he has COVID-19," the nurse informed.

"No, I did not know."

She said that he was moved to a COVID-19 ward. I was in a state of dismay and called on all my family to pray. Each day I called the hospital but got no reply. Finally, someone answered and connected me to the doctor in charge of Andy. He said that Andy was now free of COVID-19 and that I should speak to Gloria for further updates. Gloria called me saying that the doctor said they were working on Andy to bring him back to full health.

GLORIA DISTRAUGHT

Poor Gloria always sounded very distraught. She was never able to inform me properly, so I continued to ring the hospital. One day a nurse answered but she kept conversing with another. In the end she said, "We cannot help you."

"But one of you helped me the first time I called. All I need to know is how my son is doing."

"Yes, but we cannot tell you anything now. We will put you on to his carer."

This she did, but the carer also said that he could not tell me anything as he was only the carer, not a doctor. From then I became suspicious that something was wrong and that they were hiding or trying to cover the truth about Andy's health.

MY WAITING DAYS

My waiting days were wrapped in prayer. I set up a prayer table, on it I placed a white candle, my Easter palm cross, Fitz's wooden cross, a glass of water, a picture of Andy, my Bible and a box of matches. Each time I went to pray I lit the candle to remind me that there is light in the darkness. The palm cross reminded me of my Saviours suffering, Fitz's cross made me reflect on how close he held it through his days of suffering, and, to me, the water represented life. Each prayer time I said the words from the 23rd and 27th psalms, they brought me comfort and hope. During one of my prayer sessions, Gloria called to say that the doctor said Andy was doing well and they wanted her permission to work on his kidney to improve its function. I called Ian for a quick chat on the matter. We all thought that it was a general dialysis and that it would be good, so we agreed to go ahead and looked forward to good news. Two days after that treatment the doctor rang Gloria again asking for her permission to perform another dialysis, as the first one did not do well. We trusted the doctor to do the best for Andy as he promised, so once again we agreed to further treatment. Two days later on 13th April, Gloria received another call from the doctor saying, "Sorry, Andy did not make it." Gloria said that the post-mortem later showed that Andy died from natural causes. I would love to know what was the natural cause.

THE FINAL CALL

I was deep in prayer when Gloria rang. I knew from her bawling that she was about to tell me that she had received the final call from the doctor saying that Andy was no more. She could not find the words, but I needed to hear them and when she did, I too broke down. However, I found the strength to call all my people and inform them of Andy's death. What an awful time, so much pain and suffering with no one to hug and hold. I continued to write, for it was in writing that I hid myself. Past memories kept me going. The present made me think that God no longer heard my prayers. I found it difficult to continue to offer prayer for myself and for others. The thought also came to me, *it was my fault why Andy died.* I blamed myself for the awful things I said to him when we were last together, but instantly that soft and gentle voice from within said, *Andy's death has nothing to do with the things you said. Remember when you forgave each other? I also forgave you both. Don't you forget that I knew him before he was formed in your womb, and as with everyone his days were written in my book. Today, I have called him, his number is up, he is now safe in my arms.* I knew that the voice was the blessed Holy Spirit.

COMFORT

This message was very soothing and sustaining but I was still so sad at my loss, and prayer did not come easily. However, I knew that I had to be strong to comfort Gloria and everyone else. Family and friends called and prayed with me on the phone, some offered consolation. Not every word was helpful, but I appreciated their thought and care. The many cards and flowers I received made me smile. I was sitting in the garden one afternoon when I heard a voice, calling out my name. I rose and as I walked towards the gate, there was Selda's friend, the florist, who made the arrangements for Fitz's funeral. She came towards me with a large box of beautiful flowers, a gift from Selda and family. As she presented it to me, she wanted to give me a hug when suddenly we both remembered the lockdown rule to keep the two-meter distance! Yet through the distance I felt her love. That lifted me.

ASSURANCE

Gloria rang me several times each day. It was hard trying to keep her calm, especially as a funeral home could not be found for Andy's body to rest. We dreaded the thought of him being buried in a trench with hundreds of others who died from Covid-19. Thankfully, Darren located one of his cousins who knew someone that owned a funeral home within walking distance from where Gloria lives. When the director heard of our troubles, he immediately said to look no further, he will take care of everything. His compassion eased our pain. I then organised a memorial service to be held via Zoom nine nights after Andy's death, in keeping with my Vincentian custom. I made just one call to my newly ordained vicar and friend about the service, and he happily agreed to doing everything. All I did was forward him all the necessary information. We had a beautiful uplifting service with relatives from around the world, over one hundred participants joined.

THE FUNERAL

The funeral service took place on 11th May 2020 at the Perfect Peace Funeral Home where Andy's body rested. I sent the layout for that service but because of Covid-19 and the many deaths that followed, the order of service had to be shortened to allow for all the funerals taking place that day. Lockdown rules restricted funeral attendees - there were just nine in all, including Gloria and his two daughters. Myself and many others, watched it live on Facebook. Andy's body was cremated on 13th May, and on Saturday, May 23rd with the help of my niece, Victor's daughter, my nephew, Selda's son, and Stacy, I organised a Zoom thanksgiving service to God for Andy's life, and for helping and strengthening us through forty days and nights of mourning. We are praying that this pandemic will soon end so that Gloria can take Andy's ashes back to St Vincent for burial, to fulfil his wish of resting with his beloved grandmother. Rest in Perfect Peace my dear Son.

Christmas 2020 was unlike all others. According to government rules we were not supposed to meet. Some members from each household took the COVID-19 lateral flow test. We all tested negative, so the family sneakily arrived at my home. Our Christmas was lovely but quiet. Most of all having the family with me after months of isolation was heart-warming.

CHAPTER 45

2021

It was such an unexpected blow when my dearest sister Christa also passed on 25th January 2021 after a very short illness. Larry, Karen's husband closely followed her. And on 21st February, Dingi, who had been suffering for many years, outlived doctors' expectations by three years and passed away on 14th March. All occurred during lockdown restrictions, but this did not deter family and friends from paying last respects at the gravesides. I did my utmost where necessary to assist with funeral services. The very best send offs were given, under the circumstances.

With the help of my children and grandchildren in England after one year of Andy's passing which would have been his birthday, we had a service on zoom in memory of him.

Amid these sorrows, on 26th February 2021, I received a letter from The Right Reverend Dr John Inge, which read; I am delighted to inform you that the bishop of your diocese has submitted your name to be one of this year's Maundy Recipients and I very much hope that you will feel able to accept this honour.

It would be usual for The Queen to distribute the Maundy gifts of specially minted coins to recipients at a service on Maundy Thursday. Regrettably, owing to the current ongoing pandemic, this Royal Maundy Service was not allowed to take place. However, the letter stated that The Queen would not wish for my Christian service in the community to go unrewarded and would be sending me the Maundy gift by post during Holy Week, and that they would like me to confirm acceptance and to present a short paragraph about myself, that they may submit to The Queen for Her Majesty's information.

The paragraph had to be handwritten on the specially designed page. I was excited to receive this invitation and was sad that the service had to be cancelled due to the pandemic. I gladly replied and gave the information about myself that was required, which hopefully I shall reveal in my follow-on book.

I was thrilled to receive the Maundy gift with a letter signed by Her Majesty expressing personal thanks to me for all that I have done to enrich the life of my community. There are also some notes from The Right Reverend Dr John Inge giving information about the history of The Royal Maundy Service. Not wanting to boast I kept all this good news to myself for a while.

The recent birth of another beautiful great granddaughter born to Lee and his partner on 28th June has also brought great positivity. A precious granddaughter for Patsy, and a wonderful gift to our family. In the August bank holiday we celebrated Hailey's 3rd birthday in style. It was funny to listen to her little story that when she was a baby, she played football on the same grounds where we had the party, pointing to the ground. She said, "Now that I'm big," lifting her foot in demonstration, "I wear big shoes!"

The lifting of the lockdown allowed seven of us to have a long weekend break in Bournemouth, where we had many trips and enjoyed the scenery, showing that life has finally opened up again to embrace each other and the beauties of life once more.

EPILOGUE

Dear readers, I have travelled a long way down memory lane. Through my years of joys and pains I have learnt to accept the things I cannot change. Bad experiences have taught me lessons which I am still and always will be learning. The good ones brought me joy, peace and love. With the birth of my newest great granddaughter and the world opening up again, God shows that there is always positivity right around the corner.

I bless the Lord for bringing me through to this present, and I thank him for enabling me to weather every storm so far. I also thank all who have helped me on along my journey. Hopefully, something from my story will be of help to you.

I end by borrowing a verse from the following hymn from Ancient & Modern New Standard because it was one of Mammatee's favourites, and I believe that it connects well with my life story.

'THROUGH ALL THE CHANGING SCENES' Psalm 34 in New Version (TATE and BRADY, 1696)

Through all the changing scenes of life,

in trouble and in joy,

the praises of my God shall still

my heart and tongue employ.

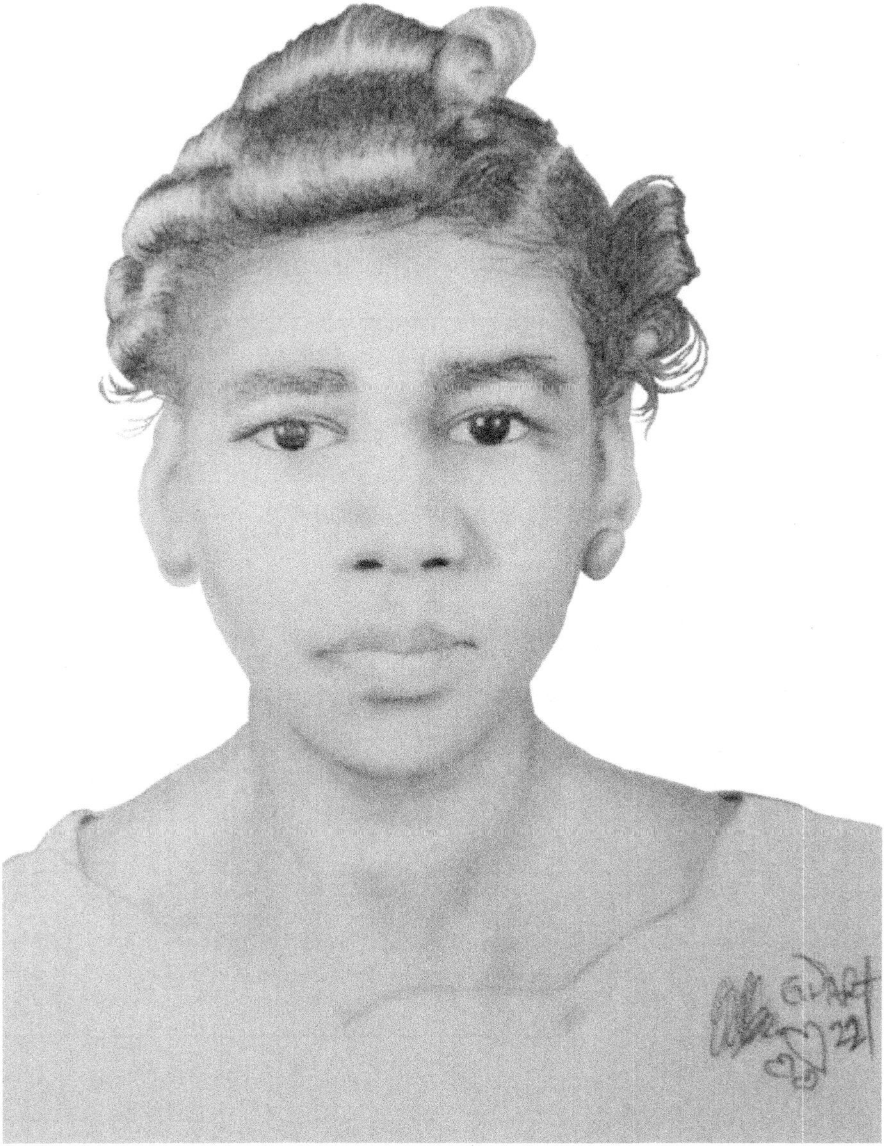

Portrait of Sheva Williams

Artist: Grant Da silva Williams (grandson)

Finally, if you enjoyed this reading, stay tuned for the next episode!

ACKNOWLEDGEMENTS

Many thanks to all who have helped me to remember dates and places of events.

Special thanks to my children and grandchildren for their generous support and encouragement.

Thanks also to:
Ella Tunstall (granddaughter),
Colleen Williams (daughter)
and
Marsha Mattis (great-niece),
who helped me to publish this book.

Printed in Great Britain
by Amazon

33875850R00178